MOST UP TO DATE TRACK N. POW

POPULAR LEISURE IN THE LAKE COUNTIES

In memory of my parents

LYN MURFIN

Popular leisure
in the Lake Counties

Manchester University Press

Manchester and New York

distributed exclusively in the USA and Canada by St. Martin's Press

Copyright © Lyn Murfin 1990

Published by Manchester University Press
Oxford Road, Manchester M13 9PL, UK
and Room 400, 175 Fifth Avenue, New York, NY 10010, USA

Distributed exclusively in the USA and Canada
by St. Martin's Press, Inc., 175 Fifth Avenue, New York, NY 10010, USA

British Library cataloguing in publication data
Murfin, Lyn
  Popular leisure in the lake counties.
  1. Cumbria. Leisure activities
  I. Title
  306.48094278

Library of Congress cataloging in publication data applied for

ISBN 0 7190 3001 3 *hardback*

Typeset by J&L Composition Ltd, Filey, North Yorkshire
Printed in Great Britain
by Bell & Bain Limited, Glasgow

CONTENTS

ILLUSTRATIONS

ABBREVIATIONS

Barrow P.L.	Barrow Public Library
B.H.	Barrow Herald
B.N.	Barrow News
B.T.	Barrow Times
B.R.O.	Cumbria County Record Office, Barrow
C.J.	*Carlisle Journal*
C.N.	*Cumberland News*
C.Pacq.	*Cumberland Pacquet*
C.Pat.	*Carlisle Patriot*
C.R.O.	Cumbria County Record Office, Carlisle
Ec.H.R.	*Economic History Review*
H.J.	*Historical Journal*
I.R.S.H.	*International Review of Social History*
J.Contemp.Hist.	*Journal of Contemporary History*
J.E.F.D.S.S.	*Journal of the English Folk Dance and Song Society*
J.Soc.Hist.	*Journal of Social History*
K.M.	*Kendal Mercury*
K.R.O.	Cumbria County Record Office, Kendal
P. and P.	*Past and Present*
P.O.	*Penrith Observer*
T.C.W.A.A.S.	*Transactions of the Cumberland and Westmorland Antiquarian and Archaeological Society*
T.R.H.S.	*Transactions of the Royal Historical Society*
V.C.H.	*Victoria County History*
Vict. St.	*Victorian Studies*
W.C.T.	*West Cumberland Times*
W.G.	*Westmorland Gazette*
W N	*Whitehaven News*

INTRODUCTION

The history of leisure and popular culture more generally have in recent years received a great deal of attention from historians. Because the subject area had only recently begun to receive academic attention, however, the pioneer studies in the field,[1] which set the themes for the debate in national terms, suffered from the absence of detailed local studies from which to draw evidence and comparisons, and the typicality of their examples and the applicability of their arguments to all areas was therefore questionable. This deficiency has to some extent been rectified by the many local studies of particular aspects of leisure which have recently been undertaken, and also by the national studies of particular themes, most notably the music hall, which have been published in recent years.[2] Nevertheless many regions remain almost entirely undocumented, and apart from a perceptive but necessarily tentative chapter in J. D. Marshall and J. K. Walton's study of the region,[3] no work on popular recreations in Cumbria has previously been undertaken. My study of leisure in the region between the mid-Victorian period and the eve of the Second World War is intended to meet this deficiency, and also, by making available information on a large, remote, semi-rural area, to further the wider debate.

Initial work on the history of leisure identified two main themes. These were, firstly, the importance of leisure to the question of social control, and secondly, the related question of the commercialization of leisure. While accepting that the question of social control was, without any doubt, an aspect of the re-shaping of popular culture in the nineteenth century, I was however influenced by E. P. Thompson's argument that people take an active part in the creation of their culture,[4] and I began my research with the premise, as since articulated by J. M. Golby and A. W. Purdue, that popular culture 'broadly express(es) the aspirations and desires of most men as most men are'.[5] I set out to investigate the extent to which 'aspirations and desires' in the matter of leisure activities changed in Cumbria during the period concerned, and to assess the factors, not excluding attempts at social control and the development of the leisure industries, which influenced change. A particular attempt was made to address the question of women's leisure, and to integrate it into the pattern of development in leisure as a whole. I sought also to assess the distinctiveness of the Cumbrian experience, and the extent to which it was, or became, integrated into the broader national leisure culture during the period in question.

The book is based partly on documentary and partly on oral evidence. The main printed source used was the local press, which from the late nineteenth century on was a mine of information on recreational activity, although coverage is obviously biased towards commercial entertainment and the more respectable and improving pastimes. A variety of other printed sources were also consulted, including parliamentary papers, parish magazines and papers relating to church organisations, licensing records, and documents and ephemera relating to the theatre. This evidence was supplemented by a programme of interviews with elderly Cumbrians.

My informants gave me a wide range of information which could not otherwise have been obtained, and the chapter on leisure activities within the home, for instance, is heavily reliant on oral evidence. Equally importantly, my informants gave me some understanding not only of the 'aspirations and desires', but also the restrictions and conventions which governed recreational life for the individual. The press, broadly, could tell me what recreational activities were available to people, how well attended certain events were, and even sometimes the names of those who participated. However, 'it is vital to the historian to know, as far as he can, not only what the people he is writing about actually did, but what they thought about what they were doing',[6] and in this respect, oral and documentary sources complement one another.

Thirty-seven people were interviewed, of whom twenty were women and seventeen were men. They were born between 1887 and 1921, and at the time of interview were resident in three areas: Penrith; Workington and Whitehaven; and Dalton-in-Furness, Ulverston and Urswick. Some of them, however, had previously lived elsewhere in the region. My informants did not form a scientifically chosen sample of the population. As is inevitably the case with any but the largest of oral history projects, there were far too few of them to constitute any such a thing. Nevertheless, every effort was made to contact as representative a selection of people as possible, in terms of class, occupational background and religion.[7] Ultimately, however, one is limited by the willingness of people to be interviewed, and there are certainly a disproportionate number of female teachers (five) among my informants. There may also be an excess of Anglicans, although such information as we have suggests that the Church of England was the major denomination in the region.[8] There seems also to be an unusually large number of single people. Twelve of the thirty-seven people interviewed had never married, eight of them women. It may be that solitary old people are more likely to attend the day centres and coffee mornings where many of my contacts were made, and they may also be more likely to welcome visitors. Five of the unmarried women were, however, old enough to have had their marriage prospects marred by the First World War, and so they may not be as untypical of their generation as they seem at first sight. The region also had an unusually high percentage of single people in the population in the late nineteenth century, and this pattern may have persisted.[9] As oral evidence has not been used statistically, the possible untypicality of those interviewed does not detract from its value.

The area chosen for the study comprises the old counties of Cumberland and Westmorland, together with Lancashire 'north of the Sands'. These form the present-day county of Cumbria, and although the term is anachronistic, it has been used throughout the book, for the sake of simplicity, to describe the region as a whole. Despite the fact that it has only recently become an administrative unit, the region, which is bounded by the sea on three sides, and by the Pennines in the east, has a geographical unity and has always, in addition, possessed a degree of cultural homogeneity. It is pointed out in the preface to Marshall and Walton's study of Cumbria that the founders of the Cumberland and Westmorland Antiquarian and Archaeological Society, in 1866, adopted the whole region as their area of study, and it is suggested that 'an area so readily recognised by a great learned society, however pragmatically, as having some kind of inherent unity can be treated, also pragmatically, as a fit and suitable subject for examination'.[10] There was, nevertheless, much economic diversity within the region. Although throughout the period of this study agriculture remained the most important single industry, there was a great deal of industrial development during the second half of the nineteenth century, when West Cumberland and Furness emerged as centres of heavy industry. There were also obvious differences between urban and rural life, and the experience of Cumbrians in Carlisle,

Whitehaven or Barrow differed in many ways from that of those who lived in the region's remote rural areas.

Cumbria has a mountainous centre surrounded by a coastal plain, particularly wide to the north, and a further lowland area in the Eden Valley between the lakes area and the Pennines. The variety of terrain gave rise to differences in the nature of agriculture, although, overall, pasture predominated, hill farms concentrating on sheep while the lowland farmers favoured mixed farming or dairying. Most of the region's farms were unusually small, family-run affairs, and where labour was employed, it was usual for live-in farm servants to be hired by the six-monthly term. This practice declined along with the number of agricultural employees during the period under study. Because of their diversity and their minimal dependence on grain, the region's farms withstood the late Victorian and inter-war depressions in agriculture rather better than those in most other parts of the country, but in part productivity was maintained by reducing the labour force, and the farming community provided much of the outflow of migrants from the region which continued throughout our period.

Cumbria's other industries were concentrated for the most part in the coastal plain, although there was mining of various commodities in the Lake District, and lead-mining in the Pennines at Alston and Nent Head, as well as diverse small-scale industries scattered throughout the region. Much of this industry was in a less healthy state than agriculture in the late nineteenth and early twentieth centuries. Coal-mining had long been established in West Cumberland, but by the mid-nineteenth century the combination of lack of investment, thin, difficult to work seams and the unsuitability of the coal for iron-smelting had caused the industry to drift into difficulties which were not alleviated by the arrival of the railways. The development of iron-mining, iron and steelmaking and shipbuilding saved the West Cumberland economy and developed that of Furness, drawing in migrants from other regions. There were, for instance, concentrations of Cornish miners at Moor Row near Cleator Moor and Roose, near Barrow. In common with that in other areas, however, much of the region's heavy industry collapsed between the wars, and many Cumbrians suffered long-term unemployment. The Furness town of Dalton, home of a number of informants, was particularly hard hit by the collapse of iron-mining in the district. West Cumberland also suffered badly, and only in Barrow did shipbuilding survive until the Second World War.

Urban growth in the region was mostly steady and unspectacular, but Workington, thanks to its iron and steelworks, grew rapidly in the late nineteenth century, and Barrow-in-Furness expanded from a small village in the mid-nineteenth century to a town with a population of over 50,000 by 1891.[11] Barrow was developed, largely by the Dukes of Devonshire and Buccleugh, as a terminus port for the Furness Railway and an industrial centre. The town's isolation ultimately told against it, however, and this century the port, and much of the town's industry as well, stagnated. Carlisle grew steadily to a little under 50,000 by the beginning of this century, and had the most varied economy in the region. It was important as a railway centre, but had in addition biscuit manufacture and food processing, light and heavy engineering, and brass and iron founding. It was also a commercial and market centre for a wide area, and offered a wider range of female employment than most Cumbrian towns. Other market centres, such as Cockermouth and Penrith, barely held their own in the absence of industrial expansion. The population of Penrith stagnated, a significant proportion, as in rural areas, migrating, while that of Cockermouth rose only marginally. Urban development of a rather different nature took place in the lakes area, where Windermere, and to a lesser extent Keswick and Ambleside, developed as centres of tourism, and became residential enclaves for the wealthy settlers who increasingly became a feature of Lakeland life during our period. There was also some small-scale seaside resort development, notably at Grange-over-Sands and Silloth.

Despite urban growth and out- and in-migration, the population of the region was virtually static during the period under study. The number of people who derived their livelihood from the entertainments industry, however, grew markedly in the late nineteenth and early twentieth centuries. In Cumberland and Westmorland, in 1891, just 114 people were listed in the census as actors, musicians or showmen. By 1911, 550 people in the two counties were employed in the entertainments industry,[12] probably reflecting, in particular, the development of the variety theatre and cinema. Thereafter, the number engaged in entertainment seems to have remained roughly constant, there being 671 people so employed in 1931, when the census category also included professional sportsmen.[13] This growth in the numbers of professional entertainers reflects the widening variety of recreational activities which became available to the Cumbrian public during the period of this study. It should not be thought of as a measure of it, however. The region had long had a thriving leisure culture which, although it provided relatively few with a livelihood, catered for the Cumbrian's need for sport and pastime, and this culture evolved during our period. Amateur recreational activities developed alongside professional ones, the churches played an important recreational role, and the range of pastimes available to the individual in his or her own home also expanded. Shorter working hours, and in particular the increasingly adopted Saturday half-holiday, aided this expansion in recreational provision, although many people, notably domestic and farm servants and married women, did not see their leisure time increase. For the majority, however, leisure became an increasingly important part of life during the period under study.

NOTES

Place of publication London unless otherwise stated.
1 Robert W. Malcolmson, *Popular Recreations in English Society 1700–1850* Cambridge, 1973; Peter Bailey, *Leisure and Class in Victorian England,* 1978; James Walvin, *Leisure and Society 1830–1950,* 1978.
2 Three collections of studies are: J. K. Walton and J. Walvin (eds), *Leisure in Britain 1780–1939,* 1983; E. and S. Yeo (eds), *Popular Culture and Class Conflict 1590–1914* Brighton, 1981; R. D. Storch (ed.), *Popular Culture and Custom in Nineteenth-Century England,* 1982. On the music hall see: Bailey, 1978; P. Bailey (ed.) *Music Hall. The Business of Pleasure,* Milton Keynes, 1986; J. S. Bratton (ed.), *Music Hall. Performance and Style,* Milton Keynes, 1986.
3 J. D. Marshall and J. K. Walton, *The Lake Counties from 1830 to the mid-twentieth century,* Manchester, 1981, Ch. 7.
4 The argument pervades E. P. Thompson's writing. See particularly 'Patrician society, plebeian culture', *Journal of Social History,* Vol. 7, No. 4, Summer 1974, pp. 382–405.
5 J. M. Golby and A. W. Purdue, *The Civilization of the Crowd,* 1984, p. 13.
6 George Ewart Evans, *Where Beards Wag All. The Relevance of the Oral Tradition,* 1977 edn, p. 23.
7 See Appendix.
8 See Chapter V below.
9 Marshall and Walton, 1981, p. 80.
10 Marshall and Walton, 1981, p. viii.
11 Marshall and Walton, 1981, table p. 25.
12 Marshall and Walton, 1981, pp. 173, 174.
13 This figure excludes persons engaged in horse-racing and bookmakers, but other sportsmen were not separately listed. 1931 Census, Occupational Tables Volume.

CHAPTER I

Domestic and family leisure

It is generally accepted that by the early nineteenth century the culture of the middle classes was to a great extent centred on the family and home. Hugh Cunningham has suggested, further, that throughout the century there was a strong middle-class desire to extend the ideal of domestic leisure to the working classes. Motivated partly by the perceived need for social control, and partly by guilt at the unequal way in which the recreational cake had been divided by class segregation, they sought to 'refine the privatization of (working class) leisure by centering it in the home as a place of family affection and quiet pleasures'.[1] Commentators in Cumbria, as elsewhere, painted an idealised picture of the affectionate family gathered around its fireside and cited a largely mythical past when this domestic ideal had existed. A columnist in the *Whitehaven News* in 1875, for example, writing under the heading 'Home and Happiness', said: 'Recreation is a necessity of hardworking overstrained life. Men and women need it and will have it. But should they go from home to find it? Is home nothing but a place to sleep, eat and drudge in?' He went on:

> The old happy home life is disappearing – and with it is vanishing not only the truest enjoyment, but also the greatest safeguard of our social state. Miserable or guilty is the man who quits home to find enjoyment. Lost is that woman who does it. Unhappy is the son or daughter who does not find home the happiest spot on earth.[2]

Mayhew had, of course, pointed out the irrelevance of this ideal to many people. 'It is idle and unfeeling,' he said, 'to believe that the great majority of a people whose days are passed in excessive toil, and whose homes are mostly of an uninviting character, will forego *all* amusements and consent to pass their evenings by their *no* firesides reading tracts or singing hymns.'[3] Nevertheless, Gareth Stedman Jones has argued that in London from the mid-nineteenth century a popular culture 'oriented towards the family and the home' began to dominate.[4] Similarly there is evidence to suggest that, from the later nineteenth century on, the ideal of domestic and familial leisure was being recognised, and to a great extent internalised by the working classes of Cumbria.

Although the theme of the increasing domestication of leisure will reappear elsewhere in this book, the present chapter will be concerned with the pattern of domestic and private leisure which week by week formed the background to the seasonal, public and commercial recreations which Cumbrians also enjoyed. A number of domestic activities, notably needlework, gardening, or the keeping of domestic animals, occupied an ambiguous position between work, or what have been described as 'non-work obligations'[5] and recreation proper. I will examine these activities first of all. Secondly, I will consider what might be described as domestic entertainment, the diversions of members of the family and visiting friends and relations in the home. The last section of the chapter will be an examination of the pleasures and restrictions of the domestic Sunday.

QUASI-WORK ACTIVITIES

Within the home, the distinction between activities which might be classified as work and those which might be classified as leisure is very hazy. In some families the work ethic impinged on leisure time to the extent that productive activities such as sewing and gardening were actively encouraged or even enforced in preference to reading or playing games. One informant, for instance, was made to do an hour's knitting or sewing before she was allowed to pick up a book.[6] In some cases these 'work' activities were viewed primarily as worthwhile hobbies. 'We were always encouraged to have hobbies', a teacher's daughter told me. 'Mother always provided wool for knitting. She taught us. ... In the garden we all had our own little bit. And you could grow in there what you wanted. ... Then we always had pets. We always had cats. We had rabbits. ...'[7] Others, however, saw at least some of these activities more nearly as work, but as work from which it was nevertheless possible to derive great pleasure and satisfaction. The variation in attitude can best be explored by considering some of these activities separately. Gardening was an important pastime in the families of the majority of oral informants, although not in all of them. There were gardeners and non-gardeners of all social classes and occupations. There were however, few women among them. In Cumbria the pastime seems to have been almost entirely restricted to men and boys, the garden not being considered a woman's sphere. There was a handful of women among the prizewinners at horticultural shows, but they formed only a tiny minority of the whole and apart from the teacher's family already mentioned, in which children of both sexes were provided with a garden plot, only two female informants did any gardening.

Middle-class houses generally had gardens but working-class urban dwellers often did not, and allotments were, according to some oral informants, not always available,[8] although a number of interviewees had them. Parliamentary returns show that there was some provision in the area. Prior to the 1892 Smallholdings Act, which enabled local authorities to provide allotments, there were some 1,125 available in the county of Cumberland, all but 64 of them less than a quarter of an acre in size. The majority of them were in Carlisle, Workington and the mining areas of West Cumberland. Westmorland had 950, all but 22 of them of less than a quarter of an acre and of these, 640 were in Kendal. Lancashire north of the Sands had 1,001, over half of them in Barrow-in-Furness and most of the remainder in Ulverston and Dalton.[9] This concentration in urban areas suggests that most rural dwellers were provided with gardens, and interviewees confirmed that this was generally the case. It also suggests that the interest in gardening in urban areas was quite considerable, even though, as oral evidence makes clear, it was not universal. After the 1892 Act some Cumbrian Local Authorities began to provide allotments, but many more seem not to have done so.[10] Those who did tended to be in areas where allotments were already available. Those Sanitary Authorities who had made no provision at the time of enquiry, shortly after the Act came into force, all gave lack of demand as their reason for not doing so. The return for Bootle district, for instance, stated that 'The cottagers generally have plots of land along with their houses and there is no demand for additional allotments', whilst the Whitehaven Authority said, 'There does not appear to be any desire on the part of the inhabitants to acquire allotments.'[11] This last statement, of course, comes from an area in which there was already some allotment provision, and if it is true, then it would seem that the existing supply was sufficient to meet the demand. The return could, conversely, simply reflect official inertia.

Stephen Constantine has suggested that the middle classes found in gardening a solution to the moral dilemma which their leisure brought them. It required 'physical effort and some intelligence' and so enabled them to avoid the vice of idleness. It was also a home-centred occupation, 'taking place in the sanctuary they had created for themselves. The garden was for the enjoyment of the family', he continues, 'and for strengthening attachments to the family. Gardening was in brief, a "rational recreation" fostering those physical, mental, spiritual and familial values the middle class believed important.'[12] It is clear from informants that the middle-class garden was an extension of the home, used for domestic recreation, games of croquet and the like. Middle-class informants were the only ones to mention lawns, which might be considered a form of conspicuous consumption of space. Vegetables for domestic consumption were also grown, and their cultivation should probably be viewed as further evidence that the values of hard work and thrift were prevalent among the Cumbrian middle class.

The working-class garden seems to have been less a sanctuary for the family than the middle-class equivalent. No working-class informant has spoken of children playing in the garden or of time being spent there in idleness. Children played in the street or the fields while the garden was made productive. As far as the garden was concerned it would seem that the middle-class ideal of family leisure in the home had failed to take root. The working-class garden's importance lay in its productivity, and it is not difficult to find practical reasons why this should have been the case. A supply of home-grown fruit and vegetables would obviously be more important in the domestic economy of the less well off, who except in rural areas, probably had, on the whole, less garden space at their disposal. A larger garden would, of course, allow space for recreation as well as cultivation. Additionally, as has been mentioned above, many working-class gardens were in the shape of allotments, away from the house. Not actually being attached to the home, they could not form an extension to it.

Although there were working-class gardeners throughout the period under discussion, it was in the inter-war years that gardening apparently took on a new significance. This may, in part, have resulted from the increasing provision of working-class houses with gardens. By the mid-1930s there were apparently flourishing horticultural societies in, for instance, the Newtown and Raffles estates of Carlisle.[13] Another important factor was undoubtedly unemployment, which left many Cumbrian men with time on their hands and a shortage of money in their pockets. A rural informant, with a large garden of which he was passionately fond, used it during a three-year period of unemployment not only to feed his family, but to provide himself with pocket money and above all, to maintain his self-esteem. His work, from which he normally derived his self-respect, was replaced by this other masculine work activity. He talked with great pride of his success with vegetables and his standing in the community as the supplier of the finest tomatoes and the most magnificent chrysanthemums. Plants and cuttings were obtained in time of economic stringency by exchanges with other gardeners, or as payment for services rendered. He was given a grapevine as payment for sweeping a chimney.[14]

Flower and vegetable shows took place all over the region throughout the period, but they seem from press reports to have greatly increased in number after the First World War, while the average number of entries also increased. Perhaps surprisingly, however, none of my informants, or their menfolk, keen gardeners though many of them were, appear to have exhibited produce in shows.[15] This suggests that, large as they often were, numbers of entries in shows reveal only the tip of the iceberg of gardening activity. For the great majority of gardeners the straightforward pleasure to be obtained from growing produce of a high standard appears to have been sufficient. While there was evidently friendly rivalry between friends and neighbours, cuttings and advice seem to have been exchanged more or less freely, and the desire to compete formally with one another was apparently not very strong.

Stephen Constantine has suggested that horticultural societies and shows were the product of middle-class enthusiasm,[16] and this does seem to have been the case in Cumbria. It is clear from newspaper reports that even allotment societies and council estate horticultural societies had organising committees whose social class was higher than that of the membership. Directories show that there were also a number of seedsmen and market gardeners apparently combining business and pleasure by filling the role of secretary.[17] The increasing tendency, by the 1930s, for prizes to be given by gardening magazines is probably further evidence of the involvement of business interests, although even at this time, the bulk of the prizes were still supplied by the local upper and middle classes. Shows usually had open, amateur and cottager classes, the latter apparently part of the middle-class drive to extend the practice of home-centred and rational recreation further down the social scale. Those prizewinners who can be traced were a mixed bag, with the middle classes and tradesmen predominating. Working-class competitors are probably less likely to be listed in directories, however, and so they may have formed a considerable part of the untraceable majority. The existence of cottager classes suggests a working-class entry, but the definition of cottager seems to have been somewhat hazy, particularly in the earlier years, including, on one occasion, a bookseller and clerk to the Board of Guardians, a builder, and a farmer's daughter, as well as various skilled craftsmen.[18] By the inter-war period, however, the council estate and allotment society shows undoubtedly had large numbers of entries from working men, as newspaper reports occasionally made clear.[19]

The reasons this minority had for wishing to make gardening a competitive hobby can only be guessed at. Prizes seem to have been of a token kind and not sufficiently valuable to encourage entry on financial grounds, although winning must have brought with it a certain status, especially among members of a society. It is possible to reconcile the need to compete with the working-class concept of the garden as an area to be made productive, although simply growing for home consumption might be expected to make exhibition superfluous. However, the rather ambiguous status of the middle-class garden – required to be productive, but intended also to function to some extent as a shield from the competitiveness of the outside world – is somewhat harder to reconcile. Clearly for the minority, the need to display expertise, advertise a lifestyle, or perhaps to 'keep up with the Joneses' was either stronger than, or in conflict with the ideal of the domestic haven.

If we now move on to consider pet-keeping we will see that the pattern is in some ways comparable, although certain differences are apparent. Evidence for the nineteenth century is hard to come by, but newspaper reports of shows, of which there are a great many, indicate that, by the 1870s, there was already a widespread interest in domestic animals and birds in Cumbria. What relationship the numbers of entries bore to the actual number of pets in the region can only be guessed, but it seems likely that, as in the case of gardening, shows reveal only the tip of the iceberg. The more exotic kinds of poultry and cage-birds were probably kept mainly for exhibition purposes and shows during the period seem to have attracted increasingly large entries, probably accurately mirroring the growth of the fancy. At the same time, however, there must have been many pet canaries and egg-supplying hens which were never put on public show. Entries in dog shows were generally low, and there does not appear to have been any increase over the period, although it seems likely that the number of dogs rose. John Walton has suggested that dog fanciers of all classes increased steadily in number in the late Victorian period,[20] and it seems from the evidence of oral informants that numbers were still being added to in the twentieth century, several families acquiring their first dog in the inter-war period, although the most common pets were cats.

The middle-class attitude towards pets was more or less straight-forward. Domestic animals added to the comfort of the home. The cat by the fireside or the canary singing in its cage were part of the domestic idyll. In addition, caring for animals encouraged responsibility in children and required a certain amount of skill and knowledge, so that time expended in this way could be considered to have been rationally spent. The president of Carlisle Cage Bird Society encapsulated the idea when he said in his speech at the annual show in 1936 that 'efforts (of the kind represented by the show) showed . . . how they were endeavouring in this country to solve the great problem of what to do with leisure. For he knew that anyone who was going to succeed at bird rearing and exhibiting certainly had to give great time attention and devotion.'[21]

With the partial exception of poultry, middle-class pets were completely unproductive in an economic sense. Dogs, cats, rabbits, goldfish and canaries were the species kept by oral informants, but the use of directories to trace show winners indicates that poultry, fancy pigeons and a wide variety of other cage-birds were also kept by the middle classes, who were well represented among those successful.

The pet-keeping activities of the working classes were to some extent limited, in the same way that working-class gardening was, by the shortcomings of their housing. Small overcrowded houses must have militated against the inclusion of animals in the family circle, and the cost of food, particularly for dogs, was often an inhibiting factor. 'You see, there again, it was the cost of feeding them. That was the trouble you see. They couldn't afford to. To do that.'[22] Nevertheless many working-class informants, even the poorest, did keep pets, and although none of my informants seems to have done this, poultry and pigeons could, of course, be housed on allotments.

The majority of working-class informants' pets were as unproductive as those of the middle classes, particularly when they belonged to children, and they were apparently viewed in a similar way. The range of species kept by informants, cats, dogs, rabbits, and canaries and poultry, was also similar. Traceable prizewinners at poultry shows include a fair sprinkling of the working classes, but there were fewer among the winners at cage-bird shows. However a cage-bird show at Millom in 1905, which was confined to local exhibitors, had 'fifteen well filled classes', which surely indicates a sizeable working-class entry.[23] The working classes also kept a variety of animals for economic and sporting reasons. Among the latter were whippets, trail-hounds and gamecocks, and these will be considered later in the chapter on sport. Animals kept primarily or partly for economic reasons were pigs, poultry and poaching dogs, but among oral informants domestic animals were a less important source of food than gardens. Only four interviewees kept animals for this reason. A much greater interest in self-sufficiency was however noted in Barrow by Elizabeth Roberts, and it may be that my oral evidence underestimates the extent to which working-class people kept hens and reared animals for food.[24] It does nevertheless appear that the working-class attitude towards domestic pets was closer than the working-class attitude towards gardening was to prevailing middle-class opinion. Whilst the working-class garden was by and large not part of the domestic sanctuary as the middle-class garden was, pets, especially those kept by women and children, were seen as very much an intrinsic part of domestic pleasure. Poultry and pigs provided food and birds of various types were exhibited competitively, but these appear to have been only minor aspects of working-class pet-keeping.

If we now, lastly, turn to the domestic pastimes of knitting and sewing, we are able to extend the argument a little further. These activities were, of course, very largely confined to women. No man would have considered doing anything so effeminate as needlework.

These crafts, like gardening, had some economic importance to the family and this was stressed by the elementary school system which, particularly before the First World War, required girls to spend a considerable part of their time in knitting and, more especially, sewing. Carol Dyhouse suggests that the subject was more symbolically than economically important, however. 'Proficiency with a needle implied femininity, it implied thrift.'[25] As early as 1874 it had been argued by Emily Shirreff that 'needlework is not of universal importance to women'.[26] However, 'Suggestions for the teaching of needlework', a circular issued by the Board of Education in 1909, still maintained that 'it should be looked upon as a matter of shame that any girl should reach woman's estate without a practical knowledge of what use she can make of her needle'.[27]

It was, of course, not necessary for any family in Cumbria to provide all its own needlework. Mass-produced goods were available and, in addition, travelling dressmakers still moved around the rural areas, staying in the houses of customers until they had carried out the required work.[28] In only two families was most of the children's clothing made by the mother, and in both cases she had been a dressmaker prior to marriage.[29] More families, however, were partially clothed by the mothers' and daughters' efforts. The knitting of stockings and jumpers was particularly common. In other working-class families, the mother's sewing skill made a direct contribution to the family budget. A Workington informant, for instance, explained that 'my mother was very clever at sewing and she'd perhaps make a dress for a neighbour's little child . . . and get perhaps 1s 6d for it. For making it.'[30] As the informant's father was frequently kept away from work by ill health, these earnings were often crucial.

Most of the needlework which was done in the families of oral informants was of a practical nature. However, fine quality decorative needlework was produced by some Cumbrian women. One oral informant showed me beautiful embroideries which had been done by her mother and grandmother.[31] In Brampton, in 1921, a 'Town Club' was formed, the principal aim of which seems to have been the encouragement of craftwork as a rational recreation. The club's annual show in 1936 had classes for *broderie anglaise*, appliqué, quilting and many other skilled crafts. It was opened by the Bishop of Carlisle's wife, who said in her opening speech: 'There is imagination in this work done by Brampton women; a sense of individuality and personality. There is a sense of industry too, of valuable work done in leisure hours on winter evenings, when otherwise time would hang heavily on the hands and would eventually be frittered away in useless pursuits.'[32] At this time the club had 135 members in addition to its committee. Unfortunately we have no details of who these women were, and their class can only be guessed at. The Women's Institute, which spread widely in Cumbria in the inter-war years, and similarly encouraged women's crafts, did however attract both working-class and middle-class women. At the end of 1927 there were 131 WI branches in Cumbria, and by 1937 the figure had increased to 172.[33] The great majority were formed in villages, and women living in towns were rarely members.

Many agricultural shows and fêtes had classes for women's craftwork, and this points to a widespread interest in encouraging the crafts, if not in the crafts themselves, although obviously there were entries. Oral evidence does suggest that, even if it was widespread, the interest was by no means general. Possibly as women's leisure time was so ill-defined, and practical sewing needs were often so pressing, many had neither the time nor the inclination to do purely decorative work. I do not mean to suggest, however, that women never derived pleasure or satisfaction from time spent in needlework. Many undoubtedly did.

To conclude I will again look at the three main types of quasi-work activity together. Although they were not asked to do so, no oral informant attempted to define these activities either as work or leisure. There were obviously elements of both in them, and no one felt the need to draw an arbitrary line between the two. The distinction between time which was the property of an employer and time which was still the property of the individual was, on the other hand, quite clear in everyone's mind. This latter time, however, remained undifferentiated. The work ethic had penetrated the Cumbrian consciousness sufficiently to make work-type activities seem preferable during this time, and its weight may have been especially heavy on married women, the whole of whose time fell into this category. The needlecrafts of women were, of all these activities, probably the closest in spirit to work proper. Working-class gardening was, however, a close second in this respect. This is not to say that the working-class gardener derived no pleasure from his labours. Most permitted themselves the extravagance of a few flowers, but attitudes towards the garden were, on the whole, severely practical. The middle-class gardener, on the other hand, was, by and large, engaging in a worthy hobby and helping to create with his own hands the domestic haven which was his ideal. Pet-keeping was also for all classes, an ingredient of the domestic idyll, and most domestic animals were pets. Dogs, of course, also acted as guards and aids to poaching, and cats as eradicators of vermin, and other animals were sometimes kept for practical economic reasons, but oral evidence suggests that most animals were admitted to the domestic circle primarily for the pleasure and companionship they gave.

DOMESTIC ENTERTAINMENT

A great deal of leisure time spent in the home was passed in the straightforward pursuit of enjoyment. The amount and quality of domestic entertainment varied with social class and from family to family, but in general, the more money there was available for non-essentials, the greater was the family's range of amusements. It is clear that quite a high priority was placed on acquiring entertainment hardware, many working-class families owning wirelesses, gramophones, pianos and other musical instruments. They were less keen to acquire books, however, only lower middle and middle-class households, and not all of them, having any sort of a library, although lending libraries were patronised by a fair proportion of the working class.

Perhaps the widest class difference was to be found in the provision of children's toys and games. Working-class children were not in the house a great deal. If they were not wanted to help with chores then they were generally sent outside to play. 'We weren't in t'house playing. . . . It had to be round in t'back streets or outside your doors', was a typical comment.[34] The limited selection of toys which the majority had reflected this. Hoops, whips and tops, skipping ropes, diabolos and marbles were all intended to be used in the street. Some informants mention playing dominoes or, less frequently, cards when they were children, but otherwise, toys or games to provide amusement in the house are scarcely met with. A few of the economically better-off remembered receiving a single toy at Christmas. Meccano, a teddy bear and a model steam engine were mentioned.[35] Many, however, did not even receive this. Lower middle and middle-class children, on the other hand, had a wide variety of toys and games to keep them amused within the family circle. Informants remembered all sorts of board games, dolls and their accoutrements, soldiers, train sets, clockwork toys and table tennis, as well as cards and dominoes. One informant even had a magic lantern with which she gave concerts to her dolls.[36] Some also remembered the hoops, and whips and tops mentioned by working-class children, as well as scooters, pogo-sticks and stilts, and it is clear that, to some extent at least, middle-class children shared in the street life of their poorer contemporaries. While working-class informants talk mainly about playing in the streets, however, those of middle-class origin talk predominantly about amusing themselves in the home and its extension, the garden.

This class difference in the provision of toys and the supervision of children's play obviously has its basis in economics and housing conditions. However, as we shall see below, shortage of funds did not prevent many working-class families from enjoying the domestic entertainment they desired. I would suggest that this dichotomy also reflects a basic class difference in attitudes towards the leisure time of children. A number of writers have shown that during the later nineteenth century the middle classes prolonged and institutionalised the period of dependent childhood for educational and social reasons.[37] At the same time, their idealisation of the concept of the family and their earnest wish to control and direct the use of leisure time brought into existence a distinctive middle-class childhood characterised by toys and rational pursuits within the home environment. The working-class child, on the other hand, spent much of his or her time outside the home in the company of the peer group. Domestic chores apart, the working-class child had more freedom, and as far as I can ascertain, did not crave the toys which middle-class children had. The familial values of the middle class had simply not penetrated the working-class consciousness sufficiently deeply to change the way in which children were brought up.

A much greater convergence of attitudes between the middle and working classes is evident on the subject of music in the home. There was a great deal of interest in music amongst all classes and while, obviously, much music-making took place outside the home environment, the domestic dimension was quite considerable. Most middle-class informants and many of the working class as well had music lessons, usually on the piano, but sometimes on the violin. In addition, a number of working-class informants, all of them men, were self-taught musicians, the most usual instruments in this case being melodeons or mouth organs. However, these were, to a great extent, played outside the home. There were also one or two girls who had singing lessons, but this was less usual. Although there was a great deal of singing as home entertainment, most of it was without benefit of tuition. There was evidently no shortage of music teachers. Directories throughout the period list them even in small villages, while most towns had several. In Barrow-in-Furness in 1908 there were fifteen.[38] There were probably also many part-time teachers who were not listed. In addition, widespread musical expertise made it possible for a number of oral informants to be taught by relatives. Although the expense of instruments was to some extent a prohibitive factor in working-class families, where the will was strong enough, a way seems often to have been found. In a Workington family, for instance, when the eldest daughter started work, her wages were set aside to pay for a piano to be played by a younger daughter.[39]

Children's enforced practice periods apart, domestic music usually took the form of a musical evening with the family, and sometimes relatives and friends, gathered around the piano singing, usually hymns or popular songs of the day. 'Mother played the piano. We used to sing all these old songs ... "The Old Folks at Home" and all that sort of song.'[40] Although a few informants were interested in classical music, and more especially opera, these were interests which were largely pursued outside the home. Traditional music and song, similarly, were more usually to be encountered in the public house or at dances and events such as sheep clippings or shepherds' meets. One musician informant did grow up in a household where traditional music was played,[41] but the most important influence on the domestic repertoire was probably the gramophone.

Gramophones and their predecessors, phonographs, tended to be owned by those families who played music themselves, although there were a few exceptions. People were either interested in music or they were not. As in the case of instruments, cost had some bearing on the matter, and the earliest models which, like the records to be played on them, were comparatively expensive, tended to be owned by the middle classes. During the inter-war period, however, when prices were more within working-class reach, most interested informants managed to acquire one. The first electric machines also appeared in Cumbria during these years, mainly in middle-class households. Few informants could remember much about the records they played, other than that, by and large, they were the popular music of the day. Harry Lauder and George Formby were mentioned, and so were the dance bands of Henry Hall and Joe Loss. The latter, and doubtless others like them, were sometimes danced to. A girl who went to service in Ambleside in 1929 remembered dancing to the gramophone as being the servants' only entertainment.[42] Other informants remember friends and relatives visiting one another to listen to the gramophone, and so it should not be thought of solely as a means by which recreation was more firmly located within the family circle. It did, however, undoubtedly help to confine it within the home.

This applied also to the other source of domestic entertainment, the wireless, particularly in the early years when there were fewer about. People would be invited into neighbours' houses to listen. Although a few informants did not own one until after the Second World War, most people acquired a set during the 1920s or 1930s. Again the middle classes led the way, but the working classes were not far behind. At least five informants had their wirelesses made by members of the family or neighbours, which suggests that the apparatus itself quickly became a hobby for the technically minded. The broadcasts provoked rather mixed feelings, but most informants agreed on the novelty value of the wireless as entertainment; 'it was a wonderful thing to hear this. I mean it was amazing',[43] and 'It was a novelty to think you could put these things on your ears and hear somebody talking.'[44] Until loudspeakers became available, listening had to be done through headphones. Some wirelesses had several sets, but where there was only one, members of the family had to take it in turns, or else contrive to swivel them in the sockets so that two people could each listen with one ear. Whatever the case, listening to the wireless was necessarily a family occupation. As the sound was only faint, complete quiet was needed: 'you sat around the fire, with these headphones on and if anybody coughed or made a noise somebody said "shh" . . . everyone decided they'd listen to the wireless and everyone sat down . . . the whole family had to be listening'.[45] After the advent of loudspeakers (which may have been a little late in reaching Cumbria), this was less the case. People were free to move around and listen to the wireless while engaged in other activities. By and large, however, the wireless remained as family entertainment in its own right in pre-war Cumbria. It did not merely become a background to other activities.

The other major domestic pastime was reading. Here, class differences are once again discernible, the middle classes, as stated above, being more likely to own books and to view reading as a worthwhile pastime. In the twentieth century the differential is only one of degree, however, many working-class informants being avid readers. The picture for the period before living memory is rather more difficult to draw. By the 1870s the great majority of Cumbrians were literate to the extent that they could sign their name in the marriage register. The rural areas had slightly higher literacy rates than the urban and industrial areas, the figures for selected districts varying between 94.9 and 76.7 per cent for men and 92.5 and 68.2 per cent for women. The lower figure in each case was for Whitehaven.[46] The figures for the country as a whole were 82.4 per cent for men and 75.7 per cent for women, so much of Cumbria was above average in this respect. By the decade 1891–1900 the percentage of people married in Carlisle who were not able to sign the register was only 1.22.[47] It is, however, difficult to assess how far this apparent literacy was put to recreational use. From the mid-nineteenth century onwards, there were private circulating libraries in existence in both towns and rural areas. Many of them were small affairs like that at Sebergham, which in 1860 had 300 volumes and forty subscribers,[48] but others appear to have been rather more flourishing concerns. It may be supposed that these institutions catered for the middle-class reader, and subscription rates lend support to this, the figures for Atkinson and Pollitt's library in Kendal, which boasted of the largest and best selection of books in the county, being 10s 6d a year, 6s 6d a half-year or 4s a quarter.[49] These libraries were declining in number in the late nineteenth century, although in places, for instance in Ulverston, they continued into the 1930s.[50] Their continuance was probably adversely affected by the availability of cheaper books from the late nineteenth century onwards.

In addition to the private libraries, there were also a great many mechanics institutes in existence during the mid-Victorian years, many of them possessing lending libraries. The one at Brampton reported in 1860 that 1,400 books had been issued during the year. Subscriptions at this institute were 1s 6d a quarter, so it is possible that there were working-class members, although a study of the mechanics institute in Carlisle found that this was not largely the case there. Lists of members are composed of 'professional and business people, farmers, shopkeepers, clerks, shop assistants and some skilled working men'.[51] These institutes were also declining in the later nineteenth century, by which time there were many working men's reading rooms and working men's institutes in existence. These were probably more genuinely working class, but not all of them had lending libraries. Many seem to have functioned more as social clubs where billiards and cards were played. However, the Kendal Working Men's Institute in 1890 issued 7,580 volumes to an unspecified number of members who paid 6d a quarter subscription.[52]

When the first public libraries were rather belatedly opened in Cumbria under the 1850 Act, from the 1880s onwards, a number of them were based on mechanics institute or working men's reading room libraries. Penrith library, for instance, which was opened in 1883, was housed in what had been the premises of the working men's reading room, its initial book stock being the library of that institution plus that of the mechanics institute, as well as certain donations and purchases.[53] Both the Carlisle and Whitehaven libraries, opened in 1891 and 1888 respectively, were based on mechanics institute libraries. The Libraries Act had also been adopted by 1891 in Arlecdon and Frizington, Barrow, Kendal, Millom and Workington.[54] Many more had been opened by the beginning of the First World War, the funds of Andrew Carnegie being instrumental in a number of cases.

The class of library borrowers in the late nineteenth century is unknown. In the twentieth century oral evidence indicates that there were a large number of borrowers from both the middle and working classes. However, those who were not library members were most likely to be working class. One or two middle-class families still subscribed to private libraries.[55]

Books borrowed from public libraries were for the most part fiction. Estimates for 1891 vary from 50 per cent in Millom to 87 per cent in Penrith and these figures are more or less in line with those for the country as a whole where, on average, roughly two-thirds of library borrowings were fiction.[56] This suggests that most books were read for entertainment as opposed to self-improvement. Few informants remember the books they read. Titles recalled were a mixture of classics and the current fiction of the day. However, one informant said that her father, a farmer, liked to read history.[57]

None of my informants was forbidden to read in the house. However, Elizabeth Roberts did find that reading was prohibited in some working-class families in Barrow-in-Furness.[58] Among my informants, active encouragement of reading was most likely to come from middle-class parents. Middle-class households were also the only ones to contain collections of books of any size. Not all of them had literary tastes. In one Penrith household the library consisted of novelettes, of which the mother was very fond.[59] At the other end of the spectrum, an Urswick family often passed the time reading Shakespeare plays around the kitchen fire.[60]

Most families took a newspaper. There was great variety in the one chosen, some families taking a national daily, others a local daily or weekly such as the *Lancashire Evening Post* or the *Westmorland Gazette*, and still others a Sunday paper only, usually the *News of the World*. Amongst informants, middle-class families were more likely to take a daily paper, but there was no hard and fast rule. The *News of the World* was apparently only read in working-class families, however, and it was generally kept from the children. 'You weren't allowed to see any scandal or anything like that in our days', explained an informant. 'They were very strict.'[61] Otherwise most informants seem to have had free access to newspapers. By the end of the nineteenth century most of the local papers had begun to print a women's column, consisting of helpful hints and comments on fashion, etc. These appear to have increased in importance in the early twentieth century, with recipes and diagrams for dress patterns being added. This perhaps indicates that the female readership was believed to have increased. Amongst oral informants, female readers of newspapers were as numerous as men, but there is no way of knowing whether this was equally true one or two generations earlier. There had, of course, been a slight gender differential in literacy. Children's columns also appeared in most papers before the First World War. The local press was, in fact, becoming more family oriented and aiming to entertain as well as inform. The addition of photographs helped in this transformation, which may in part have been a response to radio's usurpation of the news function.

Magazines were not widely read and it may be that the newspapers filled this role for the adult population. Comics were mainly read by the generation of children who grew up between the wars, although one slightly older informant remembered reading them.[62] Probably for financial reasons, few working-class children received them regularly. While some comic readers were also avid readers of books, others were not, and there is no apparent correlation between parents encouraging reading and buying comics for their children. They were perhaps, more than anything, a part of the home-centred leisure culture of the middle-class child.

By the inter-war period, Cumbrians of all classes were finding a great deal of their entertainment within their own four walls. The range of domestic pleasures was greatly widened by the technical developments which resulted in the gramophone and wireless. It was widened also by the provision of libraries which (perhaps aided by compulsory education) greatly increased the numbers of people who were able to find pleasure in reading. It is, however, difficult to assess how much of the individual's leisure time was spent in this way, and whether the amount was increasing. Did the wireless and gramophone encourage people to spend a greater part of their leisure time in the home; or was the speed with which these novelties found favour rather an indication that there was already in existence a 'captive audience' of home-centred families, waiting to be entertained? I would suggest that it was a little of both. Although the additions to the range of domestic entertainment were greeted with enthusiasm, the ideal of home and family-centred leisure was, by this century, firmly established in the region.

SUNDAY

Attendance at religious services occupied for some families the greater part of Sunday. Many others attended church once during the day and even non-attenders usually despatched their children to Sunday School. The importance of the churches in Cumbrian life will however, be discussed later on in Chapter V. In this chapter I will consider that part of the day which was not taken up by religious worship.

Although Sunday was the one full day of leisure most working people had, its pleasures were to a great extent circumscribed by Sabbatarian restrictions. Throughout the nineteenth century, argument had raged around public and commercial recreation on Sunday. Many critics maintained that the closure on Sundays of places of rational amusement had driven people to the public houses.[63] No complaint, naturally, was made about the possibility that these restrictions encouraged people to spend the day at home, but this of course was the other side of the coin. Given that the cult of the fireside was gaining ground at the expense of more riotous pleasures, it may well have been that Sabbatarianism was instrumental in the development of an essentially domestic Sunday. There is no doubt that it was, by the early twentieth century, very much, although not wholly, a day to be spent with the family, either at home or out walking or visiting. There was a widely expressed feeling that 'Sunday was Sunday',[64] and as such required a greater degree of decorum than other days of the week. That 'we didn't do what we would have done on weekdays'.[65] Informal football was banned, for instance. Two informants who as youths used to go for walks on Sunday afternoons with others of their peer group (who had become too grown up for the family walk) said that

> We just used to play a little bit of football on the sneak, when we got . . . well out of the town. Somebody'd bring a ball out and we'd have a little game on the Q.T. But our parents hadn't to get to know that we'd been playing football on a Sunday.

You'd be sent to St Helena or somewhere like that.[66]

Walks, in fact, seem to have been the only permitted outdoor activity, and a ritual which virtually all families engaged in, irrespective of class. Many informants explained that 'On a Sunday afternoon all the families used to be out walking, you know. Mothers and fathers and children.'[67] The only exceptions to the family rule were courting couples and young men, who after a certain age walked with their friends. The other usual activity, again common to all classes, was visiting the homes of friends or more particularly relatives, still usually as a family group. A Langdale farmer's daughter explained that 'Really, every Sunday was a kind of a party, in the way that, you know, cousins, aunties, uncles used to come and have tea.'[68]

Restrictions extended also to the recreational activities which took place within the home. A number of informants spoke of certain domestic pastimes being prohibited or restricted on Sundays. Those variously mentioned were reading (especially novels and newspapers), sewing and knitting, and playing games, particularly cards. No informant spoke of any prohibition of gardening or of music in any form. It is difficult to suggest reasons why certain activities should have been singled out in this way. Because of their association with gambling, cards were completely banned in some families. Perhaps where they were vetoed only on Sundays, we are seeing a modified version of the same moral objection to them. While one informant explained that 'we never played cards on a Sunday. No, we didn't. We drew the line there',[69] others drew the line rather less liberally. Reading was an activity upon which opinion was polarised. It was either a trivial pastime, unsuited to the Sabbath (hence the particular ban on novels and newspapers), or it was the preferred indoor activity of the day, quiet, restrained and improving. Knitting and sewing were perhaps too close to being work activities to be acceptable on the day of rest, but paradoxically, there was no objection to gardening. Possibly practicality overrode piety in this instance, the necessary daylight leisure hours being at too great a premium for the activity to be vetoed on Sunday. Music, whether performed or listened to on the gramophone, was essentially a family activity and as such it was a suitable diversion for the day which was devoted to family togetherness. Some informants did mention singing or listening to records of hymns on Sundays, but this was in addition to and not instead of the secular music which generally prevailed.

These Sabbatarian principles appear to have grown out of, on the one hand, religious belief, and on the other out of the general consensus as to what constituted respectability. This second force was apparently of universal importance among informants and may be illustrated by the existence of a perceived need to possess Sunday clothes whenever humanly possible. This being so, it might be expected that the family's religion would be the crucial factor in deciding on the degree to which Sunday recreation was restricted. There was, however, no apparent denominational pattern.[70] Families nominally of the same religion could differ widely in attitude. Whether the variation resulted from different depths of religious feeling is difficult to assess as informants were not questioned about their religious beliefs. It would seem however that at least part of the explanation for the differing degrees of restriction must lie in varying interpretations of, or aspirations towards, respectability. Whereas some families were apparently satisfied with showing a respectable demeanour to the world at large, others had internalised the concept to the extent that it pervaded their private domestic life.

It should be said at this point that informants were particularly prone to contradicting themselves when talking about this subject. This could indicate that there was a gap between the behaviour which was considered proper for Sunday and the pursuits which were actually enjoyed, the theory and the reality having become confused (possibly deliberately) in people's minds. Alternatively, it could mean that attitudes were being re-evaluated in the early twentieth century, and that restrictions were not being consistently applied in individual families. The second interpretation is perhaps strengthened by the testimony of middle-class informants who seem on the whole to have had a less restricted Sunday. A change in the opinions of society on such a subject might have been expected to emanate from these groups.

The middle classes were also the possessors of the first motor cars, which by the Second World War were transforming the family's day of leisure. A Penrith family, for instance, when they acquired their first car, gradually abandoned Sunday School and walks to place flowers in the cemetery in favour of the delights of Silloth.[71] It was still a family Sunday, but its dimensions had been extended beyond the range of the existing framework of behavioural rules. Slightly lower down the social scale, one or two informants possessed motor cycles, and these similarly opened up the possibilities of Sunday. Most usually they were the transport of the young and single, and once again they replaced the Sunday walk. It was, of course, this younger generation who were to take part in the transformation of Sunday leisure in the post-war period.

CONCLUSION

It is obviously not possible to ascertain whether Cumbrians were spending more of their leisure time at home in the 1930s than they had been in the 1870s. It is however, quite clear that the range of home-based recreations widened considerably for all classes during that period, and it is apparent that the concept of home-based family leisure was spreading.

For the middle classes, gardening became a highly respectable hobby, which helped them to avoid the sin of idleness, while at the same time enhancing the domestic environment and helping to make a haven of the middle-class home. Garden ownership among the working classes was extended by improvements in housing between the wars, and if for them the pastime was more closely related to the family's subsistence, it was at the same time, for many men, a hobby and a source of pride. Gardening clubs and produce and horticultural shows consequently spread and flourished in the region.

Pet-keeping also appears to have expanded as the dog fancy and, more particularly, an interest in exotic cage birds and poultry developed. This, too, was rational recreation, demanding knowledge and expertise, and occupying leisure hours within the home.

Pet-keeping was also an integral aspect of the 'domestic idyll', an ideal which, encouraged in some cases by improved housing conditions, was increasingly being subscribed to by working-class people as well as the middle classes. The keeping of animals for economic reasons appears, on the other hand, from my evidence, not to have been either a very widespread or growing pastime. Domestic animals were, it seems, becoming primarily pets.

The craft activities of Cumbrian women were never as overtly recreational, and in a number of families they continued to be of practical importance. The symbolic importance also, in part, remained, and skill with a needle was still considered a feminine virtue by some of the middle classes, and by the schools, where the subject was stressed for working-class girls. Between the wars, however, perhaps due in part to the growth of the Women's Institute, increasing recognition was given to the artistic value of women's needlecrafts, and competitions and exhibitions began to be organised, elevating needlework from women's work to rational recreation.

Domestic entertainment *per se* widened considerably in range during our period. In the early years the most usual entertainments would have been music or singing with some card-playing and reading. Domestic music continued throughout our period, and the advent of rate-supported libraries from the late nineteenth century on extended reading to those of the working classes to whom it appealed. The great developments in domestic entertainment were, however, the new inventions of the twentieth century, the gramophone and the wireless, which were rapidly and eagerly acquired by all classes. Whether these novelties increased home-centredness is difficult to assess. They probably led to an increased amount of domestic entertaining as friends or relatives called to 'listen in' or hear the latest 78s, and the wireless in particular must have brought a new dimension to 'staying in' by bringing the outside world into the domestic circle.

The cornerstone of home-centredness was the domestic Sunday, and this was probably already well established by the start of our period. Sabbatarianism appears to have merged imperceptibly into domesticity, and although some older pleasures were restricted, there were apparently no strictures against the gramophone or wireless, which were considered to be acceptable family entertainment. Sunday broadcasts were of course suited to the day. Although the motor car was beginning to transport the family beyond the confines of the home before the Second World War, the family Sunday, and home-centredness in general, were central to recreational life in inter-war Cumbria. Home was by then, for the great majority, much more than just 'a place to sleep eat and drudge in'.

NOTES

Place of publication London unless otherwise stated.

1 Hugh Cunningham, *Leisure in the Industrial Revolution*, 1980, pp. 88–9.
2 *W.N.*, 9.9.1875.
3 Quoted in Cunningham, 1980, p. 89.
4 G. Stedman-Jones, 'Working-class culture and working-class politics in London 1870–1900', *Journal of Social History*, vii, 1974, p. 485.
5 See, for instance, Stanley Parker, 'Relations between Work and Leisure' in M. A. Smith, S. Parker and C. S. Smith (eds.), *Leisure and Society in Britain*, 1973, pp. 75–85.
6 Respondent 14.
7 Respondent 2.
8 Respondents 16, 18 and 20.
9 P.P. 1890, LVII 323 (C6144).
10 Official returns peter out in the early twentieth century.
11 P.P. 1892, LXVIII 37 (310 Sess. 1).
12 S. Constantine, 'Amateur gardening and popular recreation in the 19th and 20th centuries', *Journal of Social History*, 14 (3), 1981, pp. 389–90.
13 *C.J.*, 21.8.1936.
14 Respondent 15.
15 Information relating to fathers is perhaps not particularly reliable.
16 Constantine, 1981, p. 389.
17 *Bulmer's Directory of Furness and Cartmel*, 1910; *Kelly's Directory of Cumberland*, 1938.
18 *Bulmer's Directory of Westmorland*, 1885; *C.J.*, 17.8.1883.
19 See, for example, *C.J.*, 1.9.1936.
20 John K. Walton, 'Mad dogs and Englishmen: the conflict over rabies in late Victorian England, *Journal of Social History*, 13(2), 1979–80.
21 *C.J.*, New Year Supplement, 1936.
22 Respondent 12.
23 *W.N.*, 12.1.1905.
24 Elizabeth Roberts, personal communication.
25 Carol Dyhouse, *Girls Growing up in Late Victorian and Edwardian England*, 1981, p. 89.
26 E. Shirreff, *Journal of the Women's Education Union*, 15.5.1874, quoted in Dyhouse, 1981, p. 88.
27 Quoted in Dyhouse, 1981, p. 89.
28 Respondent 33 was such a dressmaker.
29 Respondents 2 and 12.
30 Respondent 11.
31 Respondent 12.
32 *C.J.*, 3.4.1936.
33 Lynn Thompson, 'The Growth and Spread of the Women's Institute Movement in the North West during the 1920s and the 1930s', unpublished paper 1988.
34 Respondent 4.
35 Respondents 9, 31 and 25.
36 Respondent 21.

37 See J. R. Gillis, *Youth and History. Tradition and Change in European Age Relations 1770–Present*, 1974: Dyhouse, 1981, *passim*.
38 *Bulmer's Directory of Furness and Cartmel*, 1908.
39 Respondent 11.
40 Ambleside respondent Z.
41 Respondent 6.
42 Ambleside respondent AB.
43 Respondent 23.
44 Respondent 13.
45 Respondent 23.
46 J. D. Marshall and J. K. Walton, *The Lake Counties from 1830 to the mid-twentieth century. A study in regional change*, Manchester, 1981, Table 6.1, p. 142.
47 T. B. Graham, 'Some Aspects of Working Class Adult Education in 19th Century Carlisle', unpublished. M. Phil. dissertation, University of Nottingham, 1972, p. 288.
48 C.J., 13.1.1860.
49 W.G., 1.1.1870.
50 Respondent 22.
51 Graham, 1972, p. 76.
52 W.G., 4.1.1890.
53 Kelly's Directory of Cumberland and Westmorland, 1925; T. Greenwood, *Public Libraries: A History of the Movement and a manual for the Organisation and Management of Rate Supported Libraries*, 1894, p. 127.
54 Greenwood, 1894, Table of Statistics in Appendix, no page number.
55 Respondents 10 and 22.
56 Greenwood, 1894, Table of Statistics.
57 Respondent 22.
58 Elizabeth Roberts, *Working-Class Barrow and Lancaster 1890–1930*, Lancaster, 1976, p. 56.
59 Respondent 21.
60 Respondent 7.
61 Respondent 18.
62 Respondent 25.
63 See for instance Cunningham, 1980, pp. 85–6.
64 Respondent 32.
65 Respondent 11.
66 Respondents 30 and 31.
67 Respondent 13.
68 This Ambleside respondent had not been allocated a code letter when I read the transcript of the interview. The informant was born in 1912.
69 Respondent 1.
70 If one excludes Quakers, who apparently as a group imposed no restrictions.
71 Respondent 21.

CHAPTER II

The leisure calendar

INTRODUCTION

This chapter will be concerned with the annually recurring festivals, the high days and holidays, which punctuated and provided the framework for the recreational year. These festivals had not been observed in an unchanging manner during the first three-quarters of the nineteenth century. It was said by John Richardson, a Keswick man, in 1876 that 'many periodical customs have disappeared within the memory of persons now living and still more if we go back another generation or so'.[1] This was undoubtedly true. In this region, as elsewhere, seasonal observances which had become irrelevant to contemporary life were allowed to lapse, while those which offended against the standards of local elites were subject to attack and suppression. This process continued during the period of my study.

The most important festive occasions in late nineteenth-century Cumbria as a whole were the major calendar festivals, Christmas and New Year, Easter and Whitsuntide. Guy Fawkes Night was also widely observed, and rushbearing still took place in a few villages. Shrove Tuesday was, at the beginning of the nineteenth century, the occasion for 'barring out' and cockfights in the schools, but by the mid-century it was only marked, as it is now, by the consumption of pancakes. An additional holiday, August Bank Holiday, was added to the calendar in 1871, and this was observed increasingly generally during the period. As a modern development, it was given shape mainly by the leisure industries, and these also had an impact on the form of all the traditional holidays, the celebration of which was, in some cases, greatly altered by the 1930s. A number of the observances which had been associated with them had by then disappeared. Other customs continued, 'not because of inertia or of conservatism', but because they still had 'important roles to play within the contemporary social settings'.[2] Where necessary, these were modified into acceptability, and in some cases they were 'folklorised', subtly altered in form to become spectacles for consumption by a passive audience. There were also instances of a new custom being instigated apparently to fill the gap left by the demise of an older one, and these functioned in a similar way to those they had replaced.

By the 1930s, also, the summer holiday habit was beginning to spread. Although it did not become general among the region's working classes until after the Second World War, oral evidence indicates that most middle-class families were already taking an annual holiday at the seaside or in Scotland by 1914. Some even travelled abroad, and this became more usual between the wars. The spread of the holiday habit to the working classes was limited by financial considerations and by the widespread lack of a paid summer holiday, which did not become usual until the 1930s. Some working-class informants then enjoyed stays in Blackpool, Morecambe, the Isle of Man and places further afield, but there were more who did not have holidays. Nationally in 1937, fifteen million people out of a population of forty-six million were taking holidays of a week or more,[3] and the proportion of holidaymakers would seem from oral evidence to have been about the same in Cumbria. Some families were simply too poor, but others who enjoyed a reasonable standard of living apparently never considered taking a holiday. The idea was not really integrated into the region's popular culture. Enjoyment was to be had near to home of course, and local beaches and beauty spots were well used by picnickers, who perhaps felt no need to travel further afield. Because summer holidays were slow to take hold in the region, the traditional holidays remained of central importance in the leisure calendar.

CHRISTMAS

Throughout our period Christmas was the most important of all the calendar festivals. The most recent writer on the subject of Christmas, John Golby,[4] has argued that the old twelve-day Christmas festival was effectively suppressed by the Puritans in the seventeenth century. Although the holiday continued to be celebrated by the gentry and aristocracy, those lower down in the social hierarchy preferred to keep New Year as the major midwinter festival until the Victorian period, when the Christmas holiday reappeared in a recognisably modern form, initially among the middle classes, but later more generally. Golby attributes this reappearance to an increased standard of living, which enabled people to emulate the habits of their social superiors; to the paternalist distribution of charity at this season, which he believes increased during the nineteenth century, and which helped, deliberately or otherwise, to spread the habit of celebration among the recipient classes; and thirdly, to pressure from the state, which was attempting, via factory legislation, to standardise the pattern of holidays within the country. As the holiday began to increase in popularity, commercial interests, particularly the food and drink trades, sought to promote it as a time of celebration and so the festival gradually gained impetus.

This argument seems to me to be basically invalid. I would suggest that Golby greatly overestimates the extent of Puritan success in permanently suppressing the festivities associated with Christian festivals, and that he is wrong in claiming that the festival ceased to be popularly celebrated. Undoubtedly there were attacks on popular culture, but it is uncertain how widespread they were, and their impact, according to Martin Ingram, 'remains in doubt'.[5] Moving forward, William Hone in the early nineteenth century reports many customs and celebrations attached to the Christmas season, which (if their age can only be guessed at) were no part of the Victorian Christmas, and which suggest a longstanding tradition of celebration. It may be that there was, as E. P. Thompson has suggested, a florescence of popular culture in the eighteenth century,[6] and I am not suggesting that all Christmas traditions predate the Puritans. What I am arguing is that the festival continued to be popularly celebrated between the seventeenth and nineteenth centuries, and that what took place in the Victorian period was reform, not reinstatement.

There seems to be little doubt that the festival was continuously celebrated in Cumbria. Certainly there is consensus among nineteenth-century writers that this was the case. Daniel Scott, for instance, tells us that 'Befitting its importance in the calendar Christmas seems to have always held the first place in popularity among the holidays and festivals of the year.'[7] John Richardson agrees that 'Of all the seasons of the year which were marked by our ancestors with particular observances, Christmas was perhaps the most noted . . . in no part of the island were Christmas customs more observed than among the hills of Cumberland and Westmorland.'[8] Although evidence is scarce, these assertions would seem to be valid. The *Times Telescopes* for 1825 and 1829 describe Twelfth Night or Old Christmas Day parties in Cumberland at which special dishes were served and tar barrels burnt;[9] and in the later nineteenth century traces of the customary twelve-day festival are still discernible. Although the whole period was not a holiday from work, the season still has the unity associated by Golby with the pre-Puritan Christmas, which makes it difficult to distinguish between Christmas and New Year celebrations. Waits, for instance, might be in evidence on either occasion, while mummers could be out on any day within the period. Christmas Day was, as far as can be discerned, kept as a holiday. I have found no evidence of people working on this day. New Year's Day was also generally a holiday, although it was not a Bank Holiday, and Boxing Day, made a Bank Holiday in 1871, was also partly and increasingly observed, although it did not immediately become universal. We are told that in Kendal at Christmas 1887, 'several mills and workshops had two days' holiday', not that the inhabitants as a whole enjoyed a two-day break.[10] By the inter-war period the Christmas festival had been more or less reduced to the two days' public holiday, and it was firmly centred on the home and family. New Year was a separate and largely public celebration which sometimes extended to two days, notably in Scottish-influenced Carlisle, but was more usually just one.

Christmas in mid-Victorian Cumbria was celebrated on various levels. In rural areas it was usual for the gentry to entertain their tenants and poorer neighbours. On Christmas Day 1869, for instance, Sir R. Brisco, Bart., of Crofton Hall, entertained his estate employees to dinner and an evening of dancing, songs and tales, 'each guest contributing his quota to the amusements of the evening'.[11] Among farming families, house visiting seems to have been the rule, neighbours visiting one another in turn during the holiday season, to eat seasonal delicacies, drink, sing, dance and play cards, while numbers of the urban and rural working classes, women as well, gathered at public house 'Murry Neets' or 'Auld Wife Hakes' for entertainment of a similar nature.[12] Change was already taking place, however, and by the turn of the century the picture was altered. As early as 1844, William Howitt, speaking of rural England as a whole, had been regretting the privatisation of the festival and in particular the demise of the gentry's practice of keeping open house. He blamed the decline of this custom and its replacement with gifts of meat or coal on the growth of social divisions, which caused those invited to the 'big house' to 'feel it as a condescension and not as springing out of the heartiness of old customs'.[13] In Cumbria this change seems to have come later, but certainly there are signs of increasing social distinction at these events towards the end of the century. By 1890, for instance, Mr and Mrs Montaigne Crackanthorpe of Newbiggin Hall were entertaining their 'tenantry and parishioners' in the barn.[14] In the twentieth century entertainments such as these are no longer reported in the press and would appear to have died out.

If increasing social divisions were helping to bring about the demise of the old Christmas traditions, they were not directly instrumental in creating the 'modern' Christmas which was taking their place. Howitt, while regretting the privatisation of Christmas, at the same time spoke approvingly of 'jolly old Christmas – the festival of the fireside – the most domestic and heartfelt carnival of the year'.[15] What he is here describing is the middle-class ideal of Christmas, which was spreading to and being accepted by all classes in Cumbria in the later nineteenth century. In the face of this, farmhouse visiting seems very largely to have dwindled away, although this is difficult to document. Public house 'Murry Neets' likewise declined and disappeared, and although this was in part a result of the narrowing socal role of the public house and the decline in the numbers of licensed premises, it was also in some measure a result of the privatisation and domestication of Christmas. The two processes were interrelated as the modern Christmas both filled the vacuum created by the demise of old customs, while at the same time its development allowed the older pattern of celebration to fade away largely unmourned. Stang riding, the carrying of an individual through the streets astride a pole, to the derision of the local inhabitants, was, for instance, once a widespread custom in the region on New Year's Day. Elsewhere in Britain this was generally a community sanction against a perceived wrongdoer such as an adulterer or a wife-beater, but in Cumbria such information as we have suggests that, latterly at least, any individual might be seized. The custom was probably validated by the prevailing holiday spirit, and it was used as an excuse for the extortion of drink and money, the person concerned being permitted to escape if he agreed to treat his captors. The custom faded quietly away in the early twentieth century.[16] The waits, who went from house to house after midnight, saluting each person by name and collecting small sums of money, disappeared from everywhere except Milnthorpe (where they were preserved as a curiosity of folklore), having become an intrusion on domestic privacy. The Christmas mummers came to be viewed in the same way, and were, by the 1890s, said to be 'very little appreciated and ... fast dying out'.[17] At Brough, the ceremony of Carrying the Holly likewise ceased, and as an illustration of the factors which were at work, it will be useful to look at this in a little more detail.

The observance of Holly Night, as it was otherwise called, probably came to an end around 1875, although there is some dispute about this. The *Penrith Observer* for that year described the event as an extant custom, but there are no further reports, and a local directory states that it ceased to be observed around 1860.[18] The custom took place on 4 January, Old Christmas Eve. A young tree was decked with lighted tapers and carried around the town accompanied by the town band and followed by the townspeople in procession, many of them carrying lighted torches. Fireworks were let off, and when the tree was nearly burnt out it was thrown to the crowd who, having formed 'sides' based on two rival inns, fought for possession of it, the winners carrying it to the hostelry they represented. The landlord, 'who derives his benefit from the numbers the victory attracts', rewarded his supporters with 'an ample allowance of ale'. A fiddler was in attendance, and a 'merry night' ensued, with dancing till morning.[19] It was held by learned contemporaries that the Brough tree was symbolic of the star which guided the three wise men to Bethlehem.[20] They often spoke of it as a 'holy' and not a holly tree, and indeed, Hone tells us that in the early nineteenth century the tree used was an ash.[21] The origins of the festival are unknown, but Pimlott tells us that the use of lights and evergreens has always been associated with Christmas.[22] The widely held belief that the festival was originally decorous and religious enabled local elites to condemn the mid-nineteenth-century form of the festival as degenerate. The *Westmorland Gazette* in 1850 lamented that 'the exhibition has sadly degenerated. The tree is anything but a holy tree and the star only lighted its followers into the quagmires of intemperance and disorder', some of them being 'soused in the river' on the way.[23] Counter-attractions were attempted with some success. In 1849 a temperance soirée was organised as an alternative to the 'demoralizing scene, ending in drunkenness', and despite the 'alluring scene being exhibited in the street', which furnished some of the lecturers with subject matter, the room was well filled.[24] In 1860, which could have been about the time of the custom's demise, the vicar and schoolmaster began a new Christmas tree tradition in Brough, by providing a German-style tree in the school on Twelfth Day, ten feet high and laden with presents for the children. We are told that

The tree being a novelty in this town it was visited during the day by
many from a distance and in the evening the schoolroom was crowded.
After tea ... the tapers on the tree were lit and the effect of all the
lights at once seemed almost magical and fairy like. The evening was
spent in singing and social converse.[25]

Whether a counter-attraction or a substitute, this new tradition
quickly took root and became an annual event. It would seem that the
tree had been successfully tamed to become part of an increasingly
decorous and child-centred Christmas.

The press yields no evidence of police suppression of Holly Night
or of prosecutions arising from it. Press coverage of Brough is,
however, always patchy, no newspaper being printed in the town.
Changing attitudes and counter-attractions were probably sufficient to
bring about the custom's demise, although there is a possibility that the
loss of public house patronage could have been a contributory factor.
As the date of the custom's discontinuance is open to dispute there
cannot be any certainty about this, however. The rival inns, whose
supporters contended for the tree were, according to the *Westmorland
Gazette*, the Swan and the Bull.[26] Directories list a White Swan and a
Black Bull in the town until 1869, but by 1885 the White Swan is no
longer listed, and has presumably ceased to exist.[27] The loss of support
for one of the contending 'sides' would doubtless have been a blow, but
it seems likely that an alternative hostelry could have been found, had
demand from the participants been strong enough. We do not however
know whether any action was taken in the matter by the licensing
magistrates. Pressure may have been exerted behind the scenes to bring
the festival to an end.

The trend towards a privatised domestic Christmas also affected
more decorous amusements. In the later nineteenth century, many
chapels, to accommodate the faithful's wish to celebrate Christmas and
to provide rational recreation on a public holiday, held tea parties and
entertainments on Christmas Day. At Keld in 1875, for instance, two
to three hundred people took tea in the Independent Chapel, after
which 'an excellent sermon was preached'.[28] At that time other public
social events also took place on the 25th. In 1879 at Ulpha there was a
Christmas Day entertainment of songs and recitations in the schoolroom.[29] After the turn of the century, such gatherings as these are no
longer taking place on the 25th. The general adoption of a Boxing Day
holiday meant, of course, that events could take place on that day

instead, and a wide variety of social and sporting events did come to be held on the 26th. Christmas Day at home with the family was clearly the norm by this time, however, and with one exception, social events did not spread over the two days. The exception was football.

Although Boxing Day matches were more usual, quite a significant number of both Rugby and Association fixtures were played on the 25th. Some teams played on both days. It is difficult to account for this anomaly. Football would, on the whole, involve young single men, who would perhaps have begun to fit a little uneasily into the domestic circle. Whatever the explanation, the ideal of a domestic Christmas Day evidently did not extend as far as the football pitch before the Second World War, or for some time after it.

No oral informant remembered going out to organised social events on Christmas Day, not even football. Some, more usually the middle classes, visited or received relatives, and to a lesser extent friends, but the majority spent Christmas at home, with the immediate family. 'I don't remember relatives coming much to my parents' home on Christmas Day. I think they mostly liked to stay in their own homes', and 'Just all of us at home. Just as a family. The traditional turkey dinner and that and just all of us', were typical comments.[30] Boxing Day was more usually the day for visiting or going to the theatre or to play or watch sport, although the poverty of many working-class families probably precluded the entertainment of visitors.

The new ideal of the family Christmas was, says J. A. R. Pimlott, 'part of the profound changes which revolutionised economic and social relationships and the general outlook on life'.[31] By the end of the Victorian period these changes had made the Christmas tree, gifts and Santa Claus into established traditions in Cumbria as they were elsewhere in the country. These newer traditions were mainly directed at making the festival a magical occasion for children (as we have seen, above, at Brough). In poorer families, parents would go without themselves in order that this should be so. Most informants had a Christmas tree, although two families retained instead the older tradition of a 'kissing bush' or 'kissing bough', a circular framework covered with evergreens and hung with ornaments and apples containing candles.[32] Every informant had hung up his or her stocking for Father Christmas, although by no means all received a toy. In poorer families the stocking was more likely to contain a new penny, an apple and an orange, and a few nuts or sweets. Pimlott has argued that the material poverty of the Christmas celebrations of many working-class families was less important than the fact that 'they shared the middle-class conception of how Christmas should be kept and did their utmost to live up to it'.[33] By the twentieth century the idea of a benevolent gift-bestowing Santa Claus figure was universal in Cumbria and despite the difference in means, Christmas was as child-centred for the working classes as it was for the middle classes. Santa Claus was an import to this country from America, whence he had been taken by Dutch settlers.[34] First making his appearance in the 1870s, he appears to have been adopted, with the help of commercial interests, as quickly in Cumbria as he was elsewhere. He was similar enough to the Father Christmas of English tradition to be familiar, but he fitted more neatly into the privatised domestic Christmas, and both fuelled and catered for the growing tendency towards a child-centred Christmas.

If Christmas became increasingly a domestic festival, New Year probably gained in importance during the period as a public celebration. By the early twentieth century it had emerged as a separate and largely adult occasion. There were many New Year's Eve balls and dances and in most towns a crowd would gather towards midnight, in the Market Square or some other central place. A band would usually be playing and people would sing and dance, apparently undeterred by bad weather. 'Oh yes, they used to have dancing! And it didn't matter how much water there was on the ground, they used to go waltzing', an informant told me.[35] Newspaper reports tell us, and photographs of the inter-war period show that these crowds were often very large indeed and composed predominantly of young people. However, at Keswick in 1930, we are told that the crowd in the Market Square contained 'folk of all ages ... young people from the Fire Brigade ball and old people from the fireside'.[36] The press is, on the whole, approving of the gatherings and the community spirit which they were felt to reflect. Many oral informants, both male and female, took part in these celebrations. The crowds appear to have been generally good-natured, although there was a certain amount of drunkenness and they were associated in a few minds with rowdyism. One informant was forbidden to go: 'I couldn't go. "Only a lot of ruffians down there."'[37] Others, mainly the middle classes and those who lived some distance from a gathering place, saw the New Year in at home. With the exception of one or two middle-class families there was little sense of occasion. 'New Year we used to sit up till midnight. Half asleep. It didn't mean a thing', said one informant; 'nothing special really, it just come and went you know', said another.[38] If the occasion was not celebrated communally, then it appears hardly to have been celebrated at all by working-class Cumbrians.

As on Boxing Day, many social events were held on New Year's Day and there was no diminution in their number during the period. Rather the reverse. Although public house sports declined in number, their place was taken by railway and other excursions, some of them to pantomimes in Manchester and Liverpool, while works' dinners, old folks' teas, church entertainments and a host of other events continued unabated. It may be that, as Christmas Day came to be considered a family occasion in the region, the New Year's holiday a week later took its place as the focus for communal festivities. There is, however, no evidence of events being moved from one to the other, and the adoption of the Boxing Day holiday clouds the issue. The celebration of New Year does however demonstrate that despite the domestication of Christmas, communal festivities had not fallen from favour altogether.

EASTER

The celebration of Easter also evolved during the late nineteenth and early twentieth centuries, and a two-day holiday became the norm. Good Friday was a common law holiday, and in this region it appears by and large to have been observed as such. In Brough in 1885, for instance, 'Good Friday was kept as a general holiday', while in Kendal in 1890 it was a holiday, 'except for the building trade'.[39] In this Cumbria appears to differ from many parts of the country, where Good Friday was, to quote Hugh Cunningham, 'an unpopular and normally unobserved holiday'.[40] Easter Saturday was sometimes a holiday – the mills in Kendal were closed on that day in 1890[41] – but probably more often it was not. Saturday was, however, a half-holiday for many. Easter Monday appears to have been partly kept as a holiday before it was made a Bank Holiday in 1871. Thereafter it was observed more readily in some areas than in others. In Penrith in 1882, 'most of the places of business were closed during the day which was observed as a general holiday',[42] but in Kendal in the same year all the shops were open, 'the Easter Monday Bank Holiday not being generally observed in this part of the country'.[43] By 1890, Kendal was beginning to fall into line. Monday was still not a general holiday but 'little business was done in the town'.[44] Kendal shops finally decided to close in 1893, 'much to the delight of their assistants and the general public'.[45] By then, the numbers of railway excursion tickets sold, in Kendal and elsewhere, suggest that Monday had become an important and widely observed holiday. There is, however, no evidence to suggest that people were now working on Good Friday; the holiday appears to have been extended. Most people worked on Easter Tuesday, although the day was partially a holiday in West Cumberland.

Easter, although to a much lesser extent than Christmas, tended to be a child-centred festival, and it was associated first and foremost with eggs. Throughout our period and in all parts of the region these were pace-eggs, hard-boiled eggs, dyed usually with onion peel or gorse flowers, but sometimes with synthetic dyes. Chocolate eggs were available by the early twentieth century, but among oral informants, only one or two middle-class children received them. The holiday centred to a great extent on the distribution and enjoyment of these pace-eggs. Among the working classes it was also the occasion for new summer clothes if these could be afforded, and it was usual for children to go dressed in their best to visit relatives or neighbours, when they would be given pace-eggs. Sunday was the most usual day for these visits. 'You used to give them out you know. Kiddies used to come to show their Easter clothes off to you.' 'And you used to give the child a pace-egg and an orange.'[46] (Oranges were also traditional to the season.) Groups of working-class children, known as Jolly Boys or pace-eggers, also went from house to house, performing a mummers' play and receiving pace-eggs and money in return. Their perambulations should perhaps be seen as an extension to the wider community of the visits to family and friends. Probably because Easter continued to be a communally celebrated festival, the Jolly Boys persisted longer than the Christmas mummers, but by the inter-war period the custom was in decline. Visits to receive eggs seem not to have been part of the middle-class Easter, and middle-class mothers provided them for their own families.

Before, or instead of, being eaten the eggs were rolled competitively or 'dumped'; that is, held in the palm of the hand and banged against another similarly held until one of them broke. For one or two middle-class informants, rolling the eggs was also a family affair. They would go out to picnic in the country, or on the beach, perhaps meeting aunts and cousins. For the great majority, however, some middle-class families included, egg-rolling was a great communal gala, taking place on Easter Monday. This was the case even when, as in Kendal, the day was not a general holiday. Then, one supposes, the crowd was largely made up of mothers and children. Every locality had its appointed place for the proceedings. For the people of Dalton and Barrow-in-Furness and nearby villages, the gathering place was Furness Abbey. In Kendal it was Castle Hill, in Workington the Mill Field, described as 'a public beauty spot',[47] and in Whitehaven the Colliery Recreation ground. The Furness Abbey gathering was perhaps the largest anywhere, as it drew people from a wide area. Informants agree that the Abbey grounds were 'black with people',[48] who walked there, usually in family groups, showing off their new clothes, whatever the weather. 'On the roads', I was told, 'there were little fruit stalls. Ice cream. And hokey pokey ... a sort of toffee stuff.'[49] Informants from all areas stressed that these gatherings were orderly and good-natured.

The main alternative to Easter Monday egg-rolling was the excursion. Throughout the period large numbers of Cumbrians set off for the day by rail, boat and latterly charabanc. Monday became the most popular day to travel, but there were also large numbers of excursionists on Good Friday and Easter Saturday. Some of these may have stayed away for two or three days. The press only reports numbers of tickets sold, so we have no way of knowing. There are no reports of Sunday trips. The numbers of those travelling by rail seem to have increased steadily down to 1914, although there were fluctuations from year to year, probably caused by the vagaries of the weather. During and after the war, the withdrawal of cheap excursion tickets makes the picture less clear. Evidently there was no falling off in demand. The *Carlisle Journal* reported in 1920 that 'the public have become so accustomed to the lack of travelling facilities they have learned to do without them and are determined to invest the Easter festival with as much of its prewar popularity as possible'. The demand for accommodation in the resorts was said to be 'as heavy as it was in the days when travelling was easier and cheaper'.[50] By the 1930s the number of rail travellers once again exceeded pre-war levels in some places, but not in others. By this time motor transport was no doubt accounting for many of the day-trippers. Easter excursionists were never as numerous as those at Whitsuntide, however.

The trippers went to the sea, the Lakes or countryside, and to sporting events such as race meetings or football matches. A few visited other towns for reasons which can only be guessed at. Some perhaps visited relatives. In 1910, to give an example, 400 people left Ulverston on Good Friday, 'chiefly to the Lakes and Morecambe'. On Monday 400 travelled to Barrow, 550 to the Lakes, 200 to Morecambe and 150 to Lancaster, Blackpool and Manchester, etc. The figures have presumably been rounded.[51] The large number travelling to Barrow doubtless includes people who intended to take the steamer to Fleetwood for Blackpool. The population of Ulverston in 1911 was 9,552, and if we assume that all those who bought tickets in the town lived there, this means that between 1 in 7 and 1 in 8 of the population went on an Easter Monday excursion.[52] Similar figures can be calculated for other places.

People of all classes and ages went on day trips. The social tone of the resorts probably to some extent determined who went where, but the large numbers going to a few places must have given the trips a communal character. By the inter-war period, many of the middle classes had cars and took their excursions privately *en famille*, leaving the excursion trains largely to the working classes. The railways did not necessarily draw people away from more traditional ways of spending the holiday, however. The crowds at the Easter football games at Workington (which will be discussed in Chapter IV) were always swelled by large numbers of excursionists from nearby towns.

Easter was still very much a communally celebrated festival before the Second World War. The middle classes were beginning to withdraw into privacy, but they had not yet done so completely. The days were becoming longer, the weather was improving, and people were more keen to be out and about than they were at Christmas. Spring was not the time of year for a 'festival of the fireside', and commercial interests drew their benefit instead from the display of new clothes and the excursion traffic.

WHITSUNTIDE

Whit Monday was made a Bank Holiday in 1871, but this made little difference to the Whitsuntide festival, which was already widely observed in Cumbria and often extended to several days or a week. I have found only one reference to people being required to work during the holiday. This was in 1890 at an Aspatria colliery and this was nevertheless 'thrown idle on Monday and Tuesday, owing to all the lads who drive the ponies attending Cockermouth and Wigton hiring fairs'.[53] There may have been others at work, but the vast crowds who attended events during this week suggest that most people were on holiday. A festive atmosphere prevailed and the occasion was put to a wide variety of uses, having much in common with a Lancashire Wakes week.

In the late nineteenth century, hiring fairs were perhaps the most important events of the week. Probably because they coincided with a popular holiday, the Whitsun hirings were much bigger events than their counterparts at Martinmas, the latter having only a limited recreational element. Most of the Whitsun fairs were great and wonderful occasions attended by showmen of all kinds. They took place in numerous towns all over the region on different days during the week, and they attracted not only farm servants, but pleasure seekers in general. In many cases the numbers attending were vastly swelled by the railways. In 1870 the Carlisle fair, on Whit Saturday, was said to have been 'unusually large', many people coming into town on 'the cheap trains'. 'On the Sands there was a much greater show than usual of menageries, circuses, itinerant exhibitions and other amusements, and they were crowded with visitors ... public houses and dancing rooms were largely patronised.'[54] Cockermouth fair, on the following Monday, was also 'very largely attended'. It was said that

> The collection of caravans was the largest that has been seen in Cockermouth for the last 25 years and comprised Wombwells No. 1 (Queens) Menagerie and a number of other establishments, containing all the wonders of the world and a great many more. There was a rather larger muster than usual of 'merry-go-rounds', shooting galleries, ballad singers and thimble riggers; and the public houses drove a roaring trade during the day.[55]

Although the numbers of farm servants declined steadily from the mid-nineteenth century, the hiring fairs were slow to diminish in importance. Some of the smaller ones like Millom and Keswick did dwindle away by the turn of the century or shortly after; a number of others, for instance Maryport and Workington, continued solely or mainly as pleasure fairs, but many of them survived, in little reduced form, until the 1920s, and a few continued as hiring fairs until the Second World War. Because of the length of the holiday, the fairs were not, on the whole, adversely affected by competition from other attractions. In Carlisle, for instance, the fair was on Saturday, but the great day for excursions from the town was Monday.

Such decline as there was probably stemmed partly from the relegation of fun-fairs to the category of non-respectable entertainment, but also from increasing sophistication. By the 1930s, the 'wonders of the world' were no longer to be found at the fair.

Another day of the holiday was, in the later nineteenth century, often taken up by Friendly Society processions. As a rule all the societies in a town or village would march to church together in one grand procession behind banners and brass bands, afterwards separating for dinners. Sometimes there was a gala and sports after or instead of the dinner, and these became increasingly common in the 1880s. Although the Friendly Societies themselves continued to flourish until the early years of this century, many of the club walks, as they were called, began to decline rather sooner. At Hawkshead in 1890, the procession was reduced to one lodge, the female union failing to process after having done so, it was said, for 100 years. The numbers in the procession were barely equal to those in the band which led it, although the sports afterwards were still quite well attended.[56] At Askam in 1900, neither the Rechabites nor the Mechanics marched, while the Foresters could only raise a turn-out of about thirty men out of a membership of 167. 'Evidently,' said the *Barrow News*, 'Friendly Society Whit demonstrations are becoming a thing of the past.'[57] In Brough, by 1910, the procession was of children, although the sports afterwards were for both children and adults,[58] and this may be a clue to the decline. Processions in the later nineteenth century were, I suggest, coming to be considered beneath the dignity of respectable adults, and when people put themselves on display as a community, on occasions such as this, they increasingly did so through their children. They were becoming a community of families.

As might be expected, no Friendly Society galas survived the First World War, although some of the sports were taken over and continued by independent committees, for instance at Hawkshead.[59] In a number of places, committees were also formed to organise children's processions and treats, sometimes with May queens and maypoles. On Whit Monday 1920 the children of Broughton in Furness were assembled in the square and marched to church behind Barrow Silver Band for a service, after which they were given tea by the Public Treat Committee. In the evening the Committee held a dance in the Town Hall, in aid of its funds.[60] The procession may have been an attempt to emulate the Whit Walks which took place in more southerly parts of Lancashire, but it was perhaps also intended to fill, in a suitable way, the gap left by the end of the club walks. The hiring fair had also been abandoned in Broughton. By 1930 this children's treat had become a fancy-dress gala.[61]

At Askam, the Friendly Society procession was also replaced by a children's May Day parade, financed by public subscription; while at Brough the children's procession continued between the wars under the direction of the British Legion.[62] At Great Clifton a committee organised a children's carnival with girl morris dancers, a May queen and maypole dancing, as well as a procession behind Cockermouth Industrial School Band.[63] None of these things – children's Whit walks, maypoles, morris dancing, etc. – were Whitsuntide traditions in Cumbria. But they quickly became so, mirroring as they did the increasing tendency for children to be made the centre of public festivities.

The new treats apart, children had always had their Sunday School outings to look forward to at Whitsuntide, the great majority of them taking place during this holiday. In Kendal, the excursions of all the rival denominations annually occupied several columns of the *Westmorland Gazette*, as well as every available means of conveyance out of the town. These were, for children, one of the great events of the year, and they are fondly remembered by oral informants.

Children never totally dominated the week's events, however. Whitsuntide was a peak time for sports and fêtes of all kinds. Public houses, temperance societies, Liberal and Conservative Associations, cricket clubs, bodies of every description, organised events during the holiday, and these almost certainly increased in number during the period of my study. Many of them were aided by the railways' willingness to bring in the crowds by running excursion trains to them. Excursions were already an important part of the holiday by 1870, and railway bookings, with the exception of the war years, remained fairly constant between then and the Second World War. Given that motor transport would be increasingly in use in the twentieth century, this suggests something of an increase in the number of trippers over the period. Monday was the most popular day, although Tuesday was not far behind, and people went to much the same places as at Easter, in slightly larger numbers.

Whitsuntide remained an important holiday throughout the period. Until summer holidays became usual, and this did not really happen in Cumbria until after the Second World War, it was, in effect, the annual summer break, gregariously enjoyed in as many ways as possible.

GUY FAWKES NIGHT

The only other calendar festival which was generally observed in Cumbria was 5 November, Guy Fawkes Night. By the 1870s the festivities over much of the region were low-key affairs, mainly for juveniles, with a bonfire and a few fireworks in a field. In some of the towns there were memories of glories now faded. The *Whitehaven News* in 1878 reported that the occasion

> which used to be fruitful of a good deal of horseplay and disorder in Whitehaven, passed off quietly this year. A couple of tar barrels did indeed make their appearance ... and had a brief but glorious career; but with this exception and a few toy fireworks here and there in the town, there was nothing to indicate that a once famous anniversary had come round again.[64]

At Orton, a year earlier, the occasion was remembered as being 'formerly a great day', on which the parish bellringers 'used to visit the public houses and sing "Britons to Arms" and other national songs'. It was lamented that 'of late years this memorable anniversary has dwindled into insignificance'. That year, 'The children had some diversion by dragging an effigy of Guy Fawkes in a conveyance around the town and collecting subscriptions.' The ringers (who received their stipend on 5 November rang the bells at intervals, and 'the little folks in the evening kindled a fire upon some waste land and all passed off very quietly'.[65]

In a few places, however, the festival was still very much alive. At Middleton, for instance, the schoolchildren had a holiday which they spent in collecting subscriptions in aid of 'a great parish fire (which) took place in the centre of the township with a grand display of fireworks and a gingerbread feast'.[66] Ulverston, Penrith, Brough,

Appleby, Sedburgh and (just over the border in Yorkshire) Dent also continued to have large-scale popular celebrations. It was usual for huge bonfires to be lit at some central point in the town. In Dent it was reported that those visiting the fire had to be sure to lock their doors, otherwise their furniture was likely to be taken and broken up for the fire.[67] Squibs and other fireworks were thrown, guns were fired, and tar barrels were kicked and rolled or, less frequently, carried through the streets. There was not always a guy. If there was, it was, with two exceptions which are mentioned below, always an effigy of Guy Fawkes. At Brough, in 1884, there was a Mrs Guy Fawkes as well, and the couple were paraded in a landau, in the manner of a *charivari*.[68] There is, though, no evidence of effigies of local wrongdoers being paraded and burnt, as was the case in the towns in the south of England which were investigated by Robert Storch.[69] And the only case of a national figure being burnt in effigy was at Ulverston in 1881, when Parnell (who was at the time in prison for his Land League activities) was the victim probably of the anti-Catholic feeling associated with the occasion.

It is difficult to assess how important militant Protestantism and, by association, patriotism were in the popular celebrations. The essentially minor nature of the festivities in Barrow and parts of West Cumberland may reflect the Irish presence there, although Barrow was a new town, with no established tradition of celebration, and West Cumberland also had a large number of migrants. In the early part of this century, the Catholics among my oral informants did not take part in Guy Fawkes celebrations. They felt that the occasion was directed against them.[70] Where a town's elites were involved, patriotism and the defence of Protestantism tended to be to the fore, but in other places it was the bonfire and tar barrels which were the important elements in the event, which was essentially a fire festival and an opportunity for a spectacular celebration at a gloomy time of year.

Where the 5th was still celebrated in a full-bloodied manner, it led to conflict with the police, magistrates and local elites generally. By the 1870s the occasion was everywhere under attack. In some places, for instance Appleby, the police and magistrates were quickly successful in suppressing the popular celebrations.[71] Elsewhere, as at Ulverston, the conflict smouldered on for decades, to erupt into violence again in the early twentieth century.

There, 'More or less serious conflicts between the youthful

populace and the police, were matters of common occurrence' in the 1870s and 1880s,[72] after which the celebrations became quieter and more restrained, but continued to take place in the town. In 1905, which was the 300th anniversary of the gunpowder plot, the celebrations were revived on a grand scale, and seem to have been intended as much as an attack on the police as a patriotic demonstration. The police had been warned of a revival by the number of reported thefts of combustible material, and as the 5th fell on a Sunday and the date of the expected demonstration was uncertain, extra police were drafted in for three nights. The confrontation began on Saturday, when the police tried to prevent the rolling of tar barrels. On the Sunday night, after church, the battles continued, although it was reported that many of the adult onlookers loudly protested by cries of 'It's a disgrace to civilization', and 'they ought to be ashamed of themselves', at the 'discreditable disturbance on the Sabbath'.[73] By the Monday the affair had clearly become an anti-police riot. Bags of flour were used as missiles and an effigy 'supposed to personate a constable holding a manx kipper' was burnt while the crowd joined hands and formed a circle round the fire and sang 'Auld Lang Syne'. The Manx kipper defies analysis, but the singing of 'Auld Lang Syne' was perhaps a token of solidarity among those involved. Huge demonstrations continued in the town until the First World War, although thereafter they became more restrained again. The police avoided further confrontation, even though by-laws were being broken. In 1907, 'Whilst carefully watching that no damage was done to property (they) remained passive spectators of the scene.'[74] The final disappearance of the riotous celebrations was probably brought about by the increasing sophistication of the inter-war years.

Alongside the popular celebrations there had always been a few displays organised by paternalist local gentry in defence of patriotism, Protestantism and, by extension, the existing social order. Perhaps the most noted celebrations were those at Graythwaite Hall, the residence of Colonel Sandys, a popular local hunting figure. From some time in the 1880s until the Second World War and possibly beyond, the Colonel, and latterly his descendants, provided an immense bonfire (in 1901 it contained 50 tons of timber and was 60 feet high and 40 feet across), a fireworks display, and hot food and drink for hundres of people from the surrounding parishes, and for his own guests who were there for the pheasant shooting. His stated object was 'to draw the people from the adjoining villages together to remind them of the diabolical plot of 1605 and to distribute literature recording the happy frustration of it'.[75]

Oral informants' memories of the event are of bonfires built by rival gangs of children who, then as now, raided each other; of penny-for-the-guying, which perhaps stems from the parading of guys and subscription collecting of earlier years; and of private bonfires and fireworks in the back garden. The communal bonfires still vastly outnumbered the private celebrations before the Second World War however, the latter being favoured only by some of the middle class, and the timid. The festival did not really lend itself to becoming a family affair and, of course, it has never entirely become so. It was, though, well and truly tamed. Suppression by the authorities and the downward spread of polite middle-class standards of behaviour probably combined to end the riotous behaviour once associated with the festival. Even before the turn of the century the Middleton parish fire and gingerbread feast, referred to earlier, had come to be considered by the parishioners, or some of them, as 'primitive', and the collection diverted to a children's Christmas tea.[76] The large-scale celebration of Christmas was socially acceptable, but Guy Fawkes Night had, by the twentieth century, largely been relegated to minor status in the festival calendar. Only Colonel Sandys and, until the First World War, the young men of Ulverston, seem to have been in disagreement.

RUSHBEARING

Rushbearing was a custom which easily lent itself to refinement and folklorisation, and in Cumbria this was to be its fate. After the mid-nineteenth century it was observed only in two pairs of villages in Westmorland – Ambleside and Grasmere, and Warcop and Musgrave. In the latter place the ceremony had been revived in the 1820s at the wish of the Revd Septimus Collinson, Provost of Queen's College, Oxford and a native of the village, after being extinct for about thirty years.[77] At about the same time, the rushbearing at Orton ceased to be observed when the church floor was flagged. This had been a simple affair. 'On a day previously arranged, the parishioners, both old and young, assembled in the village and then went forth to the moors, where they gathered bundles of rushes and then returning with them to the church, were regaled in the porch with ale and Orton cake.'[78] Langdale rushbearing came to an end in 1752 when the chapel was rebuilt, and similarly, in about 1826, Urswick rushbearing ended. At Langdale an attempt to revive the festival in 1889 was unsuccessful,[79] but at Urswick the custom was revived in 1908 by the parish's eccentric antiquarian incumbent. It seems probable that other rushbearings had quietly ceased to take place in the eighteenth and early nineteenth centuries, but if this is so, no record of them remains.

I described the rushbearing villages as two pairs, because in each couple the two are geographically close together and their rushbearings were very similar. The custom in Grasmere and Ambleside, however, differed in a number of ways from that in Warcop and Musgrave, while the Urswick revival was different again. None of them bore much resemblance to the basic custom at Orton, nor to rushbearings in Lancashire, which really had little more than the name in common.

In Clarke's *Survey of the Lakes* in 1770, Grasmere Rushbearing was noted as taking place towards the end of September. The bearers were said to be 'women and girls'.[80] In 1827 when Wordsworth was involved in the custom, the date was changed to the Saturday nearest to 20 July, which is St Margaret's Day, the significance of which is not known. At this time the rushbearings were described as 'tall poles decked with rushes and flowers'.[81] They were carried by boys and girls up to the age of about fifteen. Rushes were brought by cart and the church floor was strewn before the procession, which was led by the village fiddler. The bearers were presented with gingerbread by the churchwardens, but there was no church service. In the evening there was a dance in the loft of the Red Lion Hotel until midnight, at which hour the rector sent his servant to confiscate the fiddler's bow.[82] Wrestling also took place during the evening in a nearby field. The event was partly a church and partly a popular celebration, and despite numerous changes in the form of the event during the next 100 years, and attempts by the church to shear the festival of its secular aspects, it remained so. It changed, however, from a festival of church and parishioners to a children's festival organised by the church and a committee of villagers, and watched by vast numbers of tourists.

In 1839, which was the last occasion on which rushes were spread in the church, it being flagged shortly afterwards, only nine rushbearers made an appearance.[83] To prevent the custom dying out, a local gentleman, Mr Thomas Dawson, gave each rushbearer 6d.[84] He continued the practice in subsequent years, during which numbers revived considerably, there being fifty in 1840. It seems likely that, had it not been for his interest and the keenness of the parish clergy that it should continue, the rushbearing would have ceased to be observed.

During the next forty years the clergy had a free hand with the event, altering the proceedings as they thought fit, successive rectors discarding or reversing changes made by their predecessors. In 1871 a church service was introduced on the Saturday afternoon. Then in 1884 the feast of the dedication of the parish church of St Oswald was revived by the incumbent, and an octave, or eight-day festival, beginning on St Oswald's Day, 5 August, was instituted. The following year the rushbearing was moved to the Saturday after 5 August, so that it fell within the octave. This caused Mr Dawson to discontinue his sixpences and so, from then on, a children's tea was given in lieu, the expenses being collected in the parish. Every household contributed what it could, or so we are told.[85] By this time the rushbearers had become much more numerous, and much younger children of both sexes. They carried more varied and elaborate devices – crosses, serpent and poles, harps, the white hand of St Oswald, and so on – which must have necessitated a great deal of help and encouragement from proud parents. The picturesque procession was a great source of attraction to visitors to the area.

In 1891, the religious side of the festival was separated from what had now become the children's treat, when the latter was moved to the Monday. The Red Lion dance was abandoned, although a band was in attendance for dancing at the children's treat. The wrestling, however, persisted until the First World War.[86]

In the twentieth century, the rushbearings became ever more elaborate – Moses in the bullrushes, the orb and crown, the wishing gate, even a Noah's Ark, and it became usual for baby rushbearers in decorated prams to take part in the procession, which numbered between 150 and 200 children. The occasion drew people from a considerable distance. In 1937 it was reported that

> Hundreds of holiday-makers swelled the ranks of the villagers, who left their homes en masse to line the route of the procession, and in the midst of such a typically English scene, it was strange to hear sentences in German, Dutch and French from interested foreign onlookers. The nasal tones of Americans from across the Atlantic were no less evident.[87]

This is a long way from a rustic procession behind the local fiddler. It is a village on display; to the visitors who are economically important, but culturally rather threatening; to the people from neighbouring towns and villages, between whom friendly rivalry always existed; and to each other, every family competitively displaying its well-dressed children and the rushbearings which had taken so much time and trouble. It has been argued by Peter Burke that, in early modern Europe, popular festivals 'celebrated the community itself, displaying its ability to put on a good show'.[88] They also provided an arena for competition, both between individuals within the community, and between one community and another. Grasmere rushbearing clearly fulfilled these functions, and in the 1930s it was still a popular festival, even though increased sophistication had dictated that those actually taking part should be children.

The rushbearing at Ambleside developed on very similar lines, altough due to the size of the place, the numbers involved were always greater. There, the element of competition was institutionalised, prizes being given for the best rushbearings, and in 1930 the event was filmed and circulated around the cinemas, which was a matter for great local pride, and doubtless a boost to the tourist trade.[89]

At Warcop and Musgrave, far fewer changes were made in the custom between the mid-Victorian period and the 1930s. Although it was called rushbearing, there were no rushes involved in the ceremony in these villages until 1939, when at Musgrave, boys carrying rush crosses were introduced.[90] The rushbearers were young girls from the villages concerned, wearing floral crowns. In Musgrave, the festival's date varied between 22 June and 6 July, Old Midsummer, finally settling on the latter. It enjoyed considerable gentry patronage. In 1882 the patrons included the Earl of Bective, MP and the Hon. W. Lowther, MP, and there were always a large number of visiting clergymen present.[91] The crown bearers, as they were called, assembled in the village and were treated to wine and cake. They then marched in procession to the church, for a service. The crowns were hung in the porch, and the girls then adjourned to a barn where they were served with tea and presented with a gift, usually a book. Sports were usually held in the evening.[92]

At Warcop, where the proceedings took place on St Peter's Day, 29 June, the crown bearers' procession went first of all to Warcop Hall, the residence of the Lord of the Manor, where they were given wine and cake, and thence to church for the service and presentation of the crowns. After church they returned to Warcop Hall for a fête, with tea and dancing. A collection was taken and divided between the crown bearers. Sports took place on the same day, but under separate management.[93]

In both cases the rushbearings were organised by committees. In the case of Warcop this was composed of members of the village reading room, the 'respectable' element in the village, but in Musgrave the composition of the committee is not know.[94] In these villages there was a very strong Methodist presence and the support given to the rushbearing by gentry and clergy may have been intended to counter this. Certainly, many of the sermons and psalms at the rushbearing services suggest that this was so. At Musgrave in 1884, for instance, the anthem was taken from the 133rd Psalm, 'Behold how good and how joyful a thing it is for brethren to dwell together in unity', while in his sermon the vicar reminded those present 'that this beautiful ceremony was an ancient church custom in which the *entire parish* combined to glorify God and adorn his temple'.[95] Nonconformists on occasion attacked the rushbearing. In 1875 at Warcop, while the congregation were leaving the church after the service, 'two men, connected with some religious sect in Penrith, stationed themselves close to the church gates and . . . pressed tracts upon each person who had joined in the services of the morning'.[96] Counter-attractions were more usual. In the late nineteenth century a temperance demonstration was usually held in the village on the same day, and the Band of Hope marched in procession around the village, headed by a band, after which tea was served in the Temperance Hall.[97] The Band of Hope could, of course, include Church of England children, but as the daughters of the church were otherwise engaged (and being treated with wine), this should probably be seen as competition from a rival religious community.

By the early twentieth century, the element of religious competition seems to have faded and the occasion was becoming more of a village fête. In the inter-war period, the crown bearers were organised by the school, and may have included Nonconformist girls, or girls from neighbouring villages, as the numbers involved became much greater.[98]

Because they were not in the part of Cumbria favoured by tourists, Warcop and Musgrave never drew such large numbers of spectators as Grasmere and Ambleside. Nevertheless they were locally a great attraction, and a chance for the villagers to 'put on a good show',[99] in competition with the rival village, and enjoy themselves as a community.

The revived rushbearing at Urswick, although a church festival led by the churchwardens, did initially include the local Nonconformists. The rushbearing queen and her attendants, four boys carrying swords, were chosen at the school and might be of any religion. However, by the 1930s it was said to be 'mainly for people who went to the Sunday School and parents who went to Church'.[100] This event was never really a popular festival, and there was no secular side to it; no tea party and no sports. The children marched in procession, sometimes behind a pipe band from Barrow, carrying a white sheet containing bundles of rushes. These were thrown out (still in bundles) as the procession walked up the aisle of the church, and later picked up again. The event excited little interest outside the immediate area. It was very much the creation of an eccentric antiquarian.[101]

Elsewhere, rushbearing, where it continued into the later nineteenth century, was a custom which, while largely directed according to the wishes of local elites, was able to not only retain, but increase its importance as a popular festival. Although 'folklorised' and diverted from its original form, it still enabled communities to co-operate in a day of enjoyment and self-celebration.

CONCLUSION

Between the mid-Victorian period and the second World War, the celebration of popular festivals changed in a number of ways. Firstly, any events which were in any way disorderly or riotous were brought to an end. Although the suppression of such events had begun long before the mid-Victorian years, it continued during our period, and Brough Holly Night quickly passed into oblivion for reasons which are not altogether clear, but which included counter-attractions and disapproving attention in the press. If there was any sort of fight to continue the custom, it has left no trace, and it seems probable that the custom had lost its relevance as Christmas became a home and child-centred festival.

The riotous celebration of Guy Fawkes Night proved more difficult to eradicate, but by-laws and prosecutions were ultimately successful, the recrudescence at Ulverston being the only exhibitions of noteworthy proportions, apart from those which were under the superintendence of local elites, to take place this century. The by-laws doubtless reflected the views of many, as there is no doubt that tar barrels and huge bonfires in narrow urban streets were dangerous.

Rushbearing on the other hand, evolved, remaining meaningful in a changed social environment. Originally a festival of and for the parish community, it developed, where it survived into our period, into a celebration of the specialness of the villages concerned, most other places by then having no such festival. Tourists and people from neighbouring villages provided an audience for the displays, which also allowed for competition between and within the villages concerned.

New traditions which developed during the period were the Christmas tree and Santa Claus, and children's May processions. These underline the growing trend towards child-centredness at holiday times, particularly at Christmas, which during the period became established as a festival of the family and home. Egg-rolling, probably the only tradition to continue unaltered and undiminished during the period, was also, probably not coincidentally, child-centred. This and the May processions were, like rushbearing, community events, and these were evidently still important in the 1930s, although people were by then increasingly functioning as communities only through their children. The community was becoming a federation of families, who also enjoyed parts of the holidays independently. Excursions had, by the early years of this century, become a major feature of Bank Holidays, and their popularity may have presaged the abandonment of the communal celebration of festivals in favour of the family holiday, although excursions were for the most part gregariously enjoyed, and people still apparently liked to be on holiday together.

NOTES

Place of publication London unless otherwise stated.

1 John Richardson, 'Old customs and usages of the Lake District', *Transactions of the Cumberland Association for the Advancement of Literature and Science*, Part II, 1876–77, p. 112.
2 Abner Cohen, *Two-Dimensional Man*, 1974, p. 3.
3 Stephen Jones, *Workers at Play*, 1986, p. 28.
4 John Golby, 'Christmas. A case study' in *Popular Culture: Themes and Issues*, Milton Keynes, 1981, Vol. 1.

5 Martin Ingram, 'Ridings, rough music and the "reform of popular culture" in early modern England', *Past and Present*, 105, Nov. 1984, p. 80.

6 E. P. Thompson, 'Anthropology and the discipline of historical context', *Midland History*, Vol. i, No. 3, 1971–72, pp. 53–5; 'Patrician society, plebeian culture', *Journal of Social History*, Vol. 7, No. 4, Summer 1974, *passim*.

7 Daniel Scott, *Bygone Cumberland and Westmorland*, 1899, p. 201.

8 Richardson, 1876–77, p. 113.

9 A. R. Wright, *British Calendar Customs. England Vol. II: Fixed Festivals*, Liechtenstein, 1968, pp. 84–5.

10 *W.G.*, 31.12.1887.

11 *C. Pacq.*, 4.1.1870.

12 See *W.G.*, 1.1.1870.

13 William Howitt, *The Rural Life of England*, 1844, reprint 1971, pp. 461–2.

14 *C.J.*, 7.1.1890.

15 Howitt, 1844, p. 451.

16 Wright, 1968, p. 36.

17 *W.N.*, 1.1.1920.

18 An account of the event was given in the *Penrith Observer* on 5.1.1875, but this is very similar to that given by Scott, 1899, p. 205, who took it from a pamphlet, and the custom may in fact have already ceased. *Kelly's Directory of Westmorland* for 1910 states that the custom was discontinued about 1860. W. Whellan, *History and Topography of Cumberland and Westmorland*, 1860, p. 730, states that the custom was still continued.

19 *P.O.*, 5.1.1875.

20 *W.G.*, 12.1.1850; *P.O.*, 5.1.1875; Scott, 1899, p. 205.

21 William Hone, *The Table Book*, 1832, Columns 26–7.

22 J. A. R. Pimlott, *The Englishman's Christmas. A Social History*, Sussex, 1978, p. 97. A similar custom, 'The Stromness Yule Tree', persisted in Orkney until 1937: John Robertson, *Uppies and Doonies. The story of the Kirkwall Ba' Game*, Aberdeen 1967, pp. 161–5.

23 *W.G.*, 12.1.1850.

24 *W.G.*, 13.1.1849.

25 *W.G.*, 14.1.1860.

26 *W.G.*, 12.1.1850.

27 *Mannix's Directory of Westmorland*, 1849; *Slater's Directory of Cumberland and Westmorland*, 1869; *Bulmer's Directory of Westmorland*, 1885.

28 *P.O.*, 5.1.1875.

29 *B.T.*, 3.1.1880.

30 Respondents 24 and 14.

31 Pimlott, 1978, p. 133.

32 Respondents 18 and 14.

33 Pimlott, 1978, p. 133.

34 Pimlott, 1978, pp. 114–15.

35 Respondent 4.

36 *C.J.*, 3.1.1930.

37 Respondent 9.

38 Respondents 23 and 16.

39 *W.G.*, 11.4.1885, 5.4.1890.

40 Hugh Cunningham, *Leisure in the Industrial Revolution*, 1980, p. 142.

41 *W.G.*, 5.4.1890.

42 *P.O.*, 11.4.1882.

43 *W.G.*, 15.4.1882.

44 *W.G.*, 5.4.1890.

45 *W.G.*, 8.4.1893.

46 Respondents 16 and 17. The daughter finished her mother's sentence.
47 Respondent 11.
48 Respondent 30.
49 Respondent 30.
50 *C.J.*, 2.4.1920.
51 *B.H.*, 2.4.1910.
52 It is possible that children's tickets were counted as half in the figures given. If so the proportion of the population travelling would be rather higher, although some travellers undoubtedly lived outside Ulverston.
53 *W.N.*, 29.5.1890.
54 *C.J.*, 7.6.1870.
55 *C.J.*, 7.6.1870.
56 *W.N.*, 29.5.1890.
57 *B.N.*, 9.6.1900.
58 *W.G.*, 21.5.1910.
59 *B.N.*, 14.6.1930.
60 *W.N.*, 27.5.1920.
61 *B.N.*, 14.6.1930.
62 *B.H.*, 25.5.1910; *W.G.*, 14.6.1930.
63 *W.N.*, 27.5.1920.
64 *W.N.*, 7.11.1878.
65 *P.O.*, 6.11.1877.
66 *W.G.*, 9.11.1901.
67 *W.G.*, 10.11.1894.
68 *P.O.*, 11.11.1884.
69 Robert D. Storch, 'Please to Remember the 5th of November: Conflict, Solidarity and Public Order in Southern England 1815–1900' in R. D. Storch (ed.), *Popular Culture and Custom in 19th Century England*, 1982, pp. 71–100, *passim*.
70 Respondents 2 and 20.
71 For 5 November at Appleby see my PhD thesis, 'Popular Leisure in Cumbria, 1870–1939, University of Lancaster, 1987, pp. 75–6.
72 *B.N.*, 11.11.1905; *B.T.*, 12.11.1881.
73 *B.N.*, 11.11.1905.
74 *B.N.*, 9.11.1907.
75 *W.G.*, 9.11.1901, 13.11.1937, 14.11.1891.
76 *W.G.*, 9.11.1901.
77 F. B. Chancellor, *Around Eden*, Appleby, 1954, p. 68.
78 *Bulmer's History and Topography of Westmorland*, 1885, p. 252.
79 *W.G.*, 24.8.1889.
80 Anon. (Miss E. G. Fletcher?), *Rushbearing*, Manchester, 1897, p. 12.
81 Anon., 1897, p. 12.
82 *W.G.*, 13.8.1910.
83 *W.G.*, 4.8.1923; M. L. Armitt, *The Church at Grasmere*, Kendal, 1912, p. 222, says that there were only seven.
84 Nothing is known about Mr Dawson except that he was a London man, who owned Allan Bank, a house in the area. Armitt, 1912, p. 222.
85 Anon., 1897, p. 13.
86 *W.G.*, *passim*, especially 4.8.1923, 'A Retrospect'; Anon., 1897, *passim*.
87 *W.G.*, 14.8.1937.
88 Peter Burke, *Popular Culture in Early Modern Europe*, 1978, p. 200.
89 *W.G.*, 3.8.1907; 5.8.1911; *B.N.*, 8.8.1930.
90 C.R.O. PR/110/1/310, *Parochial Magazine*, August 1939.
91 *P.O.*, 11.7.1882.

92 J. W. Braithwaite, *Guide to Kirkby Stephen*, Appleby, 1884, p. 59; P.O., 11.7.1882; C.J., 9.7.1880; P.O., 6.7.1895; W.G., 8.7.1911.
93 Whellan, 1860, p. 770; P.O., 8.7.1884; W.G., 1.7.1911; C.J., 6.7.1917.
94 P.O., 3.7.1877; C.J., 8.7.1870; 10.7.1860; P.O., 1.7.1884.
95 P.O., 8.7.1884.
96 P.O., 6.7.1875.
97 P.O., 6.7.1875.
98 W.G., 5.7.1930.
99 Burke, 1978, p. 200.
100 Respondent 22.
101 Respondent 7.

CHAPTER III

The public house

INTRODUCTION

In mid-Victorian Cumbria the public house was central to popular recreation; it served as a gathering place, and a venue for events of all kinds. Many public houses had club rooms in which friendly societies and other organisations met, and others had dancing rooms, often over the stables, which were used by itinerant dancing masters, and were the most usual venue for dances.[1] A form of public house dance which was a longstanding part of the popular culture of the region was the 'Auld Wife Hake'. Two such events organised by the licensee of the Brown Horse at Winster at Christmas 1869 and Whitsuntide 1870 were said to have been attended by 120 people of both sexes who partook of tea and currant cake and danced until the small hours.[2] In rural areas hunts met at public houses, returning afterwards for refreshments and an evening's sociability.[3] Shepherds' meets – annual occasions for the exchange of stray sheep, combined with a day or two's sports and festivity – were also held at rural inns. Many publicans promoted recreational events themselves. The licensee of the Wheatsheaf Inn at Wigton held wrestling and a 'velocipede' race at Whitsuntide 1870 for instance, and 'a good company' gathered together in August the same year at the annual sports organised by the landlord of the Punch Bowl at Crosthwaite.[4] Pigeon-shooting was very widely promoted, and there were also sparrow and glass ball shoots, rabbit-coursings and hound trails.[5]

The everyday recreational role of the public house at the start of our period is less easy to document, but here as elsewhere pubs must have been places where men could find warmth, companionship and relaxation. The extent to which women used pubs, apart from special occasions such as 'Auld Wife Hakes', is unknown, but evidence for later in the period suggests that there were some female customers at this time. All classes appear to have used the region's public houses, although it is probable that there was little class mixing. A police return of the forty-four public houses in Kendal, dating from the 1880s or 1890s,[6] describes the class of customers who used each house, and although this is for a slightly later period, the information given is probably equally relevant to the period under discussion. It may also be supposed that the situation was paralleled in other towns. Four houses were described by the police as 'superior'; ten as 'middle' class and five as 'low'. One pub was described as the 'market house', and the remaining twenty-four as 'mixed'. Class mixing could have occurred in the latter, but it seems more likely that, as was the case later, different classes were catered for in separate rooms, the majority of pubs having a tap-room, a parlour and so on.[7]

During the later nineteenth and early twentieth centuries, the centrality of the public house to Cumbrian leisure was greatly reduced. It is difficult to separate cause from effect in this process of change. Official suppression of licences and public house entertainment, the development of chapel and temperance culture, the economics of the drink trade and a more general and ill-defined change in the way the public house was viewed in a changing recreational environment, all played their part. Linked with these changes was a great reduction in the number of public houses in the region, and this decrease will be examined in the first part of the chapter. The restriction of opening hours and official attitudes towards recreations on licensed premises will be considered next, and the third section will be an examination of a peculiarity of Cumbrian public house history, the State Management Scheme. This was in operation in the Carlisle area from 1916 until the Second World War and beyond, and it brought a mixture of negative and positive influences, drastically reducing the number of public houses and undermining the city's old rough pub culture, while providing a model for the 'improved public house' which was to become the licensed trade's policy in the 1930s and post-war years. Fourthly, I will consider the question of women in public houses, and finally, the recreational role of the public house in the inter-war years, and the extent of change during our period, will be assessed.

PUBLIC HOUSE CLOSURES

The number of public houses in Britain and in Cumbria had, by the inter-war years, been greatly reduced from its mid-Victorian level. In England and Wales, numbers fell from 112,884 in 1871 to 75,528 in 1935, and 73,365 in 1940.[8] Around 11,000 were closed before the 1904 Licensing Act, which was intended to reduce numbers and introduced compensation for loss of licence, came into force. For

Cumbria, figures in the oficial returns are often contradictory, but the trend and the approximate proportion of the diminution in numbers is quite clear.[9] In the county of Cumberland almost half the 'on' licensed houses disappeared between 1869 and 1935, numbers falling from 1,423 to 786. Before 1904 there was a decrease of around 250 houses. Figures for Westmorland show a smaller decline of a little over a third, from 323 'on' licences in 1869 to 201 in 1935, approximately eighty of them disappearing before 1904.[10] Although the proportionate decline in Westmorland was around the national average, it occurred mainly during the late nineteenth century, while in England and Wales as a whole, the main period of reduction in numbers was after 1904. Cumberland saw an above average decline both before and after the 1904 Act, the number of closures in the later period being increased by the activities of the State Management Scheme.

There was no apparently coherent pattern to the closures, which varied nationally from county to county, and within Cumbria from one petty sessional division to another. The decrease might be a fifth or slightly less, or over a half.[11] In Cumbria, one or two areas maintained or even improved on their public house density. The Workington division gained seven licences between 1874 and 1932, making a total of seventy-seven while Barrow-in-Furness Borough had eighty-seven licensed houses in 1874 and eighty-three in 1935, having reached a peak figure of ninety-six in 1907–08. The population of both these towns was growing in the late nineteenth century, and this probably prevented any decline in numbers during that period, but there is no obvious explanation for the stable numbers in Workington during this century.

The decline in numbers resulted in part from legislation and in part from economic and social changes which affected the viability of many licensed houses. In the period before 1902 the latter were probably more important, but after closure on the grounds of redundancy was introduced, the withholding of licences became the major cause of closure.

Under the 1828 Alehouse Act the granting and renewal of licences were placed in the hands of licensing justices. Despite increasing concern about the social evil of drunkenness, in the period before 1902 they appear not to have used their powers with very great severity. Parliamentary returns show only a very few cases of non-renewal. For 1882–86, for instance, only two refusals to renew on the part of magistrates are shown.[12] A return for 1900 shows that the North Lonsdale bench refused to renew a beerhouse licence on the grounds that the applicant had failed to provide satisfactory evidence of good character, and that his house was disorderly, and not qualified (i.e. in rateable value) as by law required, but this was the only instance reported for Cumbria in that year.[13] Although an undetailed return for 1875–83 shows a rather greater number of refusals, these were partially offset by a suspiciously large number of new licences issued, and I suspect that transfers to new tenants might be clouding the issue.[14] It may, however, have been that benches were weeding out the worst houses and allowing others to replace them.

It appears then that official suppression of licences was not the major cause of the great decline in the numbers of public houses before 1902. It is probable that there was a movement away from public house-based leisure in this period. The growth of Methodism in the region, and the creation of a whole recreational life centred on the chapel, must have affected the viability of public houses in certain areas. Temperance organisations were also widespread, although their effectiveness in educating people away from the public house must be questioned. Discussing a decline in drunkenness prosecutions in Kendal in 1895, the *Westmorland Gazette* asserted that 'Fifteen years ago public opinion was less severe towards the drunkard than it is now. ... In the interval ... temperance reformers have been more active and more influential in the borough. Much of the credit for the improvement undoubtedly belongs to them.'[15] It will be seen in Chapter V, however, that temperance organisations for adults were not widely successful in the region, although the influence of the Band of Hope on the rising generation cannot be completely disregarded.

At the same time economic factors were against the licensee. There were, in the early 1870s, probably too many public houses to be viable, even though the 1830 Beerhouse Act did not make a very great impression in Cumbria.[16] Population per 'on' licence in 1874 was, for instance, 141 in Eskdale, 154 in Carlisle, 177 in Bootle division, 228 in Westmorland East Ward and 274 in Kendal.[17] The national average in 1871 was 201, so Cumbria appears to have been fairly typical.[18] It is generally accepted that the national figure represented a great deal of over-provision. Even E. A. Pratt, the critic of official policy, concedes this.[19] The number of persons per 'on' licence is not necessarily a measure of economic viability, firstly because it takes no account of travellers, market customers and the like, who did not live locally, and secondly because many publicans did not rely on their houses for their livelihood. Directories show that many also had secondary (or primary) occupations, especially in thinly populated rural areas, and it may be supposed that the public house was mainly the responsibility of the landlord's wife. Farming was the most usual second occupation, but there were a variety of others: a shoemaker, a blacksmith, a wheelwright, a mason, and a contractor for the county bridges being a selection drawn at random from an 1885 directory of Westmorland.[20] Plans of public houses very frequently show pigsties, byres, orchards, etc., and many had land attached.[21] Bearing this in mind, there must, even so, have been areas in which the ratio of public houses to population was such that the least favoured among them did insufficient trade to justify the work involved in keeping them open. At the Leath Ward sessions in 1895 it was noted that four licences had not been renewed as the owners had declined to apply.[22] These could have been owner–occupiers abandoning an uneconomic trade, or alternatively breweries rationalising their outlets.

The growing tendency for brewers to buy and 'tie' public houses may have increased the number of closures, because if one brewer owned all the houses in an area, he could afford to close the least profitable without any loss of custom. Wilson suggests that, by 1890, probably some 70 per cent of 'on' licences were held under a tie of some kind,[23] but virtually no information on the matter is available for Cumbria. A return for Brampton, Longtown and Eskdale in 1892[24] shows that out of ninety-four houses, only twenty were tied, but I suspect that this figure might be unusually low. Alternatively, it could be that the main period of 'tying' in this area was the 1890s. Wilson pinpoints the period 1892–1900 as one of frantic activity amongst London brewers.[25] Certainly by the time closures under the 1904 Act began to take place, the majority of the owners appear to have been breweries, and the situation cannot have arisen overnight. In Carlisle in 1905, only seventeen of the 116 'on' licences were not tied.[26] Monckton claims that nationally in 1914 brewers owned 95 per cent of all public houses.[27] Rationalisation of the trade must therefore be considered as one probable factor in bringing about the reduction in numbers of public houses.

Both the majority and minority reports of the 1896–98 Royal Commission on Licensing found in favour of compensation for loss of licence on the grounds of redundancy.[28] This recommendation was not incorporated in the 1902 Act, and subsequently a number of benches took it upon themselves to refuse to renew licences on the grounds of redundancy without compensation being payable. In Cumbria in 1904, there were seven cases of refusal of licence on this ground.[29] It was therefore largely pressure from the trade, which by then to a great extent meant large public breweries with many shareholders, which brought about the 1904 Act. Many breweries were not in a healthy state at this time,[30] and there was a great deal of co-operation with licensing benches in the matter of redundancy, especially as the bulk of compensation went to the owner and not the tenant. The licensed trade's opponents described the Act as the 'Brewers' Endowment Bill', but publicans who either lost their licence or had to contribute to the compensation fund nicknamed it the 'Mutual Burial Fund'.[31]

The compensation authority was the County Licensing Committee at the Easter Quarter Sessions, and houses recommended for closure on the grounds of redundancy were referred to them by the licensing benches in the petty sessional divisions. For Westmorland and Lancashire, only limited information is available as the meetings of the compensation authority appear not to have been open to the press, my main source.[32] For Cumberland, the minute book of the County Licensing Committee is available. This shows that between 1905 and 1939 there were 205 closures under the Act.[33] The years immediately following 1904 saw the greatest number of referrals, there being 136 between 1905 and 1911, of which 115 were closed. The peak year for closures was 1906, when compensation was paid in forty-three cases. A great many referrals were not contested, the only argument being over the amount of compensation which was paid. Those owners who did contest closure frequently succeeded in gaining renewal of their licence, especially after 1910. Probably the worst houses were closed in the early years, and those referred later were less undesirable and easier to defend. It appears also that owners and their solicitors became more adept at putting convincing cases for renewal. By the inter-war years the licensing committee may also have been becoming more liberal in its attitude towards public houses, and more willing to listen to their arguments.

Houses closed might be fully licensed or beerhouses, although, given that there were far fewer of them in existence, there seems to have been a proportionate bias towards the latter. Bootle division, which had thirty fully licensed houses and ten beerhouses in 1905, referred just five of the beerhouses for compensation before 1919. Most divisions, however, referred numbers of their fully licensed houses as well.

Compensation cases probably accounted for most of the public house closures in Cumberland after 1904, although it has not proved possible to obtain conclusive figures for the inter-war years. Between 1905 and 1919, forty-two of the forty-three closures in the Whitehaven division were brought about by the 1904 Act, for instance, and in Allerdale-below-Derwent, sixteen of seventeen. However, in Leath ward there were thirty-four closures between 1905 and 1917, of which only twenty-one received compensation.[34] It is not known whether the remainder resulted from official closures on grounds other than redundancy, or from reasons not directly connected with the administration of the Licensing Acts.

In Westmorland only about forty public houses closed after 1904, and the majority of these seem to have ceased to do business before the First World War, when a steady trickle of referrals to the compensation authority are reported in the press.[35] The number of public houses in Barrow fell by thirteen between 1908 and 1935 and North Lonsdale lost fifty-five houses between 1905 and 1925,[36] many of them, it would seem from press reports, under the 1904 Act.

The number of closures which could take place was restricted only by the amount of money in the county's compensation fund. The only legal ground for referral was that the house was redundant, but obviously, the question of redundancy turned on the number of licensed houses in an area, and the authorities were free to choose the ones they wished to see closed. Rather oblique evidence of this can be seen in the names of some of the houses which were closed. It was surely not a coincidence that the Red Flag and the Shamrock in Whitehaven were considered surplus to requirements, for instance.[37] Nor does it come as a surprise that the Black Boy beerhouse in Barrow, where the landlord had been convicted for an assault on a policeman, was not necessary to meet the requirements of the district.[38] Similarly, the statement of a witness at the Kendal County sessions in 1906 makes it clear that the Duke of Cumberland at Farleton had been referred for compensation because it was believed to be a meeting place for poachers.[39] At the Appleby sessions in 1910, the renewal of the

Golden Fleece at Kirkby Stephen was objected to by the superintendent of police, who considered the house to be redundant because
it 'was principally frequented by footballers and their friends – chiefly
young men'. Witnesses were called, who stated that the licensee made
the house attractive to young men, which was not conducive to their
moral welfare, and the licence was referred for compensation.[40]
Wilson argues that the 1904 Act reduced the power of justices to close
houses they considered undesirable, but which remained within the
law, as they could only refer houses for compensation if they were
actually redundant.[41] He does not appear to have realised that the
notion of redundancy was capable of a highly subjective interpretation.
There do seem, however, to have been houses chosen for referral at
random, simply because those in authority were expected to reduce the
number of licences in the area.

The extent to which this reduction in the numbers of public
houses reflected public opinion is difficult to assess. The temperance
lobbies were doubtless pleased, but even in strongly Methodist areas
there must always have been at least a minority who made use of the
public houses and had no wish to see them close. In places there was
strong opposition to closures. In 1906, for instance, a petition in
support of the Nook Tavern at Preston Patrick signed by 'all the
inhabitants' was given to the Kendal County bench, and in the
previous year a 'largely signed petition' in favour of the continuance of
the Plough Inn at Silecroft was handed to the justices at Millom.[42]

The impact of this reduction in public house availability on
leisure patterns is likewise impossible to measure. It may be supposed that, unless all the houses in an area were closed, the effect
would not have been too great, although the loss of a dancing room,
or the departure of a licensee who was particularly keen to promote sporting activities, would obviously have had a detrimental effect
on recreational provision in the locality. Cases of closure of the only
public house in a village appear to have been few, but they did occur.
In such places, more particularly this century, the provision of village
halls may have partly filled the gap, but the possibility that some
villages were left without any gathering place cannot be ruled out.

OPENING HOURS AND ENTERTAINMENT

If the diminution in the numbers of public houses had, in itself, only a
limited effect on their recreational role, this was further undermined

by the curtailment of opening hours and by the imposition of other limitations by licensing justices. Restrictions had been placed on Sunday opening hours in 1854, and the first general restriction on opening hours came in 1872, a further Act being passed in 1874 to simplify its provisions and remove anomalies which had arisen under it. Sunday opening hours were now reduced to 12.30–2.30 p.m. and 6–10 p.m., a restriction which must have seriously interfered with social gatherings on the only full holiday of the week. Weekday hours were still very long, however, from 6 a.m. until 10 or 11 p.m., and would only have interfered with the public house's recreational function in that closing time would, if the law was enforced, have prevented people from dancing until the early hours at events such as 'Auld Wife Hakes', although it is unlikely that in remote rural areas closing time could have been enforced.

The public house's everyday function as a gathering place was probably not affected by legislation until the First World War, when the licensed trade was drastically curtailed, and all-day opening was brought to an end. People did use public houses from very early in the morning before the war. Men called in on their way to work, and they also began drinking early on holidays, as the daughter of a Dalton publican recalled: 'I can remember, 6 o'clock on an Easter Monday, holiday time, "Come on, get up, it's time you were open!" They wanted to be in all day.'[43] Wartime conditions enabled the government to do what in peacetime would probably have been unacceptable, and opening hours were reduced to around five hours a day, with a break in the afternoon. In addition, all public houses were permanently short of beer during the war, often having nothing to sell, and this must have helped to accustom the public to spending their leisure time elsewhere. After the war the 1921 Licensing Act, which returned the trade to a peacetime footing, retained the period of closure in the afternoon and reduced hours to half their pre-war level. These reduced hours apparently met with widespread acceptance among the general public. This was certainly the case by 1930, as witnesses to the Royal Commission on Licensing made clear.[44] The public house had by the inter-war years undoubtedly lost much of its centrality to leisure time. The per capita consumption of alcohol had fallen markedly after the turn of the century as real wages stagnated, limiting the amount of money available for alcohol, while at the same time a widening range of alternative places of entertainment drew people away from the public houses.[45] The pubs were functioning less as entertainment centres by the First World War, and although this must in part have reflected declining public demand, part of the responsibility for bringing this about lies with the licensing justices who, in the early years of this century, frequently imposed restrictions and prohibitions on public house entertainments.

Magistrates in the latter part of the nineteenth century were obviously keen to uphold the letter of the licensing laws, and a serious view was taken of drunkenness and infringements of licensing hours. Public house recreations were not legally proscribed, however, and sporting events at least appear to have been viewed on the whole with tolerance. In 1869, when a Flookburgh innkeeper was charged with permitting drunkenness in his house, 'a mitigated penalty' was inflicted by the justices when they learned that there had been a foot race on the day in question.[46] Public house sports continue to be widely reported throughout the century, and there is no evidence of any objection from licensing benches. The attitudes of justices towards public house dances are less clear, and there may in places have been a degree of disapproval. For instance, in Barrow in 1882 magistrates refused to grant a music and dancing licence to the Brewery Inn. The grounds for the refusal are not known.[47] Nevertheless, public house dances were undoubtedly taking place in the late nineteenth century, as a variety of fragmentary evidence, ranging from the activities of dancing masters to reports of hiring fairs and convictions for drunkenness, makes clear.[48] The reduction in public house numbers, the growth of Methodism, and the influence of the anti-drink lobbies may have lessened the numbers of dances, but it would seem that, over much of the region, justices either had no power or no wish to forbid them.

In the early years of this century, when the 1902 and 1904 Acts had strengthened the power of magistrates, judicial attacks on public house culture became commonplace. Drunkenness was a live political issue, and the public house tended to be regarded by justices as simply a drink shop. With rates of drunkenness conviction in mind, they opposed anything a licensee might do to encourage custom, and any practices which could possibly lead to excessive drinking. Some of these restrictions had no basis in law, but in view of their vulnerable position, landlords appear to have felt bound to acquiesce. At the Kendal Borough Licensing Sessions in 1910, for instance, the Chief

Constable reported that 'in consequence of the hint thrown out at the last brewster sessions, he had reason to believe that the practice of giving free drinks and cigars on Sundays had been almost entirely stopped. There may be one or two exceptions, but as a rule the publicans have given up the practice.' The justices said that they were glad to hear it, and 'hoped all the publicans would fall into line'.[49] Early twentieth-century justices clearly objected to music and dancing in public houses. Licences were now evidently required in many places, but these appear to have been granted only to better-class hotels, such as the Furness Abbey Hotel, which was licensed by the Barrow bench in 1908. Numbers of publicans applied for licences, but were refused. In 1904, for instance, the landlord of the King's Arms in Dalton applied, but 'the police did not think it was desirable to have dancing generally on a Saturday night at this place', and the justices refused the licence.[50] Two years later a music licence was sought for the Cavendish Arms in the same town, 'but the bench declined to accede to the request'.[51] At the Wigton sessions in 1905, the police superintendent complained that the licensee of the Board Inn at Pelutho, near Silloth, 'promoted dances and other entertainments to induce young people to the house', and the renewal of his licence was adjourned. It was eventually granted when the landlord's solicitor gave an assurance that dances were no longer held in the barn, and 'there had never been any dominoes or games of any kind in connection with the house'.[52] A dancing licence had presumably not been necessary in the area concerned. The disapproval of public house entertainments was again made explicit in Barrow in the same year, when the transfer of a licence to the previous holder's widow was being considered. The police 'mentioned' to the bench 'that this was the house where they were always playing gramophones and permitting other music, a practice of which the bench had frequently complained'. The transfer was granted on the understanding that the music would cease.[53] The Barrow bench had, at the brewster sessions that year, 'passed a resolution against music in rooms at public houses and desired that the practice should be discontinued'.[54]

There is no evidence of attacks on public house sports by justices, but they nevertheless became few after the turn of the century. The press still carries occasional advertisements for pigeon shoots (now sometimes clay), and the occasional hound trail, and some houses had bowling greens, but there is nothing more. Developments in sport generally brought about a decline in the types of sport promoted by publicans, and this added to the growing tendency to spend leisure time away from the public house.

Public house entertainment, whether from official repression or other factors, was at its nadir in the decade before the First World War, but it never entirely disappeared. Cards and dominoes were played, there were bagatelle tables,[55] and despite official disapproval, there must still have been a great deal of informal music. There was certainly singing in the Dalton public house in which an informant grew up, her father being a noted singer, who regularly entertained his customers.[56] Singing also continued in rural inns after hunts and at shepherds' meets. If the days of the publican as entertainments entrepreneur were over, he or she still provided a place where people might gather for society and amusement. Clubs and societies of all kinds also continued to meet in public houses.

STATE MANAGEMENT

In 1915 the building of a huge munitions factory was begun at Gretna, north of Carlisle. Between October that year and June 1916, between 10,000 and 12,000 hard-drinking navvies arrived in Carlisle, and 2,000 to 4,000 more were sent to Gretna and neighbouring villages.[57] Accommodation was a problem, and many men apparently had to walk the streets till bedtime. There were fights, and the number of drunkenness convictions rose. In Carlisle there were 564 in the first six months of 1916, as against seventy-two in the corresponding period of 1915, and this despite restrictions on the licensed trade which severely curtailed drinking hours. To deal with the problem, the Liquor Control Board, which had been created in 1915, compulsorily purchased all the licensed premises and breweries in Carlisle and the majority of those in an area which, on the English side of the border, stretched by 1917 as far as Maryport.

The Control Board pursued a policy of closures and changes in the nature of public house premises and management. In Carlisle in July 1916 there were 119 public houses. By the end of 1920, fifty-two of these had been closed, and two new licences had been issued, so that sixty-nine remained. Six houses were closed within twelve days of the commencement of the scheme, and at the end of four months, twenty of the 'worst' licensed premises had been closed down.[58] Of the

340 licences in the whole State Control area of Cumberland, 123 had been suppressed by the Board by the end of 1920. In those public houses which were kept open by the Control Board, disinterested management was introduced. In most cases the existing licensees became the Board's managers, and they were paid a flat wage, unrelated to alcohol sales. The supply of non-intoxicating drinks was insisted upon, and managers were paid a bonus on the sale of refreshments and for general good management. As a result, food was on sale at twenty-eight public houses in Carlisle by the end of the first year of State Management. Alterations were also made to many premises. Small snugs, and jug and bottle departments where people had been in the habit of drinking, were knocked out to make supervision easier, and large, rather bare and unwelcoming rooms took their place. These 'improvements' were intended to make public houses more respectable places, but they were greatly disliked by the majority of customers, so much so, that during the inter-war years the policy was modified. The Board's General Manager had been forced to accept by 1918 that 'the British drinker does not appear to like too large an open space'.[59] There was criticism of the early State Management houses from many quarters. A trade union delegate at a State purchase meeting described the State houses in Carlisle as 'about as cold and uncomfortable as a third class waiting room at a country railway station',[60] while another observer thought they were 'about as cheerful in appearance as an undertaker's shop, in the hands of the official receiver, on a wet day'.[61]

There was, however, some approval. A journalist said in the *Daily News* that he had 'visited some of [the State houses] last night and found, on the whole, more customers in these bright homely places than in the narrow stand up bars which remain in some cases merely across the street'.[62] The emphasis on the provision of non-intoxicants was also praised by a teetotal trade union delegate who toured the Carlisle houses in December 1919.[63]

> The disadvantages of the old system as distinct from the conditions prevailing in Carlisle, are that it almost compels the abstainer to part company with a non-abstainer in nearly the whole of his social life. I have always felt that it would be a great advantage if my friend and I, whoever my friend happened to be, could enjoy ourselves together, each following his own tastes and that problem is solved here.

The great reduction in the numbers of public houses coming, as it did, in the wake of numerous closures under the 1904 Act, undoubtedly caused a shortage of public house accommodation, even though some of the 'improved' houses were larger than they had been previously. In the Longtown division two parishes, Kirkandrews Nether and Westlinton, lost their only public house,[64] and in Carlisle the number of public houses was apparently reduced to a level at which it could no longer meet the recreational needs of the population. By February 1919 the situation had become so difficult that a meeting of local social and sporting societies was called by the Carlisle and Cumberland Society of Yorkshiremen, and a deputation was appointed to see Sir Edgar Sanders, the General Manager of the Control Board.[65] Sir Edgar denied that there had been any reduction in facilities, and said that smoking concerts had been held 'on frequent occasions' in the Victoria, Bowling Green and Bluebell Hotels. The complaint was evidently heeded, however, as the following week the Control Board announced that a building adjoining the Gretna Tavern, which had recently been acquired by them with no particular purpose in mind, was to be converted 'into premises suitable for dinners, suppers, smoking concerts, small dances, social gatherings, whist drives, etc.'[66]

By the end of the First World War, the Board was strongly in favour of recreations on licensed premises, as they were considered to be a distraction from the consumption of alcohol. This was the direct opposite of official policy in the region during the early part of the century, and heralded a change which was to influence licensing benches in the region. It met with criticism both as policy and for the sometimes inept way in which it was carried out. The attempt to provide an 'improved public house' at Rockcliffe by converting the village reading room brought ridicule from, among others, the *Daily Mail*.[67] On visiting the place their reporter found

> Three gloomy countrymen sitting in a tiny uninviting room, sadly regarding a portrait of the late Sir Wilfrid Lawson. In a larger room was a library of uninteresting books and a deserted bagatelle table. The place was as cheerful as a morgue. The intention had (he finished) been to make a workmen's club; the effect – a Sunday school with a licence.

Criticism also came from 'Sister Lillie Davis', who wrote to the *Cumberland News* in 1920 to express her fears that the provision of music would lead young girls astray by encouraging them into public houses. The numbers of young men under twenty frequenting them had, she said, already increased.[68] This complaint followed the announcement that music was to be provided in the Gretna Tavern on Tuesday and Friday evenings, when Mr Haddow's Orchestra were to perform selections of music and vocal items between 7.30 and 9.30 p.m.[69] Admission was to be free, and if the experiment proved successful, music was to be offered in other houses. How success was to be measured in a house where large drink sales were not sought is unclear, and it is not known whether music was ever made available elsewhere. There was, however, singing among customers in State houses,[70] and the wireless was made widely available. In the Blue Bell in Carlisle, in the mid-1920s, there were 'six sets of wireless headphones hanging on hat hooks on the walls'. It was reported that 'No charge is made for the use of the 'phones, neither is there any obligation to buy as a condition to listening in.'[71] The wireless was very popular, and in 1925 the provision was extended from Carlisle to Longtown and Aspatria.[72]

A number of the State houses had sporting facilities. The St Nicholas Arms in Carlisle, a house which prior to conversion had been the residence of an MP for the city, had a large lawn which was used as a putting green.[73] Other houses had bowling greens, and billiard tables were provided, for instance in the Blue Bell and the Irish Gate Tavern in Carlisle.[74]

The policy of the 'improved public house' was being followed by many brewers throughout Britain by the 1930s.[75] The brewer Sir W. W. Butler said in August 1925, for instance, 'It is certain that the younger generation will not be content with the conditions which satisfied their forefathers. They have been educated up to a higher standard of comfort and they will expect to obtain it.'[76] The State Management scheme was one of the pioneers of the idea, and in this region their activities helped to give the public house a more respectable image. The 'improved' houses found an early champion in the Bishop of Carlisle. In February 1925 he was reported in the *Manchester Despatch* as saying that he

> had entertained the whole diocesan conference in one of the licensed houses, and he did not notice in the afternoon any undue exuberance in their demeanour, or that their morals had deteriorated. His wife too, had entertained the Mothers' Union Council there, and none of the

mothers protested against glasses of beer, now and again, being consumed by working men.[77]

Official support for the 'improved public house' was given by the Church of England Assembly in 1936.[78]

The introduction of State Management in the Carlisle area resulted in the disappearance of many of the small low-class public houses which had been a home from home for working-class men and women. In their place were put larger café-style premises with good facilities, which were increasingly found acceptable by the respectable classes, although in working-class areas, working-class public houses remained. The new houses had in many ways a similar social function to the larger rural inns at the start of our period. They pointed the direction for the public house in post-Second World War Cumbria and influenced the policies of licensing benches in the inter-war years. They also helped to make public house attendance by women respectable, although this change was only beginning to be felt in the region before the Second World War.

WOMEN IN PUBLIC HOUSES

'Auld Wife Hakes' and other more modern forms of dance which were held in public houses presuppose the presence of women, and it is clear that the region's public houses were never wholly male preserves. The extent to which women participated in pub culture in general is however difficult to assess. There were always a minority of women among those convicted of drunkenness. In 1903, for example, 296 men and forty-two women were proceeded against in North Lonsdale division, and twenty-two men and four women in the Kendal County division.[79] The relationship of these figures to the numbers of men and women in public houses is, however, a matter for conjecture. The barring of children from licensed premises under the 1908 Children's Act would have made it more difficult for women to be there, but the extent to which mothers had previously taken their families into public houses is unknown. A Home Office return of the numbers of women and children frequenting public houses did not concern itself with Cumbria, but in all the towns surveyed, women and children were found on licensed premises.[80]

Oral evidence suggests that in the years immediately before the First World War, few women were to be found in public houses in

Cumbria. An informant whose father became licensee of a small beerhouse in Dalton in 1911 said that, initially, 'we never used to have any women. My father would never have any women to come in at all.'[81] Women who frequented public houses were generally considered to be 'low', but it appears that financial considerations could also keep women out of public houses. A Maryport woman, who married in 1908, said that apart from the stigma, 'There wasn't money. I mean even when they had a job, there wasn't money to let two people go to drink.'[82] Women who did frequent public houses usually did so furtively. They did not usually mix with the men. Sometimes a small room was set aside for them, or alternatively they would gather in jug and bottle departments. The Chief Constable of Barrow complained of the latter practice to the licensing justices in 1907:

> In some fully licensed houses people were served with drink to be consumed on the premises in the ... jug and bottle department. Although there was no absolute law about it, he thought it would be against the wishes of the licensing justices, and further, he should remark that it appeared the people found in those houses were women.[83]

The Chief Constable of Carlisle made a similar complaint two years earlier. He was afraid that drinkers thus concealed from public view 'could get more than is good for them'.[84]

Furtive drinking among women was evidently well established in Carlisle at the start of the State Management scheme. The knocking out of snugs was aimed principally at eradicating it, and this was not appreciated by the women who had used them. One woman, 'a poor shrivelled little body', who was questioned by Ernest Selley in February 1917 about the alterations to her 'local' which was in a 'very poor quarter', said that the Control Board 'had properly spoilt the place. Before they altered it, I could nip in and have a glass and come out again without anybody knowing. Now you has to go in and have your drink with all the rabble!' Another woman, referring to the same house, said 'There's no privacy now. If a woman wants a drink she has to go where she's seen and she doesn't like it.'[85] Women drank in privacy partly because of the social stigma of being seen in a public house, and partly because men would not tolerate their company. The General Manager of the State Management Scheme said 'that the men in certain parts of the city would not have the women drinking with them'.[86] One house mentioned in this respect was the Goliath. 'Patronised largely by coal carters and railway workers', it was 'the place where the Caldewgate and Crown Street factions met ... and brawls were frequent'.[87] Evidently there was, in places, a violent male pub culture in existence which was neither willing nor able to accommodate women.

The response of the Control Board was to comply with custom and officially designate certain rooms as women's rooms. These were included in many of the early conversions undertaken by the Board, and as with most of the Board's activities, they met with a mixed response. Most criticism seems to have come from outside the region, which perhaps suggests that in some parts of the country, women's bars were an unknown social custom, although it could simply be that middle-class observers were not aware of their existence. Selley noted that snugs where women congregated were to be found in all the areas he visited while researching his book.[88] The writer of a letter to the *Weekly Westminster* in 1924 nevertheless commented unfavourably on the 'herding together of women in one compartment'.[89] The *Daily Mail* asserted that in these bars women were only permitted to have one drink, but the truth of this has not been ascertained.[90]

It appears that the majority of those who used the women's bars were older women. Younger women were perhaps kept at home by children. Perhaps also, they were more influenced by the growth of home and family-centredness, and spent more time with their husbands than older women who were more accustomed to keeping the company of their own sex. Miss Mary Ellen Creighton, of the State Management Advisory Committee, giving evidence before the 1930 Royal Commission on Licensing, said that 'on the whole she believed that women's bars were an advantage for older women. It was a kind of club for them.'[91] Lady Horsley, giving evidence as 'a woman citizen' to the same Commission, said that when she visited one women's bar, 'about fifteen women were there, all singing at the top of their voices. They were mostly poorly dressed, middle-aged or older.'[92] The *Birmingham Post* claimed that the separate bars were much appreciated by country women on market day.[93]

Many of the State Management Scheme's later 'improved public houses' did not have women's bars, although those in earlier houses for the most part remained. The General Manager, giving evidence to the Royal Commission on Licensing in 1930, told them that 'opinion had now become modified considerably and in the latest building schemes it had not been thought necessary to provide separate accommodation'.[94] Bars in these houses were instead often designated as first or second class, and they were either for men only, or open to both sexes.[95]

It was claimed that the number of women frequenting public houses in the State Management area was increasing between the wars, and this was blamed both on the provision of entertainment and, more particularly, on the increased respectability of the houses.[96] This increase probably appeared greater than it really was, due to the ending of invisible, furtive drinking among women, but it does nevertheless appear to have been real as far as young women were concerned. The Bishop of Carlisle, addressing the Church of England Temperance Society in 1925, maintained that there was an increased tendency for young women to drink, but that this was not a result of the increased respectability of State Managed houses. Drinking by women was, he said, a post-war trend, which was affecting the whole country.[97] Selley also asserted that more women were visiting public houses in all parts of the country. It was, he said, 'a change in social habit'.[98] He suggested, probably correctly, that the war had 'brought out women and girls to a great extent', and they were now more willing to take their place alongside men socially.

Away from the State Management area, however, change came very slowly in Cumbria, and conditions similar to those in Carlisle before 1916 persisted. The daughter of the Dalton beerhouse-keeper mentioned above said that the first sign of change came during the First World War:

> After the war broke out they brought a lot of Manchester girls and such like (to work in munitions). Well they'd been used to going in you see. I remember one man . . . he brought one or two of these Manchester girls in with him. . . . My father ordered them out. He said he wouldn't serve women. But you see, you'd got to get used to it, because . . . it got all going then.[99]

Women continued to be suffered unwillingly on licensed premises, however. Possibly the fear of being accused of harbouring prostitutes was at the root of it, and the negative attitudes of licensing benches must also have been influential. The presence of women on licensed premises was still considered reprehensible by the authorities in Kendal in 1920, for instance. The police drew the attention of the magistrates to it, and they 'desired to ask the licensees to stop drinking amongst women and girls'. The Chairman 'asked them to consider these women as their own daughters, and treat them accordingly'.[100] They seem to have failed to comprehend that a publican might treat his daughter differently from the way a JP treated his. Mass Observation described attitudes such as these as 'a continual inhibition, a conservatism from necessarily aged persons who are also automatically too high up the social scale to know much, if anything, about ordinary pubs'.[101] An informant whose mother held the licence of a large fully licensed house in Dalton said that women were permitted on the premises, 'but mother wouldn't let the women go with the men. And she was very strict. There was a smaller room and women could go in there.'[102] Women customers were, however, very few, and the majority bought what they wanted in the jug and bottle department (where drinking was not permitted) and took it home. Similarly, in another house in the town, 'there was a little room at the back where they could go if they wanted to', although the informant, the licensee's grandson, never remembered seeing any women there.[103] This may be explained by the fact that furtive drinking continued in the inter-war years. Another informant said of women in public houses in Dalton, 'you never seen them. I'm not saying that they didn't go in them, but you never seen them.'[104] An Urswick informant said that women, 'just odd uns . . . used to go t'vaults at Ulverston. Casey's Vaults. Up back entry. You see, they used to drink out o' sight like.'[105] The same informant said that before the Second World War, public houses were not places you took your wife or girlfriend to.

Only one female informant went into public houses before the Second World War, and she did so while in farm service near Preston.[106] She would not have considered doing so in her home town of Dalton, where drinking still carried a decided stigma for women, particularly young ones. 'I'll tell you one thing,' she said, 'they weren't called ladies.' In Workington and Penrith, the majority of male and female informants insisted that no respectable woman would have entered a public house between the wars. 'Oh, you were no class at all if you went to a pub', said one woman.[107] A Penrith informant did say, however, that it was not unknown for a man and his wife to call at a country pub while out for a Sunday walk,[108] and it may have been that rural houses had a slightly more respectable image, as refreshment houses, than those in towns.

It is apparent that public house culture was one aspect of leisure in which women did not fully participate in the first forty years of this century. Despite the pioneering efforts of the State Management Scheme, drinking was still in the 1930s considered to be a bad habit which was not indulged in by the respectable classes, and the weight of respectability fell more heavily on women than on men. A man might, up to a point, rub shoulders with undesirables without losing status, but a woman lost her reputation much more easily. Sitting drinking also implied time and money wasted, and this, too, was more reprehensible in a woman than in a man. Although it was accepted that women might venture on to licensed premises for dances and other special events, calling in for a bottle of stout or glass of port was, in most parts of the region, a matter for shame and secrecy. Whether this had been the case in the latter part of the nineteenth century is a matter for conjecture. The fact that those women who frequented public houses were usually at least of middle age perhaps suggests that the habit had been more acceptable in their youth, although younger women would always have been limited in their leisure activities by children. The writing was on the wall, however. Young women were making an appearance in public houses. A Workington informant remembered the 'uproar' in the town when 'a young lady . . . just walked in' to a public house.[109] Though she may have been an object of scandal at the time, she and others like her did ultimately, after the Second World War, force Cumbria's licensees, justices and male drinkers alike to 'get used to it'.

CONCLUSION: THE PUBLIC HOUSE BETWEEN THE WARS

After the First World War, the attitudes of justices towards the public house became more liberal and accommodating. This did not happen immediately in all areas. The Kendal County bench in 1919, for instance, refused to grant a music and dancing licence to the Punch Bowl Inn at Crosthwaite. The police had objected to the licence on the grounds that dances could be held in the village club and reading room, which was in their eyes a preferable venue.[110] By 1930, however, the Barrow bench, which had previously been so restrictive in this matter, licensed thirteen public houses for music and singing, 'to cover wireless entertainment'. In 1935 the number had increased to twenty-two, and a further two were licensed for dancing.[111] The policies of the State Management Scheme were probably influential, and the support given to the 'improved public house' by the Bishop of Carlisle, and later the Church hierarchy in general, probably influenced clergy on benches. The continued reduction in the number of drunkenness convictions after the First World War must also have been a factor in bringing about this change of heart. In Barrow, drunkenness prosecutions fell from 320 in 1913 to seventy-three in 1922.[112] In Kendal borough they declined from seventy-five in 1904 to twenty-four in 1929, and in Kendal County from fifteen in 1904 to two in 1929.[113]

Between 1870 and 1939 the publican ceased to be an entertainments entrepreneur. His numbers dwindled, which perhaps made it less necessary to attract people to his house by offering entertainments, while at the same time, the developing leisure industries provided forms of amusement with which he could scarcely compete. The importance of his house to leisure activity was further limited by the imposition of restricted hours. Despite all this, the basic recreational function of the public house remained fundamentally unchanged on the eve of the Second World War. It was still a social gathering place, mainly for men, but for all social classes. Bar games such as dominoes and cards (but rarely darts) were played, and although quoits largely disappeared, bowls and billiards became popular and widely available.[114] Despite the period of judicial disapproval, there was also music and singing at the end of our period, just as there had been in the beginning. In Urswick, 'we used to sing songs and harmonize and orchestrate', and in Penrith they had 'maybe an odd song or two. Hunting songs mainly. ... there were some horrible singers as well.'[115] As we have seen, there could also be singing in the women's bars, and the range of musical and other entertainment was added to by the spread of the wireless. Public house dances also flourished in the 1930s,[116] when the pastime was second only in popularity to the cinema. The public house's share of the recreational cake was less than it had been in the 1870s when the variety of entertainments on offer was much smaller, and drink featured more strongly in people's lives, but it nevertheless maintained its importance as a place where men might meet socially on neutral ground.

NOTES

Place of publication London unless otherwise stated.

1 See plans of public houses in Barrow P.L. Z900 series; J. F. and T. M. Flett, *Traditional Step-Dancing in Lakeland*, 1979, p. 8.
2 W.G., 1.1.1870, 11.6.1870.
3 See Chapter IV.
4 C.J., 10.6.1870; W.G., 13.8.1870.
5 C.J., 13.2.1880; B.H., 6.11.1869; C.Pacq., 3.1.1860.
6 Kendal Borough Police, Return of Public and Beer Houses in the Borough of Kendal, and the general accommodation, n.d. Fixed to the 1880s or 1890s from the number and names of houses listed. Licensing records, K.R.O.
7 See plans in Barrow P.L. z900 series.
8 Brian Harrison, *Drink and the Victorians*, London 1971, p. 313; G. B. Wilson, *Alcohol and the Nation*, 1940, Table 19, pp. 379–80; Annual Abstract of Statistics.
9 Figures in official returns sometimes differ from those given in Chief Constables' reports. Where there is a variation I have, where possible, taken the figures given in Wilson, 1940, as these have been generally accepted.
10 P.P. 1868–69 (429), XXXIV 309; Wilson, 1940, Table 19, pp. 379–80.
11 I only have figures for all counties from 1875; Wilson, 1940, Table 19, pp. 379–80.
12 P.P. 1889 (131), LX 715.
13 P.P. 1901 (353), LXI 215.
14 P.P. 1883 (338), LXIV 491.
15 W.G., 31.8.1895.
16 Beerhouses licensed under 1 Will 4 C64, 1830 numbered 251 in Cumberland and forty-eight in Westmorland in March 1869. P.P. 1868–69 (429), XXXIV 307.
17 P.P. 1875 (465), LXXI 621.
18 Wilson, 1940, p. 236.
19 E. A. Pratt, *The Policy of Licensing Justices*, London, 1909, Ch. VIII, *passim*.
20 *Bulmer's Directory of Westmorland*, 1885.
21 Plans Kendal R.O. and Barrow P.L. Z900 series.
22 P.P. 1896 (379), LXIX 219.
23 Wilson, 1940, p. 85.
24 Return of public houses in Brampton, Longtown and Eskdale divisions, 1892, C.R.O. new acquisition, not catalogued.
25 Wilson, 1940, p. 87.
26 C.J., 3.2.1905.
27 H. A. Monckton, *A History of the English Public House*, 1969, p. 110.
28 Monckton, 1969, p. 100.
29 P.P. 1904 (230), LXXX 201. The 1904 Act came into force the following year.
30 Wilson, 1940, p. 87 relates this to their keenness to own tied houses, even if it meant borrowing heavily and buying the breweries which already owned them.
31 Monckton, 1969, p. 111.
32 The minutes of the Cumberland County Licensing Committee record the decision to bar the press from their meetings. C.R.O. CQL/1/1. The meetings of the committees in the other two counties appear not to be reported in the press, which suggests that they, too, were closed.
33 Cumberland County Licensing Committee minute books 1873–1924, 1925– , C.R.O. CQL/1/1/
34 Minute books, C.R.O. CQL/1/1 and local press, *passim*.
35 W.G., *passim*.
36 Barrow press, *passim*.
37 Cumberland County Licensing Committee minute book 1873–1924, C.R.O. CQL/1/1.
38 B.H., 6.2.1908.

39 *W.G.*, 10.3.1906.
40 *W.G.*, 12.3.1910.
41 Wilson, 1940, pp. 112–13.
42 *W.G.*, 10.3.1906; *B.H.*, 11.3.1905.
43 Respondent 9.
44 Quoted in Wilson, 1940, p. 159.
45 See A. E. Dingle, 'Drink and working-class living standards in Britain, 1870–1914', *Economic History Review*, II, Vol. XXV, 1972, pp. 619–20; Wilson 1940, pp. 332–3; Mass Observation, *The Pub and the People*, 1970, p. 216.
46 *B.H.*, 20.3.1869.
47 J. N. Martin, *Paterson's Licensing Acts*, 1966 edn., pp. 143–4. *B.T.*, 11.11.1882. Music and dancing licences were only necessary if they were required by a local act or, after 1890, if part IV of the Public Health Acts Amendment Act had been adopted in the locality.
48 For dancing masters see Ch. IV; *C.J.*, 8.6.1900, Wigton Hiring Fair; *W.G.*, 18.2.1899, drunkenness after a dance.
49 *W.G.*, 12.2.1910.
50 *B.H.*, 5.3.1904.
51 *B.H.*, 3.3.1906.
52 *C.J.*, 10.2.1905.
53 *B.H.*, 5.4.1905.
54 *Licensed Trade News*, 18.2.1905.
55 Respondents 4 and 9.
56 Respondent 9.
57 Information on the State Management Scheme is taken from E. Selley, *The English Public House as it is*, 1927, pp. 78–84, Arthur Shadwell, *Drink in 1914–1923. A lesson in Control*, 1923, pp. 58–79 and Basil Oliver, The *Renaissance of the English Public House*, 1947, Ch. III.
58 Selley, 1927, p. 84.
59 N. Longmate, *The Waterdrinkers*, 1968, p. 271.
60 *Morning Advertiser*, 2.1.1920.
61 *Manchester Despatch*, 13.11.1920.
62 *Daily News*, 29.11.1919.
63 *Derby Daily Telegraph*, 22.12.1919.
64 Chief Constables' Returns of Licensed Houses in Cumberland, 1.1.1915 and 1.1.1923, C.R.O. QL9.
65 *C.N.*, 15.2.1919.
66 *C.N.*, 21.2.1919.
67 *Daily Mail*, 29.11.1919.
68 *C.N.*, 19.10.1920.
69 *C.J.*, 15.10.1920.
70 *C.J.*, 13.5.1930.
71 Selley, 1927, p. 100.
72 *Glasgow Evening News*, undated news clipping in 1925 file of State Management papers, C.R.O. T/CSM/2.
73 Selley, 1927, p. 98.
74 See Oliver, 1947, Ch. III. Selley, 1927, pp. 99, 100.
75 See Oliver, 1947, *passim*. There was much discussion of the idea in the inter-war press.
76 Wilson, 1940, p. 181.
77 *Manchester Despatch*, 12.2.1925.
78 Horace Keast, *The Church and the Public House*, 1936, p. 16.
79 *W.G.*, 4.2.1905, 11.2.1905.
80 P.P. 1908, C3813, LXXXIX 625.

81 Respondent 4.
82 Respondent 16.
83 B.H., 5.2.1907.
84 C.J., 3.2.1905.
85 Selley, 1927, p. 88.
86 A. E. Mitchell, in *C.N.*, 3.5.1930. He was explaining why the Control Board had found it necessary to provide women's bars.
87 *The Star*, 29.11.1919. The Goliath was listed as a house with a women's bar in *Evening World*, 23.5.1930.
88 Selley, 1927, p. 125.
89 *Weekly Westminster*, 9.8.1924.
90 *Daily Mail*, 29.11.1919.
91 *C.N.*, 24.5.1930.
92 *C.J.*, 13.5.1930.
93 21.5.1925.
94 *C.N.*, 3.5.1930.
95 Plans of many of these houses are given in Oliver, 1947, Ch. III.
96 See, for instance, *C.N.*, 17.1.1925, Wesleyan meeting at Wigton.
97 *Yorkshire Post*, 29.4.1925.
98 Selley, 1927, pp. 126–8.
99 Respondent 4.
100 *W.G.*, 14.2.1920.
101 Mass Observation, 1943, pp. 230–1.
102 Respondent 9.
103 Respondent 3.
104 Respondent 20.
105 Respondent 15.
106 Respondent 20.
107 Respondent 13.
108 Respondent 27.
109 Respondent 25.
110 *W.G.* 8.2.1919.
111 *B.N.*, 15.2.1930, 2.2.1935.
112 Shadwell, 1923, p. 148.
113 Annual Report of Chief Constable to Kendal Watch Committee, 1904, K.R.O.; *W.G.*, 11.2.1905, 15.2.1930.
114 Respondents 3, 4, 5, 6, 9, 25 and 34.
115 Respondents 15 and 6.
116 Respondents 15 and 3, dance band musicians.

CHAPTER IV

Sport

INTRODUCTION

Sport is a term which can embrace a wide range of disparate activities, from organised games to blood sports, or hiking and mountaineering. Cumbria's population was obviously well situated for activities of the latter kind. They had on their doorstep all the natural attractions which brought visitors to the region. Many oral informants enjoyed walking, and the sea, lakes and rivers were made use of for bathing, fishing and occasionally boating, especially by the young. These activities never formed the major part of adult sporting activity, however, and climbing, one of the region's main atrractions for the visitor, was not a pastime which was generally engaged in by local people. There were noted local climbers, but proximity to the mountains did not make climbing any less of a minority interest than it was nationally. Nevertheless, Cumbria did, throughout our period, have a very full sporting culture, the development of which forms the subject matter of this chapter.

In some ways sport in Cumbria differed little from that in other parts of the country. Here as elsewhere, football, cricket and other codified sports established themselves by the end of the nineteenth century. There were other sports, however, which were peculiar to the region, or which differed markedly in organisation from the same sport elsewhere. Foremost among these regional sports were hunting, wrestling, athletics and hound-trailing. In addition, despite legislation against cruel sports, cockfighting persisted in Cumbria.

COCKFIGHTING

In the early nineteenth century, cockfighting was a long practised and widely popular sport in the Lake Counties. Although it had aristocratic associations, all classes seem to have been involved. Mains were apparently held at Lowther Castle.[1] The Bishop of Carlisle is reputed to have had a cockpit at Rose Castle,[2] and clergymen often seem to have presided at mains, particularly in their capacity as masters at the Grammar Schools, most of which had the tradition of Shrove Tuesday or Easter cockfights and the payment of a 'cockpenny' by the boys.

Many towns and villages in Cumbria had annual mains and there were county and district matches. It was also the usual practice for cockfights to be held at horse-race meetings.[3] Nicholson suggests that there was a prohibitively high entry charge to urban cockpits to keep out the 'rough element',[4] and William Fleming's diary for March 1813 states that the admittance charge to a three-day main between Cumberland and Lancashire in Ulverston Assembly Rooms was 6s.[5] It would seem, though, from the ubiquity of cockpits, that only certain mains were exclusive, and that the sport itself was not class-specific during its period of legality.

The Cruelty to Animals Acts of 1835 and, more specifically, 1849, made cockfighting illegal.[6] They had little immediate success in eradicating the sport in Cumbria. Although the sport's following gradually diminished, cockfights continued to take place at least until the inter-war period. Oral informants remembered cockfights taking place in country areas outside Penrith, at Urswick and in the Workington district between the wars, and the *Westmorland Gazette* reported a main at Orton in 1938. W. M. Williams maintains that mains were also held at farms less than a mile from the village of Gosforth in the late 1930s.[7]

According to G. R. Scott, the wording of the Acts made prosecutions difficult.[8] It was necessary for participants to be apprehended whilst a fight was in progress, and this made life very difficult for the police, as those involved were quite aware of the letter of the law. As an oral informant said, 'you'd got to catch them at it! Twas no good if you didn't catch them at it.'[9] Very often the police, after lurking under hedges and tramping over remote hillsides, had to be satisfied with preventing a cockfight from taking place. For instance, a main had been arranged to take place at New Mills near Gosforth at 4.30 a.m. in May 1895. Before the battle had begun, a scout discovered a policeman up a tree. He gave the alarm and several more policemen were then found to be lying in ambush. The participants made their escape in waggonettes and the mains did not take place.[10] It was doubtless difficult for the police to remain in hiding for long enough to be able to bring a prosecution. Cockfighters also utilised the county boundaries, particularly that between Lancashire and Cumberland, moving from one county to the next if disturbed by the police.

There were convictions, nevertheless. In 1874, a man was

successfully prosecuted at Barrow following a cockfight at North Scale.[11] Again in Barrow, in 1903, two men and their three accomplices were fined after a Whit Monday cockfight;[12] and at Hackthorpe in 1938 seventeen men were fined a total of £367 following the match at Orton already referred to.[13] Successful prosecutions represent only the tip of the iceberg of cockfighting activity, however. Those prosecuted were only a minority of those present, and those cockfights which were raided were only a minority of those which took place. In the 1874 case mentioned above, twenty-nine 'accomplices' and 150 spectators escaped prosecution, and one week after the 1903 case another fight took place on the same ground 'without any interference from the authorities'.[14] Reports of numbers of undisturbed cockfights are to be found in the press, often mocking the failure of the police to prevent them. The *Whitehaven News*, reporting a main which took place on an afternoon in May 1890, informed its readers that rumour had it 'that the men in blue had got wind of the encounter and were up betimes in the early morning looking for a possible clue. The match had not begun however and the early birds had to feast on other game.' Turning the knife, the report finished by saying that 'the station platform was pretty lively after the match'.[15]

The sport's continuance was very much an 'open secret', and there was still very widespread support from all classes of the community. A Penrith informant claimed that there were still gentry and farmers involved in the sport between the wars, although the majority of fights were organized by the 'potters' and other working-class inhabitants of the Town Head area of the town.[16] Local men convicted in the 1938 prosecution were two farmers and a retired farmer, a grocer, a dentist, a haulage contractor, a painter and decorator, a mine watchman and an unemployed miner.[17] In Urswick, those involved were typically iron miners. The rather eccentric incumbent of the village, the Rev. T. N. Postlethwaite, was also reputed to have been involved early this century. Certainly he bred gamecocks.[18]

Cockfights took place at several levels in late nineteenth and twentieth-century Cumbria. Firstly there were matches between two individuals, as in Workington in 1930, where a single fight between two birds 'was the outcome of a challenge thrown out in a public house by a breeder'.[19] Similarly, fights in Penrith were said to be between rival families.[20] Then there were matches between villages or other local communities such as those which took place between Eskdale and Kirkby in 1880, and Bolton and Irby in 1907, or that which occurred in 1895 between 'the miners of Rowrah and Frizington and those of Millom and Haverigg'.[21] Lastly, there were county matches such as that between Cumberland and Lancashire which took place at Orton in 1938.[22] This was a true county match with participants from various parts of both counties. The existence of county matches suggests a high degree of organisation in the sport, but there is no hard evidence of this other than the known existence of a 'South Cumberland and Furness Cockfighting Club' in 1890.[23] This seems to have operated on the lines of a football league, matches being arranged between member villages.

Women were never involved in cockfighting. The sport was exclusively male. Women might, on occasion, be involved in rearing the birds, poultry being, by and large, the women's domain on farms, but they never attended fights. Their only other role in the proceedings was cooking the fallen, defeated cocks being generally eaten and considered delicacies because of their luxurious diet.[24] The reason for the lack of female participation in the sport can only be surmised. It may be supposed that many women would have preferred to stay away on the grounds of squeamishness, but a minority of women did (and of course still do) take part in other blood sports. Part of the answer may lie in the perhaps more negative attitude of women towards participation in illegal activities and their exclusion from such by their menfolk, but there is no evidence of female involvement whilst the sport was legal. An anthropologist who studied cockfighting in the very different environment of Bali in the 1950s[25] found that cockfights there were also exclusively male, women being expressly forbidden to attend. This exclusion of women was unusual in that country's culture.

What was the continued appeal of this illegal blood sport to the men who were involved? Clifford Geertz has suggested that in Bali gamecocks were anthropomorphic; 'it is only apparently cocks that are fighting', he maintains, 'Actually it is men.'[26] He claims that there was 'a deep psychological identification of Balinese men with their cocks', which were 'symbolic expressions or magnifications of the owner's self'.[27] (The *double entendre* is, he informs us the same in Balinese.) If it is perhaps a little excessive to suggest that this identification was exactly paralleled in Cumbria, it is nevertheless apparent that there, fighting cocks did represent the man or the community which pitted them in battle. The pride and status of the owner or his village rested on the birds.

The very large amounts of money which were often wagered at cockfights make it clear that there was more at stake than the relative merits of two birds. The main between the miners of Rowrah and Frizington and those of Millom and Haverigg in 1895 was for £50 a side, for instance.[28] Geertz has identified Bentham's concept of 'deep play' as relevant to cockfighting.[29] This is 'play in which the stakes are so high that it is, from his utilitarian standpoint, irrational for men to engage in it at all'. Loss of money was likely to result in net pain, rather than net pleasure for the participants and so, in Bentham's view, deep play was basically immoral and ought to be prohibited by law.[30] Cockfighting was so prohibited, but still it and the 'irrational' gambling on its outcome continued. Applying Geertz's ideas broadly to Cumbria we may say that, if money represented status, then the greater the amount wagered the greater was the status claimed. Defeat brought loss of status as well as loss of money. Both could be recovered in a subsequent match, but to bet only moderately was to assign low status to ones self. It is possible that it was the question of status which was crucial to the exclusion of women from the sport, as women had their own different relationship to the status of men. W. M. Williams (speaking of post-Second-World-War Gosforth, when greater secrecy was necessary), however, claims that cockfighting's 'persistence in the face of numerous hostile influences cannot be explained entirely as due to the high prestige that can be gained within the limited participating group'. 'It is,' he says, 'pursued for its own sake', an adherent telling him that 'finest sight in t'world tha knows is two birds ready to fight'.[31]

Cockfighting was not, in any case, 'deep play' for everyone involved. Spectators would attend simply, it may be supposed, for enjoyment, and the opportunity to gamble. A bookmaker was said to have been in attendance at Workington in 1930, while in Penrith someone would generally act as bookmaker for side bets.[32] There were few legal outlets for the working-class propensity to bet in the late nineteenth and early twentieth century. The sport's illegality perhaps added extra spice and there seems to have been genuine pleasure to be had from outwitting the police. Stories abound of policemen led astray by such ruses as cats in cockbags.[33] Williams tells us that in Gosforth in the 1950s 'the flouting of external authority brought added satisfaction', and that 'the discomfiture of a policeman who follows a false trail is remembered long after the contest that took place the same night'. The appeal of the sport is, he says, 'undoubtedly strengthened by the fact that it is done surreptitiously in defiance of laws to which the local community has never given its assent'.[34]

Nevertheless, the sport declined. This has been attributed by my Penrith informant to redoubled police activity during the 1930s,[35] and this assertion probably has some validity, but, as has been made clear, the police had not previously been idle. During the 1930s public opinion seems to have tilted against the sport. Perhaps it is not irrelevant that public opinion by then contained a larger female element. It was women who were heard to remark 'how dreadful and wicked' in Hackthorpe police court in 1938.[36] The sport's decline precedes the 1930s, however, and it must be seen as part of the fundamental process of change which altered the nature of Cumbrian sporting activity during the period of this study. F. Nicholson quoted an acquaintance of his, an old 'setter' of cocks who regretted the sport's decline, because there was no substitute for the 'pluck, courage, stamina and endurance' of gamecocks to lay as an example before the rising generation.[37] Increasingly during our period, these qualities were in fact sought and found in other sports which did not involve a fight to the death, but which could replace cockfighting as a focus for individual and community pride and provide opportunities for gambling. Some of these will be considered below. In the twentieth century, gamecocks began to take on a new social role as exhibits at poultry shows.

HUNTING

Cumbria's other major blood sport was hunting. Although hounds had long been used to pursue game and 'vermin' in the region, hunting only really developed as a major sport during the nineteenth century. In the earlier part of the century various quarry were pursued more or less indiscriminately with the same hounds, although otter-hunting, which took place during the summer, was always a distinct affair. The famous John Peel, who died in 1854 and who is known to the English speaking world as a fox-hunter, is said to have hunted fox, hare and mart.[38] Similarly, the Coniston Hunt was founded in 1825, 'to hunt fox, mart and hare'.[39] Mart were foulmart (polecat) and sweetmart (pine marten). They continued to be hunted until the 1890s, by which time they had become very scarce.[40] By then, fox- and hare-hunting had largely diverged. Selective breeding had produced a fast lightweight hound for fox, while hares were hunted with harriers and increasingly, from the end of the nineteenth century, with beagles.

Fox-hunting in later-nineteenth-century Cumbria had two quite distinct forms. On the one hand there were the Cumberland Foxhounds, who had adopted all the conventions of hunting in the shire counties and hunted on horseback, as the hunt's country, to the North and East of the fells, made this practicable. This pack was founded by Sir Wilfrid Lawson in 1858, and it appears to have been largely upper or upper-middle class in membership. It remained so during the period of this study, being described by an oral informant as 'a real gentlemen's outfit'.[41] On the other hand, there were the fell packs, which for reasons of terrain were followed on foot. A red coat and rather superfluous velvet riding cap had been adopted by the huntsmen of these packs, perhaps as a mark of status, while the whippers-in had to be content with a red waistcoat, but otherwise the conventions of hunting dress formed no part of fell fox-hunting. Stout boots and weatherproof clothing were the order of the day. Because little expense was involved, hunting with these packs was theoretically open to all. They should not be thought of as working-class concerns, however. The masters were frequently gentry. The Blencathra, for instance, was founded by the Crozier family of Threlkeld, and 'Squire' John Crozier was master for over sixty years, being succeeded on his death in 1903 by J. W. Lowther. Mr J. E. Hasell of Dalemain was master of the Ullswater Hounds from 1880 to 1910 and he was succeeded by Mr W. H. Marshall of Patterdale Hall.[42] Meets of both these packs were attended by gentry, as well as other classes, throughout the period, as my informant indicates: 'Mind, there was a tremendous lot of upper crust used to attend the Ullswater foxhounds . . .' And the Blencathra hounds also was a mixed pack, like you got the gentry mingling . . . with the ordinary people.'[43] It may have been that some meets were more likely to draw gentry followers than others. For instance, when the Ullswater met at Gowbarrow Hall in January 1880, the field were described as 'all well mounted'[44] which was not usually the case. Richard Clapham, however, asserted that 'the regular followers of the fell packs consist chiefly of shepherds, dalesmen and the like, comparatively few of the local gentry being sufficiently keen to take more than a passing interest in the sport'.[45] The Eskdale and Ennerdale seems to have been the least aristocratic of the packs of foxhounds. It was founded as the Eskdale in 1857 by Tommy Dobson, a bobbin turner, and he combined the roles of master and huntsman until 1910. His successor, a Mr W. C. Porter, has proved impossible to trace, but he too hunted his own hounds, unlike the gentry who appointed huntsmen. The Melbreak seems also to have had no gentry connections before the Second World War.

The social standing of the followers of the several packs of harriers and beagles is more difficult to assess. Little or nothing has been written about these packs, and the gleanings of the local press provide only a few clues. It is probably fair to say that, as with the foxhounds, some of them had a mixed following, whilst a minority were more upper class in membership. The Oxenholme Harriers appear to have become more socially exclusive after they became the Oxenholme Staghounds in 1888. Thereafter they hunted, but did not kill, 'carted' stags, the followers being on horseback.[46] This was the only stag hunt in the region during our period.

Otterhounds likewise had a mixed following. The first real pack to be established, the Carlisle Otterhounds were founded as a subscription pack by two or three Carlisle butchers and a Maryport miller. In 1905, it was said that there were 'nearly 300 subscribers ... but the donations are generally very small, and the whole suscriptions amounts to less than £140'. There were, however, occasionally gentlemen among the followers.[47] A similar subscription pack was founded in Cockermouth in 1890 with Lord Lonsdale as honorary master.[48] Another pack, well patronised by gentry, existed in Kendal until 1900, while the Lake District otterhounds, similarly patronised, had a brief existence before the First World War.[49] All these hunts drew large numbers of followers, fields of 200 being quite usual. At Whitsuntide 1880, a field of 300 to 400 was reported at a meet of the Kendal pack.[50] This suggests that a significant working-class element might have been present. It is also noteworthy that packs of otterhounds seem to have been urban based. The sport was essentially separate from other kinds of hunting, and was not integrated into the rural popular culture as was fox- and, to a lesser extent, hare-hunting.

Middle- and upper-class women took part in all the varieties of hunting, but there is little real evidence that working-class women followed hounds. Ladies seem to have been particularly in evidence at otter hunts and at mounted meets, although Lady Mabel Howard claimed that she had hunted on foot with the Ullswater,[51] and Clapham says that 'A fair number of ladies attend the meets of the fell packs during the course of the season and wonderfully well indeed do some of them get about.'[52] It is impossible to assess whether Clapham is using the word 'ladies' in a precise manner, but it seems likely that he is. Hugh Cunningham, speaking of the country in general, says that, 'Women [by which he means middle- and upper-class women] began to hunt only in the 1850s when the social exclusivity of the sport had been firmly established.'[53] In Cumbria social exclusivity was not generally established, but ladies hunted nevertheless. This suggests that mixing with lower classes, at least in the hunting field, was not here considered so undesirable for a lady. Working-class women for long lagged behind their social superiors in the question of sporting activities, partly perhaps because of the more limited leisure time at their disposal, and partly, I would suggest, because working-class attitudes towards femininity were in some ways more restrictive.

Why was hunting, and particularly fox-hunting, such an important sport in the region? Foxes were, of course, viewed as vermin (and Machell described mart and hare in the same way).[54] They were said to kill newborn lambs. The *Westmorland Gazette*, for instance, reported in May 1910 that the Coniston Foxhounds were still hunting due to loss of lambs.[55] On the other hand, Clapham asserts that foxes were imported into the region 'for restocking certain districts adjoining the fells'.[56] He gives no further information about this, but if it is true, then the 'pest control' rationale for the sport is seriously undermined. Criticism of the Eskdale and Ennerdale hunt for hunting 'tame foxes' in the Lamplugh district which appeared in the *Whitehaven News* further damages this practical justification for the sport.[57] What are we to make of these contradictions? There is no doubt that the fox was viewed as a predator and nuisance by fell farmers, and that Cumbrian fox-hunting had its origins in pest control. During the nineteenth century, however, the pursuit of the creatures developed as a sport (perhaps in part stimulated by developments elsewhere), and was carried out on a much wider scale. Perhaps at this point it became necessary to import foxes. It is certainly true that in the mid-nineteenth century foxes were scarce in the region.[58] By late in the century they were plentiful, but they were of a different variety to those pursued by John Peel. In his day they were a type known as the 'greyhound' fox, 'long in the leg, with a grizzle grey jacket covering a wiry frame'.[59] they were larger and heavier than the red fox which was either introduced or spread naturally into the area, and which interbred with them and gradually replaced them. They became sufficiently numerous to provide almost unlimited sport, but at the same time to be a continual threat to livestock.

From Peel's day on, there was a great deal of sociability attached to fox-hunting. Its aristocratic branch apart, the sport became firmly attached to the public house. The hunt often met there and it was usual to return to the hostelry for refreshment afterwards. A great deal of singing went on on these occasions, and hunting songs became the most typical of Cumbrian 'folk-songs'. The songs themselves reveal much about the place of hunting in rural society. It was an activity which brought the people living in a sparsely populated rural area together as a community with interests in common. The companionship is celebrated in these lines from the 1930s song 'Grizedale Hunt':

> With laughter and song and calling for more
> Confused and confined in one glorious uproar
> Each one a neighbour, a brother, a friend
> What a pity the jollification must end.[60]

The relief the hunt brought from the monotony of life in a remote area in winter is set out:

> In winter Mardale's dree and drear
> Away, away
> But 'tis not so if hunt is here[61]
> Away, my lads, away.

Above all the community themselves are celebrated. Hunt followers are mentioned by name, often listed for verse after verse, their exploits being admiringly or humorously referred to. The names of hounds are treated in a similar manner. In most cases hounds were billeted on farms during the summer and puppies were also 'walked' by farming families, pride and interest being taken in their subsequent performance. It was said that 'hounds were made members of the family', and 'a farmer would take it very ill if he did not have the same hound sent him at the end of the hunting season'.[62] To mention hounds by name was thus almost the same as mentioning the people. David Itzkowitz has suggested that a hunt, 'Because it was a highly visible institution and because it was identifiable with local personalities ... could become a symbol of local pride.'[63] This was clearly the case in Cumbria.

Noted huntsmen became folk heroes. John Peel's immortalisation in song is of course well known, but it is interesting to note that songs celebrating him (and there are others besides that written by John Woodcock Graves) did not become popular until after his death.[64] 'D'ye ken John Peel?', as Marshall and Walton have noted, first found success with expatriate Cumbrians in London. The song made Peel's name nationally famous and this recognition doubtless increased local pride in this aspect of their culture. Songs celebrating other huntsmen appeared, the greatest hero of them all being Joe Bowman, huntsman of the Ullswater Hounds from 1879 until shortly after the First World War, although few masters or huntsmen were without a song or two to their credit. The rural culture of which hunting was one aspect was in the later nineteenth century suffering dilution as a result of out- and in-migration. The development of tourism was probably also making it rather more self-conscious. The creation of new songs in the traditional idiom (and quite a number were reworkings of older songs) may have been intended, consciously or otherwise, to reinforce hunting culture. Nevertheless, the social side of hunting underwent a great change in the late nineteenth and twentieth centuries. The old 'Mayor Hunts' for the most part disappeared, while hunt balls and fund-raising whist drives and dances took their place.

Mayor hunts are said, by W. C. Skelton,[65] to have originated in the days when hounds were 'trencher fed', that is, kept in ones and twos on different farms and only brought together as a pack at the time of a hunt. They consisted of a hunt followed by a dinner, election of mayor and an evening of singing and drinking. The Mayor hunt at Troutbeck is known to have been already taking place in 1778,[66] and many other places are known to have had these events, which were organised by the hunt followers in the particular locality.

They took place annually, either at the start of the hunting season (St Luke's or St Crispin's Day), at the Christmas/New Year period, or on Shrove Tuesday.[67] The duties of the mayor appear to have been purely social. At Troutbeck, 'He presided over the sing song, attended to the paying and ordering of drinks from the collected

funds and made arrangements for the hunt and dinner.' His qualification for the role was that he was 'a statesman of substance and a good
fellow', although at least one woman, a Mrs Backhouse, said to have
been a keen sportswoman, is known to have held office, while Wilson
quotes the story of one unwilling candidate who was told that he would
do very well as 'any daft-like sort of a fellow would do for mayor'.[68]

Mock mayor-makings elsewhere in Britain are generally held to
be reversal rituals,[69] but this explanation does not seem to be relevant
to the custom in Cumbria. Here they were perhaps intended symbolically to weld the hunting community together under an elected leader.
The elections at Bowness and Cartmel Fell were accompanied by the
reading of a mock charter. That at Bowness was supposedly signed by
Queen Elizabeth I (at her palace of Buckingham!), while the Cartmel
Fell Charter purported to date from 1066.[70] Crosthwaite mayor-
making was also said to have been established by a charter, in this case
granted by Alfred the Great, but no such charter was produced.[71]
What was the purpose of these supposed charters? Why was it deemed
necessary to give the proceedings much greater antiquity than they
possessed? It is well known, as Bob Bushaway has argued, that 'An
appeal to the past, or at least to historical continuity . . . is implicit in
much of the customary activity of the labouring poor and of local
communities in England during the eighteenth and nineteenth
centuries.'[72] The appeal to the past was, however, usually an attempt
to reinforce the custom against attack. Unfortunately we do not know
when the charters were written. It seems likely that they were less old
than the tradition they sought to validate, and were a response to the
changes which were taking place in the organisation and following of
hunting.

Only the Troutbeck Mayor Hunt appears to have survived into
the inter-war period.[73] By then, it had become just one of the many
fund-raising events organised by the hunting fraternity. The balance
sheet of the Coniston Foxhounds for 1919–20 shows that hunt balls
brought in £109, subscriptions £149 16s 5d and donations £52 12s.
'Mr. Woodward of Ambleside collected £20-12-6d and the Troutbeck
Mayor Hunt contributed £4.'[74] This gives a total of £336 0s 11d and
gave the hunt a credit of £66 compared with a deficit of £56 at the start
of the year. The deficit perhaps reflected wartime difficulties, but it
does seem that the fell packs and also the packs of harriers and
beagles had, in general, a hard time making ends meet. Possibly the

Cumberland Foxhounds had the same difficulty, but no information is available on the financing of that pack. Itzkowitz testifies to the problems faced by most hunts in raising sufficient income. The more high class the hunt, the greater was the cost of maintaining it, and so even hunts with an aristocratic membership were likely to face problems. Sufficient money was usually raised , however, and this, says Itzkowitz 'testifies to the importance of the hunt in the eyes of local sportsmen'.[75] In the case of the Coniston, quoted above, subscriptions were clearly insufficient to maintain the hunt. Its survival evidently depended on the fund-raising efforts of supporters. As in the 'trencher fed' days, the hunt belonged to and was part of the community. If there was any anti-hunt sentiment, it is not visible. Hunt balls were probably the most important method of raising funds, but there were also whist drives, concerts and prize draws. There would not be one hunt ball, but many. Different localities in the hunt's country would organise their own events, and committees were evidently in existence for this purpose.[76] Just as there were different classes of hunt, so there were different classes of hunt ball. That of the Oxenholme Hunt in Kendal in 1890 was described as 'One of the most important social events of the season.' Windermere Harriers' hunt ball at Burneside in 1930 had a ticket price of 5s, while that of the Eskdale and Ennerdale at Bower House in 1917, was priced at 1s 6d for gentlemen and 1s for ladies.[77] Other events, however, catered for all. A concert organised in aid of the latter hunt at Seascale in 1920 offered reserved tickets at 3s, unreserved front seats at 2s and back seats at 1s.[78] The social side of hunting in Cumbria, like the sport itself throughout our period, had room for and relied on people of all classes.

HOUND TRAILS AND WHIPPET-RACING

The sport of hound-trailing developed from around the mid-nineteenth century. The earliest trails were laid by dragging a dead fox, and the sport's connection with fox-hunting was initially very close. At Warcop sports in 1860, hounds were required to hunt foxes in the neighbourhood in the morning in order to be eligible to take part in the hound trail in the afternoon,[79] and at Grasmere sports in 1866 the first three places in the hound trail were taken by 'famous Patterdale foxers'.[80] After it was discovered that hounds would follow a trail of aniseed and oil, the two sports gradually diverged and a lighter and sparer breed of hound was developed for trailing.

A mystique developed around the feeding and training of trailhounds which was very similar to that which surrounded the rearing and 'setting' of gamecocks. Both were fed on secret mixtures containing such items as sherry and raw eggs. Rollinson suggests that 'In some ways trailing seems to have taken the place of cocking in its popular appeal, and today [i.e. the 1970s] hound trails are supported by the same cross section of the community which once supported cockfighting.'[81] As far as can be ascertained, a cross-section of the community has always been involved, although information is sparse. T. Newby-Wilson, Esq., JP owned winning trail hounds in the 1890s, as did a 'Mr. J. A. E. Raynor of Ambleside and Liverpool'. In the mid-1890s Mr Stanley le Fleming of Rydal Hall bought a winning hound, Rattler, from 'a poor Ambleside cobbler named Lancaster'.[82] In early twentieth-century Urswick the usual hound owners were said to be iron-ore miners.[83] At that time entry fees for trails were typically 2s 6d per hound. This and the cost of food would perhaps have precluded hound ownership by the very poor. The entry charge for spectators at the same period was usually 4d, and so at that level the sport would have been open to virtually everyone.[84] Although originally and principally a rural sport, hounds are said to have been kept in Workington, and by the early twentieth century, trails were held in all areas of Cumbria.[85]

Cash prizes were given for hound trails, but these were typically only a pound or two, and gambling was also an important part of the sport. By the inter-war period at least, this had become formalised and bookmakers were in attendance at trails. Betting may have encouraged dishonesty in the sport, which lent itself to malpractice. An oral informant said that

> In the old days it was the biggest twist on earth the hound trailing . . . they used to run them into a barn with doors at both ends. Run 'em in so that every dog was in the barn, and then open and let one out and get on its way. And then let the rest out. There was all sorts of fiddles went on.[86]

To eradicate this dishonesty the Hound Trailing Association (according to Marshall and Walton, dominated by local notables) was formed in 1906. Despite the existence for a time of at least one breakaway association, this body effectively controlled the sport from then on, registering hounds and overseeing the conduct of trails. Thereafter, although there is no necessary connection, the sport's popularity appears to have increased greatly, lists of fixtures in the press becoming very lengthy.

An alternative to hound-trailing was whippet-racing. This sport was a little slower to develop than hound-trailing and did not rival it in importance until the inter-war period. Whippets were particularly popular in West Cumberland and parts of Furness, perhaps because, in urban areas, the organisation of a 100 yard or 150 yard race was easier than a hound trail of several miles. Additionally, many whippet fanciers were miners, and the sport may have been imported from other mining areas where it was well established. In West Cumberland whippets greatly outnumbered trailhounds. At sports held in Parton in 1920, there were twelve entries for a hound trail and 220 for the whippet race, the latter figure being not untypical.[87] There was apparently no whippet-racing in the central lakes area. Initially, live rabbits were coursed and the sport may perhaps be seen as the working-class equivalent of the upper-class coursing of hares with greyhounds. 'Running to the rag' superseded rabbit-coursing around the time of the First World War, possibly because it made the sport fairer – some rabbits did not run – and it obviated the need to net rabbits which, as the sport was expanding, were needed in increasing numbers.

Prize money in races was, as in hound trails, typically a few pounds, and again the usual entry fee was 2s 6d and admission to the ground 4d. The extent to which betting took place is difficult to gauge. Although the press makes no mention of it, it is to be supposed, in the nature of things, that it occurred. The frequently large numbers of entries for races suggests that an interest in the sport usually meant ownership, but even so, the excitement of the brief races would be greatly heightened by gambling. For the casual spectator, whippet-racing would surely have had a limited appeal without the opportunity to bet.

There does not appear to have been any mystique surrounding whippets, and there are apparently no legendary whippets as there are trailhounds. Winning whippets were not bought by gentlemen and photographed for posterity. Their role was to provide sport and win money for their working-class owners. The high level of participation suggests that the sport was important in the community.

In both whippet-racing and hound-trailing all the competitions were between individual dogs. There were no inter-village or county matches. Only individual status and money were at risk. Alan Metcalfe has asserted that the Northumberland miner was ready to 'back himself, his dog or any of his belongings against any other man in the world,'[88] and it seems likely that this was the spirit in which whippet-racing and hound-trailing were carried on in Cumbria. They were, in part at least, a legal alternative to cockfighting. Like that sport, they were, as far as can be ascertained, male pastimes, and the dogs, like gamecocks, were evidently a focus for the owners' pride and a route to sporting status within communities. The races also provided an alternative opportunity for gambling. Although the sports were not adapted to inter-community competition, this need, as we shall see below, was increasingly being met by other developing sports, notably football.

SPORTS MEETINGS – WRESTLING AND ATHLETICS

Hound trails and whippet races were very often organised as part of a sports day. These varied in size from small local or village events to great sporting and social occasions such as Grasmere sports. As well as one or occasionally both of the dog events, there would usually be wrestling and foot races. Sometimes there would also be pole vault (very much a local sport), high and long jump competitions and cycle races. Sports held in suitable locations would sometimes have a 'guides' or fell race, and occasionally there was a tug of war or horse races, and on the coast or lakeside, boat races. Horse-racing never acquired any great following in Cumbria, although Cartmel races developed into an important social event after the First World War. Earlier race meetings were not distinguished by the standard of the horses competing ('the galloping was not of a brilliant or exciting nature'[89]) and they relied on hound trails and showmen's stands to draw the crowds. Athletics, wrestling, and indeed the sports themselves experienced fluctuating fortunes during our period.

In the latter part of the nineteenth century most sports were either organized by publicans or formed part of a Friendly Society gala or similar event. There were, however, already sports which were organised by a local committee, for instance Grasmere and an important event in West Cumberland, Cleator Moor Whitsun sports.[90] Perhaps because of the decline of the friendly societies, the early twentieth century was a time of relative decline for sports. Discussing the Whitsuntide holiday in 1910, the *Barrow Herald* declared that 'At one time the principle attractions were athletic sports. Almost every town and village in North Lonsdale had its sport carnival', but now, 'Athletics in this district has become a thing of the past.'[91] In some places an effort was made to continue the sports. For instance, at Hawkshead, the sports, 'originally the Whit Tuesday walk and Gala ... were subsequently carried on by a separate organisation.'[92] Elsewhere, sports continued to be promoted by cricket clubs or the Volunteers. Grasmere sports were also largely unaffected by any decline. These sports were begun as an annual event in 1865, and they seem to have developed out of the competitions which took place at the annual sheep fair in September. The conversion of the rushbearing sports into a children's treat may have been a further stimulus. Beginning as a small event with £5 prize money, by only a decade later Grasmere had developed into a glittering social occasion attended by 6,000 people including many gentry, 300 carriages being on the field.[93] The prize money was then £120. by 1890 the prize money had reached £250 and thereafter it remained at that level.[94] The date of the sports was altered in 1870 to the last week in August, 'to enable the attendance of visitors in the Lake District.'[95] This was probably crucial to the growth of the sports. To a greater extent than any other, Grasmere sports were a product of the growing consciousness of the regional culture. On the one hand this awareness led to the desire to further traditional Lakeland sports and reinforce the local culture against outside influences. Marshall and Walton tell us that it was 'the older gentry like the Machell and Sandys families (who) provided leadership in the organization of Grasmere sports.'[96] Perhaps these local notables used their patronage of the sports to reinforce their own social position against the influx of 'new' gentry. On the other hand, the developing tourist industry demanded that the culture as well as the scenery of the lakes be made available, suitably embellished where necessary, for the entertainment of visitors.

Sport in general was disrupted by the First World War, but during the 1920s some sports days were revived, perhaps as a by-product of the generally increasing interest in organised sport. In 1929, for instance, the Old Flan Sports which had ceased in the 1880s were successfully revived by a local committee.[97] Nevertheless, in 1930 it was claimed in the press that in Millom they 'cannot now successfully run Whitsun sports.'[98] Part of the answer must be that many people now preferred to take excursions rather than watch sports on public holidays. But there was also a decline in active involvement in athletics and wrestling from the 1890s onwards.

Wrestling is an extremely old-established sport in Cumbria. Matches generally took place at social gatherings such as shepherds' meets, and in the first half of the nineteenth century there were noted 'rounds' at Greystoke, Melmerby and Langwathby, as well as Carlisle, the Flan How at Ulverston and Windermere Ferry.[99] The sport was still enormously popular at mid-century and a match between two Cumbrians for the championship of all England, which was held at Ulverston Flan in 1851, was attended by an estimated 10,000 people. Many (some, it may be supposed, Cumbrian exiles) had arrived by train from outside the region, but there were also trains from Westmorland, and a special train which was run from Carlisle via Whitehaven departed the latter place with nearly forty carriages drawn by three, and in some places four, engines.[100] Towards the end of the century the sport's popularity apparently declined, and fewer young men were becoming wrestlers. To remedy this, and to revive the sport, a Northern Counties Wrestling and Athletic Association was formed in 1899. This body co-ordinated village competitions. In addition, wrestling academies were established in many places in the early part of this century.[101]

Wrestling was a 'professional' sport in that money prizes were given. At the all England contest referred to above, the prize was the then enormous sum of £300. At Grasmere sports in 1881 the prize for the heavyweight wrestling was £10 and a cup, or £18, the winner choosing the latter,[102] which suggests that at smaller and less prestigious sports the prize in a wrestling competition in the later nineteenth century would have been a few pounds.

As in the animal sports already mentioned, there was also betting on wrestling, and this was in some cases clearly more important than the prize money or the prestige of winning, as it led to what was known as 'barneying', arranging the outcome of matches. As far as can be ascertained, dishonesty was not prevalent in the sport in the early nineteenth century and earlier. At that time, prestige appears to have been all important. Belts were traditionally awarded to winning wrestlers, and these, we are told, were worn proudly to church on the

Sunday following the contest, as a mark of status and a challenge to others.[103] Machell tells us that it was not until 1878 that 'complaints were made publicly regarding the apparent dishonesty prevalent in the wrestling ring.'[104] The practice of barneying, or at least public disapproval of it, appears to have become more marked by the early twentieth century. Wrestlers were disqualified for it at Grasmere in 1903 1904 and 1906,[105] and in the latter year the Cumberland and Westmorland Wrestling Association was formed in order 'to inoculate with a purging antidote those competitors who had become infected with the virus of dishonesty and gambling and to cleanse our northern athletes from the blots which disgusted spectators and disheartened honest rivals'.[106] The extent to which the Association controlled the sport is not certain, but Grasmere and other sports were subsequently conducted under its rules. At Grasmere some restrictions were also imposed on betting. A poster for the 1910 sports states that 'buying and selling' were strictly forbidden, and that betting was not allowed.[107] By 1930, however, 'bookmakers' stands were allowed in the adjoining field.'[108] It would, in any case, have been impossible to prevent private betting, and by the inter-war period, dishonesty in wrestling appears to have been eradicated, or at least carried out in a more circumspect manner. Skelton (writing in 1921) tells us that 'since the war there has been an honest revival in the appreciation of sport for sport's sake after the men got back home',[109] and this change in attitude does seem to be evident in wrestling in the inter-war period, as well as being reflected in the revival of sports days.

Away from the organised side of the sport, both before and after the First World War, wrestling was a yardstick for personal prowess among young men and boys. A number of oral informants had been wrestlers, although none had competed in organised competitions. Others, not wrestlers themselves, remembered seeing informal wrestling take place. 'When they'd had so much to drink they would challenge one another', said an Urswick informant.[110] Very often the challenge involved money. 'One Saturday at Swarthmoor ... there was a fellow there. "I'll wrestle for half a crown." He grabbed me, you see, so the next thing I knew like, he just put his leg out, round mine, you see, and down I went .... And we got up again, both hold and I pulled him up like that and laid him down .... Ah, I could have putten him down a thousand times! Then he would race me for half a crown'.[111] At least one of these protagonists was a miner, and one is reminded again of Metcalf's Northumbrian miner, always ready to back himself or anything belonging to him.

Some boys learned wrestling at school. The master at Pennington School, for instance, organised matches among the boys before the First World War.[112] The shortage of wrestlers and the need for wrestling academies to promote the sport suggests that this was not usual, however. Despite these attempts at revival, Rollinson is undoubtedly right to say that there has been a decline in the sport's popularity during this century.[113] He attributes this to the rise of footballers as popular heroes in place of wrestlers. Another possible factor is the growing interest in boxing, especially after the First World War. The *Whitehaven News* in 1920 commented that 'Since the war, boxing has taken a hold such as it has not had before for half a century.'[114] Later that year, the same paper reported that Messrs Sandy Porthouse and Billy Simpson had taken a room in Hensingham, 'for the purpose of teaching the correct principles of the noble art' of boxing. Meanwhile, in Penrith, a boxing booth was opened in the market hall by one Dick Edwards, a Canadian who had come to Britain during the First World War and remained here. He was something of an entrepreneur in the local entertainments industry and also promoted tennis courts. The boxing booth 'became very, very popular', and 'contenders used to come from all over Cumberland and Westmorland'.[115] There was betting 'on the quiet'. My informant suggested that pub brawls were sometimes adjourned at a later date to the boxing booth, just as many impromptu wrestling matches resulted from public house challenges. The increasing integration of Cumbria into a national sporting culture, in which boxing figured, but Cumberland and Westmorland style wrestling did not, must have been an important factor in wrestling's decline.

Very probably a similar process was at work in athletics. Until the late nineteenth century, athletics in Cumbria was a 'professional' sport which merged imperceptibly into pedestrianism. As with wrestling, cash prizes were given for athletic events at sports, and men competed to win money. Nationally, however, amateur athletics was a fast growing pastime in the later nineteenth century. At first it was a gentlemen's sport, governed from 1866 by the elitist Amateur Athletic Club (AAC). This body was anxious to disassociate itself from pedestrianism and prohibited not only professionals but also mechanics, artisans and labourers from competing.[116] In 1880, the AAC was replaced, due to the weight of public pressure, by the Amateur Athletic Association. This body removed the prohibition on working men and smoothed the way for working-class amateur sport. Success in amateur sport at the highest level led to national and international fame for an athlete. It also inexorably pushed standards up, and the more modest achievements of those competing for cash prizes at local sports became less of a route to status. Beating the record became more important than beating an opponent, and amateur athletics became more 'professional' in training and outlook than the 'professionals' had ever been. Few athletes could reach the highest standards, and I would suggest that this may be one reason for the fall-off in participation in local sports from the end of the nineteenth century onwards. Major events such as Grasmere, with sufficient prize money to draw top-class professionals, continued to draw crowds, but many small local events faltered. Another factor (as Rollinson suggests) was probably the diversion of energy and athletic talent into the game of football.

FOOTBALL

Football, in a variety of localised forms, is one of the ancient games of Britain.[117] There are references to its being played, together with other sports, on public holidays in Cumbria from the seventeenth century onwards.[118] It was also played on Shrove Tuesday, or at Easter, in some at least of the region's grammar schools.[119] Schools apart, versions of the traditional game are known to have survived into the nineteenth century in four places in Cumbria.[120] At Keswick, there was an apparently short-lived revival in 1852 of an Easter football game 'nearly thirty years obsolete'.[121] The revival may have been at the instigation of a local publican, as a 'Mr. Bowe of the Kings Arms Inn' threw the ball in. Nothing further is known of this Easter game, but football was still being played in the town in 1860, when it was reported that annoyance was caused at the Oddfellows Whitsuntide fête 'By (the) ill mannered conduct of football players who persisted in driving their not over clean ball against the ladies who were dancing and in fact against any respectable person who provoked their envy'.[122] At Seascale, Laking How was the venue for a football game on mid-Lent Sunday. The pitch was an area of common land, one goal being the sea and the other some enclosed land to the east. The game is said to have ceased around 1850 when the land was bought by the Furness

Railway.[123] Thirdly, in Carlisle, football formed part of the Easter
sports on the Sauceries at least until 1836, in which year the game was
reported in the press. However, in the 1886 *Carlisle Journal* it was
lamented that the crowds who had frequented the sports forty or fifty
yeas previously no longer did so, that the sports had evolved into a
pleasure fair and that 'the wild game of football which was the annual
event on Easter Monday evening, after the young children had gone
home, is now played no more . . .'.[124] We are told that the game had
been accompanied by a great deal of rough horseplay, but nothing
more is known about the game during the nineteenth century, or the
reasons for its demise. As the game was played on open land outside
the city it would not have been an obvious target for the reforming zeal
of the respectable classes. In 1886 it was said that 'the football played
by the present generation of young men takes a more scientific form
and is played elsewhere'. It may have been that the traditional game
was simply supplanted by the codified forms of the sport, although the
press report implies that its demise pre-dated the spread of the latter,
and William Whellan said that, around 1860 the game was unknown
in the city.[125]

The fourth place in which the game survived was Workington.
There, the game still survives today, although it probably reached its
zenith during the period of this study. The earliest press report of the
game was in 1775, when it was described as a 'long contended annual
match at football which has been played . . . for many years between
the sailors and colliers'.[126] Originally the game was played only on
Easter Tuesday, but in the second half of the nineteenth century two
further games, on Good Friday and the Saturday after Easter, were
added. According to Anthony Daglish (a member of the most
prominent footballing family), interviewed by the *Whitehaven News* in
1927, 'There never was a Good Friday game until 1865', while the
Saturday game was first mentioned in the press in 1882. The latter
game was said to have developed out of an apprentices' match to
become 'a repetition of the great match on Easter Tuesday'.[127] In the
late nineteenth century, the three games were identical in form.

As in many traditional football games, there were no limits to the
playing ground, and although the pitch was nominally the Cloffocks,
an area of meadow separated from the town by the River Derwent, the
game was played right through the town as well as in the river and
harbour. The opposing teams were the 'Uppies', originally colliers but

latterly anyone from the upper part of the town, and the 'Downies', originally sailors, but by our period also including ironworkers and others. The 'Uppies' goal was in the grounds of Workington Hall, which suggests that the game might at one time have had Curwen patronage, although there is no evidence of this, while that of the 'Downies' was in the harbour a little over a mile away. There were no limits on numbers, and players and spectators tended to merge. The latter, many of whom arrived by excursion trains, typically numbered several thousand, although in 1899 there were claimed to be between 15,000 and 20,000 spectators and in 1930, 20,000 was the reported figure.[128] Although it was principally a men's game, some women were involved. In 1885 it was reported that the ladies were 'conspicuous for the dexterity with which they pulled up their skirts and waded through the water, regardless of the colour of their stockings'. Women were again reported to be among the participants in 1915, 1920 and 1921.[129]

The game was extremely rough, and those taking part risked life and limb. 'Rough?' said an informant, 'It wasn't a "Uppies and Downies" if there wasn't somebody taken to the hospital or somebody drowned . . . [130] There were two drownings during the period of this study. A sailor was drowned in the river in 1882, and in 1932 a young labourer at the steelworks met the same fate during the Tuesday game, his funeral taking place before the Saturday match.[131] Fatalities apart, the local press, year by year, prints long accounts of wanton damage and gratuitous violence. Gardens and allotments were trampled and the crowd seems to have taken an especial delight in damaging the turf of the cricket pitch and tennis courts, which lay within the field of play. The players themselves had their clothes torn from their backs, and if they escaped more serious injury, cuts and bruises were inevitable.

Why, when similar games elsewhere were suppressed or abandoned, did Workington's football not only continue, but have the number of games increased from one to three? The press makes it very clear that the town was very attached to its Easter football. 'Workington without its annual football carnival would bear a close affinity to Rome without its Pope, or London minus its own Lord Mayor', said the *Whitehaven News* in 1885:

> It would be a bold man, indeed, who would advocate the abolition of the Easter football play. The town has been identified with the game for

many generations. The tradesmen like it; the sailors like it; the colliers like it; in fact everyone likes it; and why shouldn't they?[132]

The same paper, in 1899, said:

'Tis on the Cloffocks on Easter Tuesday that Workingtonians can boast to strangers of the muscular and brave fellows that ugly old Workington has produced. And the stranger watching the play is bound to confess that in no other town in the length and breadth of the kingdom are the hardy sons of toil so ready and willing to pit themseves against each other in the same fashion as do the Workington 'Uppies' and 'Downies'. For years past the institution has been the great source of attraction to visitors, who cannot elsewhere see such a battle of sinew against sinew.[133]

So it would seem that the town was displaying the toughness of its men for the benefit of visitors from outside the area. The game was an intrinsic part of the popular celebration of Easter in Workington, and we are again reminded of Peter Burke's argument that popular festivals 'celebrated the community itself, displaying its ability to put on a good show'.[134] Workington's industries, mining, iron and steel, and work connected with seafaring, called for hardy men and gave rise to a working-class culture in which strength and toughness were a source of pride. I would suggest that this is what is being displayed here.

Funds to pay for the ball and for the post-game celebrations were raised by a round-the-town collection, those contributing signing their name on the ball.[135] This practice would have allowed the involvement of those not physically able to take part. The game also allowed workers in the opposing industries, rivals in hardiness, to compete with each other. This, according to Peter Burke, was another function of popular festivals in the early modern period, and again the argument may be applied to modern Workington. This was also a function of the codified varieties of football, of course, and as we shall see below, these coexisted with the traditional game in the town.

The trade which the large numbers of excursionists brought to the town probably induced the town's sizeable business community to overlook the damage to property. This century, the corporation's seal of approval was set on the event by the mayor's presence as spectator. In 1931, we are told that he 'took a hand' in the game 'when the ball was on land'.[136] It would not be true to say that there was never any dissension, however. The police attempted intermittently to control the play by confining it to the Cloffocks, and they usually tried to prevent damage to property. They were successful on at least two occasions this century in preventing market stalls from being over-turned, and in 1921, the police reportedly joined in the game, playing either up or down, as the protection of property demanded.[137] Direct conflict with the police was perhaps greater in the late nineteenth century. In 1899 the ball was thrown into the brewery, where police had been stationed to keep the players out. 'One of the police constables pounced upon the sphere and then a crowd of "Downies" pounced upon the officer. Poor Robert's helmet was knocked off and he himself prostrated.' '"Uppies and Downies"', stated the newspaper calmly, 'have no respect for the law.'[138]

The belief was current (and one of my informants still believed it to be true) that the players were immune from prosecution.[139] This seems to have been a common belief where games of this sort were concerned. Robert Malcolmson makes it clear that it was current in Derby before the game there was suppressed in the early nineteenth century.[140] In Workington it seems, practically, to have been true. I have found no evidence of any prosecutions arising from the game.

Although by the late nineteenth century Workington had the only surviving traditional football matches on the grand scale, the game had only recently been played in Keswick, and it seems likely that, as Hugh Cunningham has suggested, casual games, the kicking about of a real or makeshift ball, continued.[141] Activity of this nature leaves few records for the historian, but the speed and comprehensive-ness of the spread of the new codified games certainly suggests that football was already known and popular.

Rugby was the first of the modern games to take hold in Cumbria Kendal had the first team in Westmorland in 1874, and by 1886, when the Westmorland County team was formed, it was said that 'every village and almost every works had their teams'.[142] In Cumberland, Carlisle was the first in the field with a team in 1870. Whitehaven followed in 1876, and by 1882 seven clubs – Carlisle, Aspatria, Eden Wanderers, Maryport, Workington, Whitehaven and Cockermouth – were competing in a Cumberland Cup competition. In subsequent years additional teams took part.[143] Barrow had its first team in 1875 and the first association football team in the region in 1878.[144] In Cumberland, the first association clubs were formed in Carlisle and Wigton in 1880. Others quickly followed, thirty or more teams competing annually in the Cumberland Shield competition, which was inaugurated in 1889. In Westmorland, the game did not really acquire a following until the early twentieth century, although a number of Kendal teams switched to the soccer code in the 1890s.[145]

The controversy over the payment of players which brought into being the Northern Union in the 1890s resulted in a split in Rugby football within Cumbria. A great many local teams went over to the Northern Union and the Rugby Union game in the region was permanently weakened as a result. Consequently in 1905 the Cumberland and Westmorland Rugby Unions amalgamated.[146] Although Workington and Barrow in particular had noted Rugby League teams, by the early part of this century association football had a greater following. Soccer fans among oral informants outnumbered the Rugby aficionados, although some enjoyed both, and Rugby and soccer matches alike could draw large crowds.

Professional soccer was apparently late in arriving in Cumbria. Alcock tells us that in Cumberland at the time of writing (*c.* 1906), 'almost all players are amateurs, professionals being practically unknown'. An informant who was born in 1888, and who as a boy regularly paid 3d to watch Carlisle United, said that the players were then still receiving an illicit ten-shilling note which was placed in their shoe.[147] This method of payment is somewhat apocryphal, and has been ascribed to other teams, but the informant's statement that the team were not regular professionals can probably be accepted. Carlisle, Workington and Barrow did subsequently have professional League teams, but Cumbria's soccer teams were not among the great stars of the game. There were, however, a number of local and regional leagues, and few towns were without at least one team, while a great many villages also possessed sides. The local soccer scene perhaps, to some extent, continued to flourish because there was no famous team on hand to vastly outshine local amateur efforts. Although the professional clubs had their regular supporters and drew sizeable crowds, soccer did not become primarily a spectator sport in this region before the Second World War.

In line with the national pattern, many of the earliest football players seem to have been middle class. Rugby Union players probably continued mainly to be so. The first Kendal team was at least partly middle class, with a solicitor as its first captain. In the early twentieth century the town's team seems to have been recruited mainly from ex-grammar-school boys.[148] In addition, as in other parts of the country, a number of Cumbria's football teams owed their origins to middle-class patronage, although it is not possible to assess how many. The local press reveals a number of teams whose names suggest a link with a church or chapel, or with a workplace. One of the latter were Kendal Hornets, who began life in 1876 as an employees' team from Castle Mills. They were encouraged by the proprietor, Mr Frank Wilson (described as 'a keen rugger'), who provided a football and placed 'the soldier field' at their disposal.[149] As Hugh Cunningham has argued,[150] the ball and the field were probably more important to the Hornets than Mr Wilson's encouragement. The modern game required money and facilities which the working class did not possess. How long the team remained under his patronage is not clear, but by the 1880s there was another team playing under the name of Castle Mills.[151] Here, as elsewhere, the team seems to have freed itself from patronage as soon as possible.

Once a team was established, gate money quickly brought independence. Unlike the usual practice today, some local teams at least did charge for entrance to the field.[152] Much of the money raised was used to pay for the pitch which, in the more rural areas, was usually rented for the season from a local farmer.[153] In urban areas, finding a pitch was more of a problem, even though most Cumbrian towns were quite small by present-day standards, and the surrounding countryside was within relatively easy reach. The provision of recreation grounds was probably always inadequate, but the enormous proliferation of local football teams in all areas suggests that pitches could, if with difficulty, be obtained.

In Whitehaven, the venue for much sport, including football, was the Colliery Recreation Ground. This was leased from the colliery company by the unions, on behalf of the men, who 'contributed coppers' from their wages to meet the cost. Although this ground was supposed to be for the use of colliery employees and their families, in the early twentieth century at least, this rule was not strictly adhered to and 'anybody could go in more or less'.[154] Nevertheless, an unmet demand for playing space still evidently existed in the town. In 1920, 'the clothes drying field, in Catherine Street', owned by the Earl of Lonsdale, was closed to the public because of 'the Persistent Playing of Football by Young Men', (as well as the running of whippets).[155] Carlisle was perhaps the least well served for recreation grounds. Until

1930, the Sauceries was, apart from a small recreation ground in Botchergate, the only 'lung' of the city. 'The chief public centre for the playing of ball games', it was 'extensively used', but was not 'sufficient to meet all the demands on holidays'. In that year a further three acres in Caldewgate were given by Mr Robert Creighton, a local timber merchant, for use as a playground. This was considered by the *Carlisle Journal* to be 'a real boon to that thickly populated area', as 'there is no better way of keeping boys and young men out of mischief than encouraging participation in healthy games.'[156] In urban areas, then, football continued to some extent to rely on the patronage or goodwill of the propertied classes, but this did not necessarily imply middle-class control of the game. It was sufficient to supply the land and leave the young men to keep themselves 'out of mischief'.

During the First World War, when professional and most other football was suspended, girls' or women's football matches, in aid of war charities, took place in Cumberland. A Ladies' Cup was being competed for in 1917.[157] This development apparently did not survive the return of the men, and the question of who the women footballers were, and who coached them, must remain unanswered. Women's more usual role in both Rugby and association football was that of supporter and ancillary worker. Although most spectators at football matches were men, there were a minority of female informants who took an interest in the sport, or who turned out to watch husbands or sons. The fund-raising social events for local clubs, which, particularly during this century, supplemented or replaced gate money, often relied heavily on the help of women. For instance, at a supper and dance in aid of Broughton-in-Furness AFC in 1930, it was the 'ladies committee' who provided the supper.[158]

By the inter-war period, football clubs formed a basis for social life which was in some ways similar to that surrounding the hunts, although football clubs were attached to single communities rather than whole districts, and fund-raising was in the hands of one committee rather than many. In other ways football's social role was closer to that of cockfighting, as it, too, provided for competition at county, town, village and workplace level.[159] Communities or sections of them, then as now, identified strongly with their local team. They went to a match to see them win, just as they would have gone to a cockfight to see their bird win. It is suggestive that Dalston football team were known as the 'black–reds' after the noted local breed of game fowl. A man arrested at the cockfight at Orton in 1938, which was mentioned earlier in the chapter, drew a parallel between the two at his trial, saying that he became as excited at a cockfight as he did at a football match.[160] In a similar vein, Tony Mason has described the opposing team as 'merely a sacrificial lamb on which the home team could practise ritual slaughter.'[161] Elsewhere, it has been said of football that 'even within its new structure the sport retained much of the emotional temper and spirit of an earlier society'.[162] Bailey has described spectatorship as 'an act of collective participation', and it is true that on occasion crowds could become almost as involved as they did in a traditional style football match. It might then be asked why the traditional and codified games coexisted in Workington. The answer would seem to be that the 'Uppies and Downies' was essentially a carnival occasion, an annual reversal of normal social rules, and by the late nineteenth century, of the rules of the game of football. It was a major tourist attraction, a 'larger than life' spectacle, outside the parameters of everyday sport. The codified game, on the other hand, provided opportunities for competition between the town of Workington and other places, and the development of more regular and mundane football was in no way impeded by the continuance of the traditional game.

CRICKET AND OTHER SOCIAL SPORTS

Football was not the only team sport to be played in Cumbria, of course. Cricket, its summer counterpart, was established in the region by the mid-nineteenth century when Carlisle, Maryport, Kendal, Ulverston, Barrow, Dalton and Kirkby Lonsdale are known to have had teams.[163] The visits of a professional all-England XI to Kendal in the 1860s are said to have given 'a great impetus' to cricket in that district and encouraged the formation of new teams.[164] More teams appeared in the 1860s and 1870s, but on the whole cricket's following remained half-hearted until the end of the century. In 1860 a 'depression in cricket playing' was blamed by the *Westmorland Gazette* on the activities of the Volunteers.[165] Later, in 1885, the game's 'decline in popularity' was blamed on the counter-attractions of tennis.[166] By the twentieth century, however, cricket had become a genuinely popular village game, even though it never had such a following as football.

Members of the gentry and middle class played in at least some of the nineteenth-century teams. Other teams were formed or sustained as a result of their patronage. Marshall and Walton tell us that Lord Leconfield assisted Egremont Cricket Club, and Lord Lonsdale provided a cricket ground at Castle Meadows in Whitehaven. The latter gentleman also involved himself in matches at Lowther.[167] Lindal Moor cricket club was founded in 1884 under the patronage of Harrison Ainslie & Co., iron-mine owners, and there were many other clubs attached to workplaces, such as Gandy's carpet works in Kendal, Burneside paper works, and the Furness Railway Company.[168] Cricket was also the particular vehicle for muscular Christianity favoured by the churches in the region, and sporting clergymen helped to create and sustain interest in the sport. We are told that the Lindal Moor team was always a mixture of middle-class and working-class players,[169] and it might be supposed that other workplace clubs were also partly, if not wholly, working-class. However, this century, middle-class or lower-middle-class informants were more likely to have played cricket than working-class ones. Kendal and Barrow clubs, at least, employed a professional from 1867 and 1875 respectively, but it may be supposed that village teams were wholly amateur, even though 'imported' players were extensively used during the 1930s.[170] This practice perhaps weakened the sense of identification between the villages concerned and their teams.

Despite the aristocratic patronage mentioned above, there was, as with football, some difficulty in obtaining pitches, especially in industrial areas. There is said to have been 'scarcely a suitable pitch to be obtained' in the Kirkland and Arlecdon area in 1899, and the following year the possibility of Arlecdon CC's continuance was said to have been very remote due to the loss of their ground. Dalton club, similarly, virtually ceased to exist in 1883 due to the lack of a playing field, although this difficulty was later overcome.[171]

This century most boys learned cricket at school or in the Scouts or some similar organisation. Perhaps because it needed more equipment, it was never as widely played outside school as football, but makeshift games nevertheless did take place among working-class boys.[172] McKeever tells us that between the wars, many clubs in the Furness district used grammar-school boys and 'students' in their first teams at quite a young age. No reason is given for this, but it may have reflected a shortage of players. An oral informant played in the Lindal Moor first team from the age of eleven.[173]

The game and the social life attached to it, which paralleled that of football, had a highly respectable image. Again, by the inter-war years, women were active on the social side of the game. At Lindal Moor in the 1920s they were serving teas, which had replaced the (small) post-game barrel of ale. They also spring-cleaned the pavilion, manned stalls at the annual field day, and catered for hot-pot suppers during the close season. By 1937 they were also doing 'gate duty' at the match.[174] There are a few reports of women playing cricket against men in charity games, but these seem generally to have been 'one-offs' (for instance Whitehaven Ladies *v.* Whitehaven Policemen),[175] and cricket does not seem to have been played seriously as a women's sport.

Probably the most important women's sport was tennis. This was never a working-class sport, probably due to the cost and the social ethos surrounding the game, but during this century it became a common pastime among the middle and lower-middle classes of both sexes. The game was invented, in its modern form, in 1873,[176] and as we have seen above, it was already being played in West Cumberland in 1885. A Cumberland Lawn Tennis Tournament was inaugurated in 1899[177] Tennis courts were not however widely available until after the First World War, when few places of any size were without them. In Penrith, courts were opened as a commercial venture by the local sporting entrepreneur Dick Edwards, and there were other courts in the town at the Conservative Club, and in the council-owned Castle Park. In Workington, courts once owned by the Primitive Methodists for the use of their members were, by the inter-war period, the property of an independent tennis club. At Dalton and Broughton-in-Furness there were tennis courts attached to the cricket clubs, and in Kendal, a tennis club was formed in 1920 by YMCA and YWCA members.[178] Dalton cricket club's courts were made use of by the local Catholic school.[179] Other female respondents also learned the game at school, at the Girls' National School in Penrith, Penrith Grammar School, and Ulverston Grammar School. Boys were not taught tennis at school, however.

Tennis was, of course, a socially acceptable pastime for young ladies. Although there were tournaments and competitions, it was essentially a social sport, and tennis clubs were select places which, in Eric Hobsbawm's words, 'functioned as potential or actual social centres ... for the middle class young of both sexes'.[180] It was this social exclusivity which enabled young middle-class women to take an active part in the sport. The game's cost reinforced the exclusivity. The cost of admission to Dick Edwards's courts in Penrith is said, by one informant, to have been 1s. Another informant, a shop assistant, who used the courts in the 1930s, could not remember the price, but said that, at the time, she thought it expensive.[181] In addition, there was the cost of the racquet and balls. 'All classes' are said to have used the Penrith courts, but the deterrent effect of the cost must be borne in mind.[182]

Two other sports which, by the inter-war period, were also enjoyed by young women and girls alongside their male counterparts, were swimming and cycling. Swimming in Cumbria long pre-dated the opening of swimming baths. The lakes and rivers, if not the sea, had probably always been used, though it is likely that many nineteenth-century Cumbrians, especially the working classes, were non-swimmers. However, swimming baths were built in a number of towns from the 1870s on,[183] and the natural water resources were used ever more extensively, numbers of informants swimming in them in the early part of this century and between the wars. In some places, instead of baths being built, the natural facilities were improved upon, as at Kirkby Stephen, where the bottom of the Eden was flagged, and at Brougham, near Penrith, where the bed of the Eamont was cleared and diving boards and changing rooms built.[184] Even where there were baths, some informants preferred to swim in rivers. In Kendal, deep pools in the Kent were thought preferable to the town baths in the 1930s as the latter 'hadn't in those days got a continuous water change. They used to change the water every so often (the informant explained, and) it used to get very green, after a bit . . . . They used to dump stuff in it to clear it. It smarted the eyes somewhat.'[185] Elsewhere though, the standard of the baths was not complained of ('they were very good baths considering how many years [ago] it was')[186] and many informants made use of them regularly. In Barrow in 1929 and 1930 some 2,000 people a week used the baths in summer, though in winter the figure fell to a few hundred.[187]

Before the First World War there were apparently few female swimmers. An informant who was born in 1888 and was a keen swimmer as a boy and young man said that the Carlisle baths were used only by men.

Aye, there was no mixed bathing in those days . . . There wasn't any swimming pool in Carlisle for ladies, I don't think . . . They never went to the rivers. We went and bathed in the river, in the Petteril, in the Caldew or the Eden. I did quite a lot of swimming and bathing. But I never saw any women. They never went bathing.[188]

The Whitehaven baths, however, had ladies' sessions twice a week in 1885, and an informant confirmed that these continued early this century. It may be that the Carlisle informant has forgotten that such an arrangement existed there. My Kirkby Stephen informant said that a few girls, 'not many, mind', joined in the bathing in the Eden early this century, but no female informant born before 1900 was a swimmer. A Workington lady born in 1897 said, when asked if she had learned to swim, 'No, that was unheard of when I was a kiddy. Unheard of!'[189]

Between the wars things were very different. Children were taught to swim at school, and many girls and young women, particularly the middle classes, swam regularly in the pools, while mixed groups used the bathing places. One middle-class female informant took part in competitions, the only informant of either sex to do so. However, swimming galas were frequent occurrences at this time. The cost of admission and, more importantly, the need for a proper costume, may have deterred some working-class youngsters from using the baths, as it is clear that makeshift costumes were in use at some of the bathing places.[190] There was apparently little or no class mixing at the latter, middle-class swimmers usually avoiding the crowds at the popular spots. The ease with which this could be done in a region well supplied with water, together with the provision of sexually segregated swimming in the baths, probably paved the way for female swimmers. Nevertheless, a change in attitudes towards women's sport and women's clothes were needed before swimming could become a popular and accepted sport for girls, and this change seems not to have occurred in Cumbria generally until after the First World War.

This was true also of cycling. 'Velocipedes', penny-farthings, were already known in the region by 1870. At that date they formed an adjunct to pedestrianism, races being organised by publicans, sometimes against a pedestrian.[191] By the 1880s, however, when the safety bicycle had been developed, cycling clubs were being formed and cycling races were being added to the programmes at sports. Due to the cost of bicycles, cycling at this time was a sport for the middle and upper classes.[192] Known club officials were all middle class and, as might have been expected, they were also all male. Lady cyclists must, however, have existed, as there was a ladies' cycle race, albeit with only two competitors, at Ullswater sports in 1895.[193] From the end of the nineteenth century the price of bicycles fell, and by the First World War a number of working-class male informants possessed second-hand bicycles. There is also some evidence that working-class women were cycling in the early years of this century, although none of my oral informants did so. Isabella Cooke, who was born in 1890, bought a second-hand bicycle in approximately 1907 when she was in farm service at Cliburn, near Penrith. She bought it from her sister-in-law who, it may be supposed, was also working class, for £3. Mrs. Cooke's wages at the time were £9 for six months, so this represented quite a lot of money to her. she obtained it by 'subbing' off her employer. Mrs Cooke also mentions cycling with 'another girl', and she talks of cycling as though it was a commonplace activity for a girl at the time.[194]

By the inter-war period, cycling was a popular pastime with all classes and both sexes, although there were still some girls who were debarred from it. A teacher's daughter in Dalton, for instance, told me that she and her sister were not allowed to have bicycles, although their two brothers were. A lower-middle-class informant from Penrith said that her aunt, who brought her up, would not allow her to have a bicycle either. 'She maybe thought it would take me too far from home.'[195] David Rubinstein has suggested that in the 1890s cycling helped women to escape from chaperonage and also aided the battle against conservative opinion on what women ought and ought not to do.[196] It is clear that in inter-war Cumbria the victory had still not quite been won. Many girls still had relatively little freedom compared with their brothers.

Those young men and women who did ride bicycles used them for trips to the countryside or sea, as well as for more mundane transport. There were many thriving cycling clubs in existence, although only the minority seem to have belonged to them. Similarly, cycling races were apparently still confined to a, mostly male, minority. As with other sports involving individual competition, consistent winners acquired a degree of local fame.

CONCLUSION

A number of trends are apparent in the history of sport in the region during our period. Perhaps the most obvious is the great proliferation in sporting activities of all kinds. Rugby and association football, cricket, tennis, whippet-racing, cycling and boxing all found a following during the late nineteenth and early twentieth centuries. Of these, only boxing, which was probably instrumental in the decline of Cumberland and Westmorland wrestling, had a directly adverse effect on a pre-existing sport. Other sports such as football and cricket may, as they grew in popularity, have drawn people away from, for instance, athletics, but by and large, the new and old sports coexisted. Increasing leisure time, rising real wages for much of the period, greater participation by women, the arrival of migrants from outside the region with different tastes in sport, and the growing importance of sport as an element in popular culture, probably combined to allow this to be so.

With the arrival of the new sports, Cumbria became increasingly integrated into a nationwide sporting culture, and its regional distinctiveness in this respect was somewhat diminished. The region's sport had never been entirely local, of course; cockfighting and the non-codified forms of football were to be found throughout Britain, as were swimming, foot races and so on. The important sports of wrestling and hunting were, however, peculiarly Cumbrian in their form, and hound-trailing and fell-racing were virtually confined to the region. The latter was always a minority sport, but wrestling declined in popularity during the period. Hunting, on the other hand, remained important, and hound-trailing went from strength to strength, but these nevertheless declined in importance in Cumbrian sporting culture as a whole. Football and cricket rivalled the older sports even in rural areas, while in the towns, new sports more suited to urban life reigned supreme. A growing regional consciousness helped to ensure that local sports were not completely rejected, but by the 1930s the sporting interests of the average Cumbrian had much more in common with those favoured elsewhere than those of earlier generations.

The absorption of Cumbria into the national pattern of sport was further aided by legislation, although this initially had a separating rather than an integrating effect. The favourite sport of cockfighting was legally prohibited, but it nevertheless continued to take place in the region long after it disappeared in most parts of the country. It was, however, ultimately destroyed as a popular sport. At a different level, the Amateur Athletic Association outlawed professionalism in athletics, and this ruling too was resisted, even though it separated many Cumbrian athletes from the mainstream of the sport, and helped bring about a decline in the popularity of athletic sports in the region.

A further identifiable trend in the development of sport is increasing class separation. Although there had never been indiscriminate mixing between the classes, older sporting activities such as cockfighting, hunting and hound-trailing brought the different classes together on terms approaching equality. While these sports, with certain qualifications, continued to cut across class lines, the new sports which acquired a following during the period were more narrowly class-specific. Whippets were the property of the working class, while football, although not exclusively a working-class sport, did not on the whole promote class mixing. On the other hand, a sport such as tennis naturally excluded the less well off, and consequently acquired an aura of social exclusivity, or in working-class eyes, snobbishness.

Sports such as tennis, swimming and cycling were essentially social, while cricket and football also had their social side in the dances and other related activities. Of the older sports, only hunting provided a similar basis for social mixing and other kinds of recreational activity, and it has been suggested that the social side of that sport became more highly-developed during the late nineteenth century. As this face of sport grew in importance, the aspect of challenge and individual competition receded as cockfighting, organised wrestling and professional athletics declined. Competition continued with trailhounds and whippets, but these, particularly the latter, were low-key affairs compared to cockfights. They were hobbies which offered a sense of personal achievement and an opportunity for gambling, and status was no longer at stake as it had once been. That desirable attribute was increasingly to be obtained by outstanding performance as part of a team. Although opportunities for individual competition still existed in cycling, swimming, tennis and the like, these sports did not have sufficient following for a race or match winner to enjoy the status of a star footballer.

NOTES

Place of publication London unless otherwise stated.

1 R. D. Humber, *Game Cock and Countryman*, 1966, p. 98
2 Daniel Scott, *Bygone Cumberland and Westmorland*, 1879, p. 194.
3 T. N. Postlethwaite, *Some Notes on Urswick Parish and Church*, Ulverston, 1906, p. 57. Other grammar schools said to have had cockfights include Alston, Wreay, Heversham, Kendal and Penrith. See G. R. Scott, *The History of Cockfighting*, London, 1957, pp. 58, 94, 117; A. R. Hall, *Wreay*, Carlisle, 1929, p. 43; Francis Nicholson, 'Game cockfighting', *Victoria County History Cumberland*, Vol. 2, 1905(?), pp. 476, 478.
4 Nicholson, 1905?, p. 477.
5 Quoted in William Rollinson, *Life and Tradition in the Lake District*, London, 1974, p. 169.
6 Act 5 and 6 Will. IV C59; Act 12 and 13 Vict. C92.
7 Respondents, 6, 15, 18 and 24; W. G., 18.6.1938; W. M. Williams, *The Sociology of an English Village: Gosforth*, 1964, p. 132.
8 Scott, 1957, p. 170.
9 Respondent 6.
10 P.O., 28.5.1895. See also B.T., 22.5.1880.
11 Bryn Trescatheric, *Sport and Leisure in Victorian Barrow*, Barrow, 1983, p. 17.
12 B.N., 18.7.1903; Newspaper Cuttings Z2497, Barrow Library.
13 W.G., 18.6.1938.
14 B.N., 18.7.1903; Newspaper Cuttings Z2497, Barrow Library.
15 W.N., 8.5.1890.
16 Respondent 6.
17 W.G., 18.6.1938.
18 Respondents 15 and 24.
19 C.J., 4.7.1930.
20 Respondent 6.
21 B.T., 22.5.1880; B.N., 15.6.1907; P.O., 28.5.1895.
22 W.G., 18.6.1938.
23 W.N., 18.5.1890.
24 Information of respondent 6.
25 Clifford Geertz, *The Interpretation of Cultures*, New York, 1973, footnote pp. 417–8.
26 Geertz, 1973, p. 417.
27 Geertz, 1973, pp. 417, 419.
28 P.O., 28.5.1895.
29 Geertz, 1973, p. 432. The concept is to be found in Bentham's 'Theory of Legislation'.
30 Geertz, 1973, pp. 432–3.
31 Williams, 1964, p. 134.
32 Respondent 6.
33 See, for instance, Soulby's *Ulverston Advertiser*, 18.5.1863.
34 Williams, 1964, p. 134.
35 Respondent 6.
36 W.G., 18.6.1938.
37 Nicholson, 1905?, p. 481.
38 Hugh Machell, *John Peel. Famouse in Sport and Song*, 1926, p. 105.
39 W. R. Mitchell, *Lake District Sports*, Clapham, Yorks., 1977, p. 33.
40 See Rev. J. Wilson, 'Foulmart hunting' and 'Sweetmart hunting', *Victoria County History Cumberland*, Vol. 2, 1905(?), pp. 452–5, 455–7.
41 Respondent 6.

42 PR/70/42/4Z, newspaper cuttings on the death of John Crozier, C.R.O.; Machell, 1926, pp. 69–70.

43 Respondent 6.

44 *W.G.*, 4.1.1880.

45 Richard Clapham, *Foxhunting on the Lakeland Fells*, 1920, p. 83.

46 See *W.G.*, 7.10.1916.

47 William Steel, 'Otter hunting', *Victoria County History Cumberland*, Vol. 2, 1905(?), pp. 462–3; *C.J.*, 5.6.1900; *W.N.*, 30.3.1905.

48 *C.J.*, 2.5.1890.

49 Major Arthur Willoughby-Osborne, 'Hunting', *Victoria County History Lancashire*, Vol. 2, 1908, p. 469.

50 See Steel, 1905?, p. 463; *W.G.*, 22.5.1880.

51 Lady Mabel Howard, 'Foxhunting', *Victoria County History Cumberland*, Vol. 2, 1905(?), p. 425.

52 Clapham, 1920, p. 15.

53 Hugh Cunningham, *Leisure in the Industrial Revolution*, 1980, p. 129.

54 Machell, 1926, p. 105.

55 *W.G.*, 21.5.1910.

56 Clapham, 1920, p. 24.

57 *W.N.*, 28.10.1920.

58 See Clapham, 1920, p. 23.

59 Clapham, 1920, p. 23.

60 D. C. W. Style (ed.), *Songs of the Fell Packs*, Melbreak Hunt Show Committee, n.d., p. 15.

61 Style, n.d., pp. 72–3.

62 *C. Pat.*, 13.3.1903 (cutting in PR/70/42, C.R.O.).

63 David C. Itzkowitz, *Peculiar Privilege. A Social History of English Foxhunting*, Sussex, 1977, p. 105.

64 See Machell, 1926, p. 117.

65 W. C. Skelton, *Reminiscences of Joe Bowman and the Ullswater Foxhounds*, Kendal, 1921, p. 158.

66 E. M. Wilson, 'Folk traditions in Westmorland', *Journal of the Folklore Institute, Indiana*, Vol. 2, 1965, p. 285.

67 Wilson, 1965, p. 285; Skelton, 1921, p. 158; *W.G.*, 3.1.1885, 31.10.1885, 22.12.1827; Ian Ward, 'Lakeland Sport in the Nineteenth Century', unpublished PhD thesis, University of Liverpool, 1985, pp. 119, 129.

68 Skelton, 1921, p. 158; Wilson, 1965, p. 287.

69 See R. W. Malcolmson, *Popular Recreations in English Society 1700–1850*, Cambridge 1973, pp. 81–2.

70 Wilson, 1965, p. 285.

71 *W.G.*, 31.19.1885.

72 Bob Bushaway, *By Rite. Custom, Ceremony and Community in England 1700–1880*, 1982, p. 5.

73 This event still takes place today. Tickets are sold and the profits go to the hunt.

74 *W.N.*, 4.11.1920.

75 Itzkowitz, 1977, p. 80.

76 See *W.N.*, 8.2.1917; *W.G.*, 15.2.1930.

77 *W.G.*, 5.4.1890, 4.1.1930; *W.N.*, 8.2.1917.

78 *W.N.*, 1.1.1920.

79 *Kendal Mercury*, 7.7.1860. Evidently the 'close' season was not strictly observed.

80 Hugh Machell, *Some Records of the Annual Grasmere Sports*, Carlisle, 1911, p. 22.

81 Rollinson, 1974, p. 191.

82 Skelton, 1921, p. 153.

83 Respondent 24.

84 W.N., 5.4.1917.
85 Respondent 25; local press, *passim*.
86 Respondent 23.
87 W.N., 8.4.1920.
88 Alan Metcalfe, 'Organised sport in the mining communities of south Northumberland, 1800–1889', *Victorian Studies*, Vol. 25, No. 4, Summer 1982, p. 474.
89 W.G., 31.5.1890.
90 See Machell, 1911, *passim*; C.J., 10.6.1870.
91 B.H., 21.5.1910.
92 W.G., 14.6.1930.
93 Machell, 1911, p. 31.
94 W.N., 14.8.1890; Machell, 1911, *passim*; local press, *passim*.
95 Machell, 1911, p. 26.
96 J. D. Marshall and J. K. Walton, *The Lake Counties from 1830 to the Mid-Twentieth Century. A study in regional change*, Manchester, 1981, p. 115.
97 Minute book BD50/12, Barrow R.O.
98 B.N., 14.6.1930.
99 Machell, 1911, pp. 13–14.
100 Francis Nicholson, 'Wrestling', *Victoria County History Cumberland*, Vol 2, 1905(?), pp. 487–8.
101 See C.J., 4.1.1910 for mention of Keswick, Penrith and Appleby Academies: W.G., 19.2.1910, Grasmere Academy.
102 Machel, 1911, p. 37.
103 Canon Rawnsley, foreword to Machell, 1911, p. 13.
104 Machell, 1911 p. 34.
105 Machell, 1911, pp. 63, 64, 68.
106 Canon Rawnsley, in Machell, 1911, p. 9.
107 Reproduced in Machell, 1911, opposite p. 72.
108 W.G., 9.8.1930.
109 Skelton, 1921, p. 154.
110 Respondent 24.
111 Respondent 15.
112 Respondent 15.
113 Rollinson, 1974, p. 191.
114 W.N., 22.1.1920.
115 Respondent 6.
116 See Peter Bailey, *Leisure and Class in Victorian England*, 1978, p. 131.
117 See Malcolmson, 1973, pp. 34–40, and James Walvin, *The People's Game*, 1975, Ch. I, *passim*, for a description of the traditional game.
118 See Jeremy Godwin, 'Mass Football in Cumberland and Elsewhere', dissertation, 1986, in C.R.O., *passim*.
119 Godwin, 1986, pp. 5, 34–8.
120 Godwin's claim that the game 'evidently continued into the nineteenth century' in Kendal would appear to be unsupported by any concrete evidence, although it was suggested in the W.G. in 1853 that the game ought in future to be included in the town's Easter sports. Ward, 1985, p. 121.
121 Godwin, 1986, pp. 35–6.
122 C.J., 1.6.1860.
123 C. A. Parker, *The Gosforth District*, Kendal, 1904, p. 36.
124 Godwin, 1986, p. 16 (C.J., 9.4.1836, 30.4.1886).
125 William Whellan, *History and Topography of the Counties of Cumberland and Westmorland*, Pontefract, 1860, p. 141.
126 Godwin, 1986, p. 17 (C.Pacq., 20.4.1775).
127 Godwin 1986, pp. 20, 21 (W.N., 28.4.1927).

128 *W.N.*, 6.4.1899; Godwin, 1986, p. 20.
129 *W.N.*, 9.4.1885; Godwin, 1986, pp. 17, 29.
130 Respondent 25.
131 Godwin, 1986, pp. 25–6.
132 *W.N.*, 9.4.1885.
133 *W.N.*, 6.4.1899.
134 Peter Burke, *Popular Culture in Early Modern Europe*, 1978, p. 200.
135 Godwin, 1986, p. 18 (information of Mr Denis Hepburn).
136 *W.N.*, 9.4.1931.
137 *W.N.*, 18.4.1912, 16.4.1931; Godwin, 1986, p. 29 (*W.N.*, 31.3.1921).
138 *W.N.*, 6.4.1899.
139 Respondent 25.
140 Malcolmson, 1973, p. 166.
141 Cunningham, 1980, p. 127.
142 James Clarke, *History of Football in Kendal from 1871–1908*, Kendal 1908, p. 9,
143 C. W. Alcock, (assisted by R. Westray and R. S. Wilson), 'Football', *Victoria County History Cumberland*, Vol. 2, 1905(?), p. 491.
144 Bryn Trescatheric, *Sport and Leisure in Victorian Barrow*, Barrow, 1983, pp. 20, 21.
145 Alcock, 1905?, p. 491; Marshall and Walton, 1981, p. 169; Clarke, 1908, pp. 9–10.
146 Trevor Delaney, *The Roots of Rugby League*, Keighley, 1984, pp. 82–3, 88. By the end of the 1897–8 season Millom, Maryport, Seaton, Broughton, Workington, Whitehaven, Whitehaven Recreation, Wath Brow, Brookland Rangers, Kendal, Kendal Hornets, Holme, Kirkby Lonsdale, Ambleside, Barrow, Dalton and Askam had all joined the Northern Union.
147 Alcock, 1905?, p. 493; respondent 19. The 3d admission price has not been verified.
148 Clarke, 1908, pp. 4–5, 442–5.
149 Clarke, 1908, P. 29.
150 Cunningham, 1980, p. 128.
151 Clarke, 1908, p. 29.
152 Information of respondent 15.
153 Respondents 24 and 15.
154 Respondent 32.
155 *W.N.*, 8.4.1920; *Kelly's Directory of Cumberland and Westmorland*, 1914.
156 *C.J.*, 14.2.1930; *Kelly's Directory of Cumberland*, 1929.
157 *C.J.*, 6.7.1917, 7.9.1917, 2.10.1917; *W.N.*, 31.5.1917.
158 *W.G.*, 15.2.1930.
159 For an example of the latter see *B.T.*, 14.2.1880. Match between the apprentice joiners and apprentice engineers at Barrow Shipbuilding Co.
160 *W.G.*, 18.6.1938.
161 Tony Mason, *Association Football and English Society 1863–1915*, Sussex, 1980, p. 230.
162 Bailey, 1978, p. 144.
163 Marshall and Walton 1981, p. 167; Trescatheric, 1983, p. 4; James Clarke, *History of Cricket in Kendal from 1836 to 1905*, Kendal, 1906, p. 10.
164 Clarke, 1906, p. 57. An all-England team also visited Carlisle in 1850. See Marshall and Walton, 1981, p. 167.
165 Trescatheric, 1983, p. 4; *W.G.*, 11.8.1860.
166 Marshall and Walton, 1981, p. 168.
167 Marshall and Walton, 1981, p. 167; *C.Pacq.*, 14.6.1870.
168 Mike McKeever, *Lindal Moor Cricket Club. Centenary Brochure*, Lindal, 1983, no page numbers; Clarke, 1906; *B.N.*, 9.6.1900.
169 McKeever, 1983, no page numbers.
170 Clarke, 1906, p. 55; Trescatheric, 1983, p. 5; McKeever, 1983, no page numbers.

171 *Marshall and Walton*, 1981, p. 168; *W.N.*, 29.5.1890; J. E. Walton, *A History of Dalton in Furness*, Chichester, 1984.
172 Respondents 6, 30, 31 and 32.
173 Respondent 23.
174 McKeever, 1983, n.p.
175 *W.N.*, 8.7.1920.
176 E. J. Hobsbawm, 'Mass-producing Traditions: Europe 1870–1914' in E. J. Hobsbawm and T. Ranger (eds.), *The Invention of Tradition*, Cambridge, 1983, p. 299.
177 *C.J.*, 12.8.1910.
178 Respondents 25 and 2; *W.N.*, 27.5.1920; *C.J.*, 13.6.1930, 3.1.1930; *W.G.*, 22.5.1920.
179 Respondent 2.
180 Hobsbawm, 1983, p. 299.
181 Respondents 6 and 13.
182 Respondent 6.
183 E.g. Barrow, 1876, Kendal 1884, Carlisle 1884; Trescatheric, 1983, p. 26; *Kelly's Directory of Cumberland and Westmorland*, 1934, 1938. Whitehaven baths were open by 1885; *W.N.*, 19.2.1885.
184 Information of respondents 6, 21 and 26.
185 Respondent 10.
186 Respondent 19 (speaking of Carlisle baths *c.* 1900–05).
187 *B.N.*, 4.1.1930, 15.2.1930, 14.6.1930, 9.8.1930.
188 Respondent 19.
189 Respondents 35, 26 and 11; *W.N.*, 19.2.1885.
190 Ambleside respondent K; respondent 26.
191 See *C.J.*, 7.6.1870, 10.6.1870.
192 See David Rubinstein, 'Cycling in the *1890s*', *Victorian Studies*, Vol. 21, No. 1, Autumn 1977, p. 48. Braithwaite Bros. in Kendal in 1897 were advertising cycles from £11 10s upwards. Ward, 1985, p. 279.
193 Ward, 1985, p. 278.
194 Isabella Cooke, 'A *Hired Lass in Westmorland*, Penrith, 1982, PP. 9, 10, 13.
195 Respondents 2 and 13.
196 Rubinstein, 1977, pp. 61–2.

CHAPTER V

Church and chapel

INTRODUCTION

A great deal of leisure time in late nineteenth and early twentieth-century Cumbria was taken up by activities connected with the churches. At first sight this is rather surprising, as the 1851 Religious Census suggested that the majority of Cumbrians attended neither church nor chapel of any kind. In Westmorland, on the day of the Census somewhere between 26 per cent and 50 per cent of the population attended one or more services, while in Cumberland the figure was lower, between 19 per cent and 37 per cent. Attendance in both counties was predominantly at the Church of England.[1] It is not possible to say positively whether churchgoing in the region subsequently increased or decreased. No further attendance figures are available for Westmorland. Local newspapers carried out censuses in Whitehaven in 1881 and Barrow-in-Furness in 1882, and it was suggested that 33.8 per cent of the population attended in Barrow, while between 19 per cent and 36 per cent attended in Whitehaven. This suggests a decline in attendance in the latter place since 1851, when the figure for attendance was between 26 per cent and 47 per cent.[2] A further census was carried out in West Cumberland in 1902 by the *West Cumberland Times*. The value of this census was reduced by appalling weather on the Sunday in question, which caused the cancellation of one or two services and reduced attendance at most others. In Whitehaven, between 15 per cent and 23 per cent braved the elements, but it was suggested that doubling these figures would give a fairer estimate of the usual attendance. If this were done, the percentage attending would be roughly the same as in 1851, although the area covered by the census does not exactly correspond. Elsewhere, the numbers attending varied. In Wigton, the figure was somewhere between 22 per cent and 41 per cent, but in Dearham only 8 per cent to 12 per cent turned out.[3] If the numbers are doubled, or in places trebled, as the newspaper's correspondents suggested, then, in many places an increase in attendance since 1851 is indicated. If the figures are accepted at face value, then the highest possible percentage is likely to be most nearly correct, as on such a day few people are likely to have attended twice. Perhaps the most that can be said with any degree of certainty, however, is that, in the early years of this century, many people in West Cumberland, probably more than half the population, did not on any one Sunday attend a religious service of any kind. Many more people may have been occasional attenders, however, and it must be remembered that included in the percentage of non-attenders were the sick and aged and small children. In addition, oral evidence suggests that attendance was linked to the life cycle, young people of box sexes being more frequent attenders than older women with domestic responsibilities and older men.

The relative strength of the various denominations is difficult to document, but an increased following for nonconformity is indicated after 1851. John Burgess has shown that the second half of the century was, in general, a time of expansion for Methodism, which in its various forms was the largest of the Nonconformist groups.[4] Migrants to mining and industrial areas swelled the ranks in a number of circuits, and in consequence, these were prone to collapse in times of depression. After the First World War there was a more general decline, and numbers of chapels, for instance in the Eden Valley, were closed during the 1920s. The Methodist Union in 1932 led to further chapel closures and loss of members, as people tended to fall away if the chapel in their village was closed.[5] It is difficult to assess whether the Church of England shared in this inter-war decline. Impressionistic evidence suggests that it did not; the picture gleaned from oral informants and the local press is of a buoyant Church between the wars. Research by E. Royle indicates that attendance at the Church of England in York did not decline until after the Second World War,[6] and it seems probable, though there is no concrete evidence, that the situation in Cumbria was similar. The Church of England was, overall, still the largest single denomination in West Cumberland in 1902, but it took second place to Nonconformists or Roman Catholics in a number of locations. Catholicism was strong in areas with a significant Irish population, such as Cleator Moor, Egremont and Whitehaven, where its position appears to have been stable.

The unworldliness of many branches of nonconformity and their opposition to amusements of all kinds in the early and mid-nineteenth century is well established. Wesleyans, for instance, were exhorted at their 1855 conference to 'love not the World' and 'the disposition to indulge in and encourage amusements' which could not be regarded as 'harmless or allowable' was observed with regret.[7] The Church of

England was also, by the early nineteenth century, not the friend to popular recreations it had once been, although a certain amount of ambivalence remained. In the latter half of the nineteenth century, however, the churches slowly abandoned their opposition to amusements. 'As the secular world came to offer more in the way of entertainment,' it has been argued, 'so ... the churches, in a bid to recruit and hold members, began to tolerate what they had previously condemned.'[8] They came to realise that if their members were to be kept from harmful pastimes, they would have to offer entertainments of their own. They would have to 'take pleasure and consecrate it'.[9] This change of heart caused a great deal of debate and soul-searching,[10] but by the 1880s and 1890s it was generally accepted by religious bodies that the provision of recreation was an essential part of their activities. In 1890, a writer in the Wesleyan Methodist magazine was able to say, without fear of causing a scandal, that 'We all value for ourselves innocent recreations ... it is worse than folly to create artificial sins'.[11] At the second Ecumenical Conference the following year, a speaker asserted that 'amusements had their right place in the economy of the World'. The discouragement of amusement had, he said, led to profanity and hypocrisy, and the church, in his opinion, was wrong to attack amusement for 'no-one ought to put a yoke on those made free by God'.[12] There were, however, others at the conference who spoke out against the theatre, and both the first and second Ecumenical Conferences condemned dancing.[13]

In Cumbria this change of heart is reflected in a steady rise in press reports of church and chapel recreations. Relatively few events are being reported in 1870, but by 1880 there is clearly a great deal going on, and by 1890, reports of church and chapel activities outnumber all other reports of recreational activity, particularly in rural areas. There is probably an inherent bias in this reporting, as the press was increasing its coverage of local matters during this period, and church activities are more likely to be reported than some others, but the general picture is nevertheless clear. The Nonconformist churches seem to have taken the lead in recreational provision, but the Church of England was only a little behind. The recreational efforts of the Catholic Church appear, however, to have been more limited. By the 1890s most chapels and many parish churches were fully occupying the leisure hours of many of their members, a situation which persisted until the First World War, after which Methodist activities, in particular, decline perceptibly, although church activities appear to be undiminished. The rise and decline of Methodist recreations parallel the denomination's fortunes, while the continued importance of church activities between the wars supports the suggestion that church attendance was not declining in the region during this period.

CHURCH AND CHAPEL

Both before and after the First World War, going to church was very much the thing to do on a Sunday. It was evidence of respectability. It was also, as an Anglican informant said, 'somewhere to go' on a day on which leisure activities were restricted, and 'you met your friends there'.[14] It was a weekly social occasion in which people could take either a passive or, through involvement in the choir, a more active role.

Vic Gammon has documented the decline in nineteenth-century Sussex of the old-style church bands and choirs and their replacement with organs and a musical style more acceptable to the educated middle- and upper-class ear.[15] There is some evidence that a similar process occurred in Cumbria. Old-style parish choirs are known to have been in existence in Hawkshead and in a number of places in Westmorland, one instance being Crosby Garrett where, until about 1856, the parish clerk acted as 'precentor'. He would strike the keynote with a pitch-pipe for the choir to render 'a Psalm from the Old Version in a style quite out of keeping with present day psalmody'. This would presumably have been the style described by Gammon.[16] In 1856 a harmonium was installed in the church, and the musical style was presumably reformed, although we have no details. At Troutbeck 'an old inhabitant' recalled in 1904 that (presumably in the first half of the nineteenth century) the clerk and precentor had been the village schoolmaster. Crippled in one leg, he would 'stump down the aisle ... mount the steps into the singing gallery, take his pitchpipe (previously prepared for that purpose) and give the key-note of the tune, and not infrequently find that an irreverent member of the choir ... had altered the pitch beforehand to his great confusion'.[17] Nothing is known of the social composition of these choirs, but it seems unlikely that, in such places, they could have been wholly middle-class bodies. The irreverent behaviour at Troutbeck suggests that the choir there was as autonomous and independent of clergy control as were the Sussex choirs, described by Gammon as 'distinct institutions within village society'.[18] As in Sussex, however, the old-style parish choirs appear to have been reformed or expelled everywhere in Cumbria. By the early twentieth century, the singing was apparently everywhere accompanied by an organ or harmonium, though nothing has been discovered about the identity of the organists.

The reformed church choirs seem for the most part to have been surplice choirs of men and boys, but in some places they were mixed, or became so in the early twentieth century, women replacing the boys. It is difficult to assess how widespread this development was. Lindal choir became mixed in about 1920, while that in Kirkby Stephen already had women singers before 1912, and the Addingham choir was mixed by 1910.[19] St Michael's and St John's in Workington both retained their all-male choirs during our period, however, as did St Margaret's in Dalton.[20] Possibly village choirs, or those in competition with other denominations, with fewer boy singers to draw on, were more likely to become mixed. The attitude of the incumbent, and whether the church was 'high' or 'low', would also have been relevant. Gammon has suggested that the ousting of the old parish choirs 'largely drove out the active popular element in worship in rural areas'.[21] If this was the case in Cumbria, the situation appears to have been relatively short-lived, as by the early twentieth century some church choirs at least had working-class and lower-middle-class members.[22] In a number of cases, as indicated above, they now also included women, who were taking part in the musical life of the Church for the first time. Although these choirs no longer enjoyed the autonomy of their predecessors, they did nevertheless provide an interest and an enriched social life for those involved in the weekly practices and in the choir socials and outings which are frequently reported in the press. Some of the mixed choirs also competed in musical festivals, and individuals were able to acquire status and a sense of personal achievement as soloists. Nonconformist choirs also frequently participated in musical festivals. *The Workington Wesleyan Circuit Magazine* for 1914, for instance, reported the successes of chapel soloists and choirs in the town's Eisteddfod.[23] Robert Moore has suggested that in Durham, competing choirs both represented their villages, and allowed for competition between them in much the same way as sports teams.[24] It seems likely that Cumbrian choirs functioned in a similar way, denominational communities being represented by their choirs.[25]

Stephen Yeo has argued that, in Methodist churches in early twentieth-century Reading, 'acts of worship were themselves increasingly interpreted as entertainments' in the effort to draw in congregations.[26] Music had long been important in Methodism. The Wesleys had from the start encouraged congregational singing, and particularly the use of 'Tunes which are in *Common Use*' amongst adherents.[27] There is, however, some evidence of a similar development in Cumbria, as more music for listening was introduced into services. In Penrith in 1910, for instance, the Primitive Methodists held, on the first Sunday in every month, 'special people's services . . . made bright with extra music from our own choir'. On 11 September that year, the Sons of Temperance Brass Band were brought in to supply the music for the service, in place of the usual organist.[28] Certainly, in the twentieth century, music was overwhelmingly important in Methodist services. This is underlined by the following complaint, which was made in an 'advice to choirs and organists' column in a circuit magazine, by the organist of Lazonby Wesleyan Chapel after a visit to a chapel 'not a hundred miles from Kirkoswald' in 1920.

> As I knew the tunes (he said) I should have been able to sing. Being a bass singer, I wanted to sing that part, but the organist concerned only played three notes on the bass and in many cses they were in the wrong place. Well, I had to give up singing and a good portion of the pleasure of the service was gone. Needless to say, that chapel is 'taboo', so far as I am concerned.[29]

There was clearly pressure within the Methodist Church that elite musical standards be maintained. Many Methodist chapels gave services of song and concerts of sacred music after Sunday evening services. In Dalton, such concerts at the Primitive Methodist chapel just after the First World War were avidly attended by Anglicans and Nonconformists alike.[30] Similarly at Westfield Wesleyan Chapel in Workington in 1914 a 'special musical service' in aid of church funds was 'packed to the doors, some even being turned away'. The programme was selections from Handel's *Messiah* by the choir and 'Mr. J. Dransfield's string band'.[31] The press reveals that sacred oratorios and cantatas were widely performed by Nonconformist choirs. The *Messiah* was a frequent choice, but the works of Handel did not dominate the scene to the extent that James Walvin suggests they had in the mid-nineteenth century.[32] There was much more besides. In the region's Methodist choirs, which would undoubtedly have contained many working-class people, classical choral music of all kinds had become popular culture by the early part of this century.

Preaching was also an art form among Nonconformists. At Culgaith Wesleyans' Chapel anniversary in 1920, for instance, it was reported that 'At both services . . . Mr. Simpson [the preacher] gave us of his best . . . . At the evening service [he] took as text 11 Kings v18. It was a great sermon . . . such a sermon ought to be published and circulated broadcast.'[33] An ex-farm servant and occasional attender at Wesleyan chapels in the same area around the same period said that 'There was good preachers and bad 'uns . . . . I used to like to hear a good preacher! Take notice of everything he said. Sit and listen and inwardly digest it.'[34] Another informant whose grandfather was a lay preacher, and who also attended Wesleyan chapels in the same area during the early 1920s, took a rather less respectful view of the preaching, but derived enjoyment from it, nevertheless:

> You know, some of these lay preachers were quite funny. Really entertaining. It wasn't really all dull. I remember one old chap that used to come around to preach and I always used to enjoy when he preached. He was a very emotional type . . . and when his sermon was getting worked up to a crescendo, everybody was going to be fried to hell if they didn't do this, that and the other . . . he used to start to sweat and wipe his forehead . . . he always had one of those red and white spotted handkerchiefs . . . I think it was more fun trying to restrain from laughing than if you could have a real good laugh and let it rip.[35]

As in Obelkevich's Lincolnshire, some 'preachers became virtual cult figures',[36] and, sceptical or otherwise, Methodists were often prepared to walk long distances to hear them.

Many children attended church or chapel, either with parents or with siblings and their peer group. Whether they did or did not, they were almost invariably sent to Sunday school. All major denominations except the Roman Catholics had Sunday schools, and children were expected to attend as a matter of course. Even the children of non-attenders at church or chapel were usually made to go. Catholics apart, only the odd individual never attended. 'You had to go, whether you enjoyed it or not!' said a Dalton Anglican informant. 'I mean you automatically went.' 'Me mother used to pack us off,' said another, the son of an Anglican mother and Methodist occasional attender father. 'I wouldn't say I liked gaan . . . me mother used to mak me gaa.' Others were more positive about the experience. 'It was something we looked forward to, to go to Sunday school,' said a Penrith lady who, although nominally Anglican, attended the Gospel Hall. 'We loved Sunday school.'[37] Why was attendance such a general thing? There was, as the Dalton informant quoted above pointed out, very little else to do on a Sunday. Children were not generally allowed out to play, and sending them to Sunday school kept them out of mischief and allowed time for parental relaxation. It was also visible evidence that children were being brought up respectably and that their religious and moral education was being attended to. It was a minimum standard of respectability for a family. There was, as suggested by Richard Hoggart, a widely held notion that Sunday school was 'a civilizing influence' which helped children 'to avoid "getting into bad ways "'.[38]

In return for their assiduous attendance, the children enjoyed Sunday school outings and Christmas treats. There is no evidence that children attended only when some treat was imminent. Informants insist that they attended regularly, and while Sunday school registers record fluctuations in attendance, there is no pattern to them.[39] As mentioned in Chapter II, most outings took place at Whitsuntide. Some were more elaborate than others. Christ Church, Penrith Sunday school, just before the First World War 'didn't get far. Our outings were only in a field', said an informant, 'and we thought it was marvellous.' Port Carlisle Wesleyans in the 1890s went by waggonette 'to a farmer's field at Bowness', where they had 'races and buns and lemonade'.[40] Dalton Anglican Churches, on the other hand, both before and after the First World War, 'had a rare do on'. Four or five hundred children and adults, accompanied by the town band, were marched through the town and then taken to Lakeside by train. There were boat trips and a picnic, and the band played for dancing.[41] Similarly, John Burgess tells us that, in the late nineteenth century, 'when Penrith Wesleyans went on their annual Sunday school treats they took 1,000 of their own members and children, plus up to 500 from other dissenters of the town, such was their excellent management and organisation'.[42] Christmas treats were usually a tea-party with some form of entertainment, singing, games, and often a magic lantern. Again, some were more elaborate than others. The Christmas treats tended to merge with those of the Band of Hope, about which more will be said below.

Involvement in church activity of a primarily religious nature had, for both children and adults, strongly recreational aspects. Involvement in the choir was a leisure activity which extended far beyond the call of duty at the service itself, providing the basis for both sociability and competition. At the same time, the choirs made the service a more pleasurable experience for the rest of the congregation, many of whom also enjoyed the preaching on an artistic rather than, or as well as, a religious level. Going to church was, for many, an enjoyable social occasion. Sunday school, similarly, could be a source of enjoyment and, although it was not appreciated by all, the treats were high-spots in the child's recreational calendar, and doubtless made it all worthwhile.

THE TEMPERANCE CULTURE OF CHURCH AND CHAPEL

It is often suggested that chapel culture and secular culture were mutually exclusive. Kenneth Young, for instance, insists that 'probably until the First World War, leisure life for the working and lower middle classes was either chapel or pub, God or gin. One could go to the tavern and music hall, or alternatively to the prayer meeting and service of song.'[43] There is a great deal of truth in this assertion, but in late nineteenth and early twentieth-century Cumbria, the situation was not quite so clear-cut. Firstly, there was not a rigid distinction between chapel people and others, teetotallers and drinkers. There were, among oral informants, people who, as practising Methodists or Baptists, did not drink and who spent the greater part of their leisure time in chapel activities. As in Robert Moore's Durham mining villages, the chapels in Cumbria were 'non-drinking, non-gambling social centres', and people who took part fully in a chapel's social life had little time for outside activities.[44] There were, however, occasional chapel attenders who also participated in public house culture,[45] and many chapel social events were not restricted to members. In most cases, anyone could buy a ticket and go to a chapel tea-party or concert.[46] Unrestricted attendance at social events might have had the desirable effect of attracting new members to the chapel, but this policy of openness probably resulted in part from the fund raising function of entertainments, an aspect which must not be overlooked. Chapels were often trying to raise money for, or pay off debts on, buildings. Westfield Wesleyans in Workington in 1914, for instance, gave nine public teas which, it was reported, raised the sum of £9 10s 0d towards clearing off the chapel debt.[47] Alcoholic drink was not a necessary adjunct to entertainment, and people were not automatically deterred from attending chapel socials or concerts because of the absence of it. It was accepted that chapel functions were 'dry'; they had compensatory attractions.

My second qualification to Young's statement is that the Church of England must not be disregarded as an influence on the recreational lives of the working and lower-middle classes. While there were churchgoers who frequented public houses, the Church of England, like the chapels, offered a viable alternative culture in the late nineteenth and early twentieth centuries. This was particularly so for women, many of whom would not in any case have considered entering a public house. Like chapel entertainments, many church events were open to all who wished to attend. The Church of England also needed to raise funds and boost its membership.

Church and chapel culture was effectively temperance culture, but it was not until the late nineteenth century that the churches in Cumbria came to dominate the temperance movement as such. This is perhaps a little later than in other parts of the country, as Brian Harrison suggests that nationally, 'the temperance movement had . . . acquired an almost exclusively Christian flavour by the 1870s'.[48] In Cumbria the churches' dominance of the movement developed along-side their dominance of village entertainment, and it was probably never quite complete. There was a long-standing temperance move-ment in the region, and a handful of secular societies continued to exist in the second half of the nineteenth century.[49] Temperance friendly societies, such as the Rechabites and the Sons of Temperance also enjoyed a great deal of support. The latter was enormously influential in the Eden Valley until the inter-war period.[50]

Brian Harrison has identified a tendency for the temperance movement to concentrate on children in the second half of the nineteenth century, and temperance work among adults was never as widely and actively undertaken in Cumbria as work among children. Most effort went into winning the young to the cause via the Band of Hope, but nevertheless there were some attempts to reclaim adults.

The Church of England appears to have made the greatest effort in this direction. Possibly in the absence of a denominational condemnation of drink there was a greater perceived need for temperance reform among churchgoers, but the Church of England was actively concerning itself with moral reform in the late Victorian period.[51] Harrison tells us that, nationally, the Church of England Temperance Society (CETS) was the great success story of the adult temperance movement in the late nineteenth century.[52] The evidence suggests that, friendly societies apart, it was the most important adult temperance organisation in Cumbria, although the movement *per se* cannot be claimed to have been outstandingly successful.

The viability of the temperance societies of any denomination depended on the entertainment offered. Abstention had to be made worthwhile, and the abstemious had to be tempted away from the domestic circle. Those societies which were too earnest and did not provide a sufficiently enticing programme of entertainments invariably foundered. The attractions on offer were those utilised by the churches generally; teas, suppers and concerts of music, readings and humorous sketches. The Church of England societies also held dances. As with other church and chapel events, temperance socials were often open to non-members. A CETS supper and entertainment at Tebay in 1885, for instance, was attended by about 100 'members and friends'. The society's membership then stood at about sixty.[53] Doubtless the reason was the same as with other church events. New members were desirable, but the money of non-members also aided the cause. It was in the end a lost cause, however, as by the inter-war period adult temperance was a dead issue in Cumbria. The consumption of alcohol was by then falling, temperance had ceased to be a political issue, and the public house was beginning to gain a limited respectability. Committed teetotallers, of course, remained, but temperance societies had ceased to figure as serious competitors for the leisure hours of adults.

The Band of Hope was likewise declining by the late 1920s. Until then it was, after Sunday school, the most important and consistent occupier of children's leisure hours. The organisation was founded in Leeds in 1847 and spread rapidly, although its establishment in Cumbria appears to have been a little late. There is known to have been a Band of Hope in Appleby in 1866 and in Maryport and Millom in 1870, while the Vale of Eden Band of Hope Union was formed in 1872;[54] but it was not until the late 1870s and the 1880s that Bands of Hope were mushrooming in all the towns and villages of the region. In 1880 there were sixty-five Bands of Hope (presumably all Anglican) in the Carlisle Diocese, and the Vale of Eden Union in 1885 had thirty-seven Bands of Hope affiliated to it with approximately 3,500 members.

The movement's development in Cumbria coincided with the desecularisation of the temperance movement in general, and most Bands of Hope in this region were affiliated to church or chapel, although there were some which were independent, particularly in the early years. The secular dimension appears to have faded away by the end of the century, and Bands of Hope attended by oral informants were all connected with churches or missions, the majority being Nonconformist. The movement was, however, non-denominational, and if, as was often the case, there was only one Band of Hope in a village, children from any Protestant church, or from non-churchgoing families would attend. In Urswick, for instance, where the Band of Hope was organised by the Church of Christ, the Church of England's only competitor in the village, any children who wished to attend were welcome. No one was turned away.[55] The Protestant churches considered that they were fighting a common foe in alcoholic drink, and there was a great deal of co-operation between them in Band of Hope matters. Roman Catholic children were not permitted to attend the Band of Hope, however. It was, as Lilian Lewis Shiman has pointed out, 'very protestant in spirit', and the Catholic Church preferred to run its own society, known as the Children's Guild.[56] Nothing is known about the development of this organisation in Cumbria. Catholic informants knew nothing of it, and around the end of the First World War one Catholic girl in Dalton regularly slipped into Band of Hope meetings unknown to her parents.[57]

It is rather difficult to assess the social class of Band of Hope organisers and workers, as few names are known, and the majority of them cannot be traced. Probably it depended on area and the denomination of the organising church. The class of the children attending is easier to gauge. They were working class. No middle-class informant was a member, although they did occasionally attend Band of Hope concerts. As Shiman tells us, the middle classes considered children's temperance to be a working-class movement.[58] Shiman also asserts that the Band of Hope was not successful in enrolling poor slum children,[59] and this may have been true of Britain's large cities, but in this region even the very poorest children were members. Among working-class children, attendance was practically universal. Whether or not the children's parents were drinkers was irrelevant. The Band of Hope was viewed in much the same way as Sunday school, as a good influence on children, and, if attendance was not insisted on in the same way, no child who was not a Catholic was prevented from joining. Even the daughter of a Dalton publican attended, and this was not considered strange either by her or, apparently, by the organisers.[60] Regardless of its value for adults, teetotalism was considered to be good for children. Legislation banning the sale of alcohol to children was, of course, gradually being enacted during the period of the Band of Hope's ascendancy.

The Band of Hope was 'the first English organisation to work with children in a general recreational as well as educational way',[61] and its meetings were very attractive to children. Sixty or seventy years later, informants still waxed enthusiastic about it. Some remembered and claimed to have taken to heart the temperance teaching. A Whitehaven man remembered his pledge:

> They used to stand up and say 'I hereby promise by the help of God that I will abstain from all intoxicating liquor as a beverage. Amen.' So we hadn't to take it you see. And I remember that. I've never forgot it. Because they *were* sincere people who ran the Colliery Mission you know. And they did help us. I mean when we were young we hadn't the entertainments they've got today.[62]

Harrison suggests that 'The pledge was not very onerous to children, most of whom had not even experienced temptation.'[63] It seems likely that in many cases it did mean very little, even though the nature of the evil was continually laid before them. 'You had the special singing books. Songs against Drink. All that kind of thing', and 'Before you came home you used to get a lecture. You know, the old lecture, the evils of strong drink.'[64] Few Band of Hope members became teetotal adults and many informants, when asked about the Band of Hope, recall only the entertainment and festivals. 'Every Wednesday evening to the Band of Hope', said one, 'And it was really lovely. We sang our heads off! ... And the magic lantern. Oh a magic lantern was an event you know!' 'We found it very entertaining' was the generally agreed-on verdict, and 'We all liked to go.'[65] As well as singing and watching the magic lantern, the children recited, played games and were told stories. They also prepared and gave entertainments, consisting of songs, readings, dialogues and (depending on denomination) sketches. They had annual (or quarterly) teas, and often an excursion in summer. In Workington, the Band of Hope Union held a musical festival and Band of Hope festivals in other places had competitions for choirs, recitations, etc.[66]

Most Bands of Hope were affiliated to a District Union and the annual galas were major events remembered by informants as among the great occasions of their childhood. At Appleby, before the First World War, the procession is said to have been a mile long.

> And every village had a banner with the name on it ... and they would march in procession to get a short lecture from somebody in the field and then the excitement starts. Sports and all sorts of things and a nice picnic tea. ... And their mothers and fathers were there. Oh, it was great ... They would either come on trains or they would walk to join up. ... Some would come in traps and waggonettes and all sorts of things. ... The whole town would be out ... [67]

In Workington between the wars,

> they used to have between 40 and 50 lorries. Horse-drawn lorries all decorated up. We used to have the morris dancers with the decorated costumes and all that. And it used to be one of the biggest affairs of Workington![68]

The Band of Hope galas reflected and utilised the working-class predilection for ritual. It is perhaps not without significance that the two great successes of the temperance movement, the Band of Hope and the temperance friendly societies, both made use of banners and processions. They made self-help and self-improvement a matter for pride and display, rather than joylessness. The galas also fulfilled all the functions of popular festivals which have been identified by Peter Burke in his work on early modern Europe, and which have already been applied to modern Cumbria in Chapter II.[69] They were something for the children and adults to look forward to; they provided a framework for the celebration of the community, and were a demonstration of its 'ability to put on a good show'.[70] They were also an arena for local chauvinism, allowing villages, represented by their children, to compete with each other both in display and in the races, singing competitions and other events of the galas. Results were eagerly reported in church magazines. It has been suggested in Chapter II that communities in this region increasingly celebrated popular festivals through their children during our period, and there is no doubt that Band of Hope galas were community festivals. Temperance culture for children had, by the late nineteenth century, become an intrinsic part of the region's popular culture.

The decline of the Band of Hope which was becoming apparent by the 1930s is less easy to account for than its success. The Methodist church, which was in the forefront of Band of Hope organisation, was declining between the wars, and chapel closures probably brought about the demise of their Bands of Hope. Inter-war economic conditions probably also had their effect, especially in West Cumberland. The organiser of the Workington gala recalled that, in the latter years before the event was abandoned in the 1930s, he was obliged to 'go on my hands and knees scrounging to get people to give the tea'. The cost of tea for four or five thousand children was prohibitive, and 'when the tea fell away, then the children fell away'.[71] By the inter-war period also, there were other church and chapel organisations as well as commerical entertainments competing for children's leisure time. Finally, I would suggest that, by the inter-war years, keeping young children at home within the family circle was stronger evidence of respectability than allowing them to march behind temperance banners, which perhaps suggested that they were at risk. The communal culture of respectability was by then in retreat, and the respectable classes were concerning themselves more with the cultivation of family privacy.

THE CHURCHES AND ADOLESCENCE

BOYS

J. R. Gillis has argued that the concept of adolescence was discovered by the middle classes who monopolised it until the beginning of this century.[72] By then it was also being increasingly accepted by the skilled and respectable working class. In response to a perceived stagnation in employment opportunities, they were placing greater emphasis on education and training, which extended the period of a boy's economic dependency and deferred adult status.[73] It has been suggested elsewhere that the invention of adolescence created a 'social problem', the solution to which lay in adult-supervised leisure pursuits.[74] The subjection of respectable boys to greater parental discipline has been identified by Gillis, as has their increasing tendency to spend leisure hours in the home, in commercial entertainments and spectator sports, or in the voluntary clubs and associations which sprang up for their benefit from the 1880s onwards.[75] He argues, however, that adolescence did not really become a meaningful concept for the poorest classes. Such boys were economically important to their families from an early age, and their poverty debarred them from participation in any adolescent culture other than that of the street. Nevertheless the concept was applied to them, in common with other classes, by voluntary agencies who were addressing the 'problem'.

In Cumbria almost all voluntary work with adolescent boys was linked to the churches. Here as elsewhere, much of the work was in the form of uniformed youth groups, although some of the efforts to direct the leisure of adolescent boys were of a rather different nature, especially before the turn of the century. Many attempts were made to extend Sunday school activity to older boys through Bible classes. Like the Sunday schools, these classes had outings and related social events designed to attract and retain the boys, but their success overall is difficult to assess. A class run by Holy Trinity Church, West Seaton, was flourishing between 1894 and 1896,[76] but of most classes we know nothing more than that they existed from time to time. There were also attempts to engage boys in handiwork for church funds. At Staveley-in Cartmel around the turn of the century, for instance, there was an organisation known as the King's Messengers attached to the Anglican church. Boys met to make baskets and nets which were sold to raise funds for missionary work.[77] Clubs such as this seem also to have been short-lived, while their entertainment value must have been minimal.

More obviously successful was the Young Men's Friendly Society (YMFS) which existed in at least one or two Church of England parishes in the 1880s and 1890s. This was apparently a counterpart to the Girls' Friendly Society, which will be discussed below, and its stated objects were very similar: 'To help young men both spiritually and temporally by promoting purity, temperance and general morality; befriending young men leaving home or moving from place to place; promoting thrift, independence and a healthy tone of literature and amusement among its members.'[78] Its structure of associates and members was also comparable. At Upperby, where a YMFS was formed in 1886, meetings 'for instruction and amusement' were held weekly, and there was also a weekly Bible class. In July 1887 the society acquired a cricket club which met for practice 'almost every evening', and by January the following year it had a well attended gymnastics class and a newly established library.[79] An 'annual festival' was held at Penrith in 1886, which suggests that a Penrith society (if no more) was then in existence, but we have no information about it until 1893 when a society attached to St Andrew's Church is known to have been meeting three times a week.[80] Thereafter, nothing more is known about either society other than that, in Penrith, there was no society in existence within the memory of oral informants.

The use of cricket and gymnastics suggests that the YMFS, in its strivings to promote purity, subscribed to the ethos of muscular Christianity, the cultivation of a healthy mind in a healthy body. Gillis has suggested that the pursuit of this ideal and the related rejection of qualities such as sensitivity and domesticity, which were supposed to be feminine, provides a partial explanation for the development of paramilitary youth organisations, for 'what could better preserve the differences between the sexes than the military?'.[81] Paramilitary organisations such as the mainly Nonconformist Boys' Brigade, and its Anglican counterpart the Church Lads' Brigade (CLB), did enjoy some success in Cumbria during our period, although they were never widely popular.

Both these organisations were late nineteenth-century developments, but there is no evidence of their existence in Cumbria before the early years of this century, when a marked jingoistic element in popular culture and in the attitudes of at least some of the Anglican clergy perhaps aided their formation.[82] The CLB was apparently the more widespread in the region, and although there were Boys' Brigades attached to Nonconformist churches, none of my informants had been a member. Both organisations are said by J. M. Mackenzie to have been formed with evangelical and temperance objectives,[83] but in the case of the CLB at least, it was the militarism which boys found attractive. In Whitehaven in 1907, the CLB boys organised an ambitious concert to raise money for their rifles and bugles, which they had apparently existed for a while without. The rifles were considered by the vicar to be the more urgent need, as they were 'a necessity for drill'.[84] A Dalton informant who was a keen member of the CLB before the First World War, described their activities as: 'just drilling and marching . . . we used to go on marches as far as Birkrigg and have a bit of a run round, a skirmish. And drilling in the Drill Hall at Dalton . . . . There wasn't much besides that.'[85] He explained that when they became too old for the CLB 'those that were keen would join the Territorials'. The CLB was affiliated to the Territorials as an official cadet force in 1911. 'In effect,' says Springhall, 'the Church Lads' Brigade . . . virtually abandoned their religious objectives' and became 'the largest unit of the national cadet force.'[86] In October 1914 the vicar of St James, Whitehaven informed his parishioners with apparent approval that the CLB was to be allowed to form at least one battalion from its former members. 'The Brigade (he said) though existing primarily as a religious agency has nevertheless by means of its quasi military discipline and methods supplied a training which has qualified a large number of its members for service with the colours.'[87]

It was its connection with the war and the military establishment which brought about the decline of the CLB nationally during the 1920s reaction from militarism.[88] The fortunes of the organisation in Cumbria appear to have followed the national pattern, as little is heard of it in the region between the wars. The Boys' Brigade adapted better to inter-war society and survived. Unlike the CLB, it was not an official cadet force, and in 1926 it amalgamated with its professedly anti-militaristic rival, the Boys' Life Brigade. Nothing is known of the previous development, if any, of this latter body in Cumbria. Two Boys' Brigades and one junior Life Boys existed in the Carlisle circuit at the time of Methodist unity in 1933,[89] but the number of Brigades elsewhere in the region at that time can only be guessed at. Press information suggests that boys' Brigades were few in comparison to Boy Scouts.

The Scouts were widely popular in Cumbria, many oral informants being members. One informant consciously chose them in preference to the Boys' Brigade, and changed his Sunday school from the Baptists to the Wesleyans in order to join.[90] The Boy Scouts were founded in 1908 and spread rapidly. Troops were already in existence at Kendal and Cark in 1910, and as in the country as a whole, there was rapid growth in the region during the inter-war period. In Whitehaven the YMCA ran Scouts, and in Penrith Rover Scouts were organised by the British Legion,[91] but in most cases they were affiliated to church or chapel. The Rovers, the Scouts' senior division, existed in a few places, but they appear to have had no great popularity. As a

F

Whitehaven informant put it, 'when I got to . . . 16, 17, you know, you just abandon these things'.[92] There is some evidence of the existence of cub packs between the wars, but these seem, too, not to have been very numerous. The emphasis was on work with adolescents. In Dalton between the wars, the Catholic church began an alternative organisation, known as the Knights of the Blessed Sacrament, which was run on the same lines as the Scouts and had similar activities, although uniform was apparently not worn.[93]

Informants of all classes were Scouts. It is often suggested that the cost of the uniform prevented boys from poor families from joining. 'Poor boys didn't gravitate to Baden-Powell's movement . . . the very poor hadn't money to spare for jersey and hat and belt, to say nothing of the subs.'[94] It seems likely that this would have been the case in Cumbria, but no instance of a boy being prevented from joining due to the lack of a uniform has been encountered. A Whitehaven informant said that uniform was 'not really' compulsory. 'Sometimes you just had part of the uniform, you see . . . it was only a khaki shirt you know, and a hat.'[95] The Wesleyan Scouts in Workington during the early 1930s made uniform compulsory, but

> what we used to do . . . . We used to have, unknown to the minister of course. I suppose he knew about it, but he kept his eyes shut. We used to have a sort of raffle . . . we used to put the money . . . in a fund and if anybody came to join the Scouts who could not, definitely, afford the uniforms, then we used to help them out.[96]

Wesleyans would even permit gambling, it seems, if the cause was perceived to be sufficiently worthy.

The object of the Scouts was the education of boys in 'manliness' and 'good citizenship'. Baden-Powell recognised that 'the subject to be instilled must be made to appeal' and confessed that he intended scouting as gilt with which to disguise the pill of the movement's reforming intentions.[97] As is well known, the movement stressed woodcraft and 'emphasised things rural, seeking the regeneration of the young through outdoor pursuits'.[98] In Cumbria, as elsewhere, Boy Scouts earned proficiency badges. They 'learnt knots; and first aid', 'making fires', 'climbing' and, of course, camping.[99] The latter was very much a novelty and an attraction for working-class boys in particular. It also encouraged fortitude, as one informant recalled. 'It poured down all night and the rain was coming through the tent,' he said, 'but we stuck it out.'[100] In Lindal some genuine scouting was attempted: 'we were given an exercise . . . . And we had to stalk and get to this point without being seen. And we struggled along behind hedgerows. And it took us hours and hours. And when we finally got there everybody had packed up and gone home.[101] The Scouts also organised more conventional sport, notably football, and in Carlisle there was a Scouts' football league. The success of the Scouts in inculcating their professed ideals is difficult to assess. As with the Band of Hope, the impact varied, and in some cases the seeds fell on stony ground. Of two informants who were the sons of Whitehaven colliers, one attended 'just dark nights for to put time in', while the other recognised that 'it broadened your outlook. You mixed with other boys . . . from different parts of town.'[102] Some informants remembered their scouting days with great enthusiasm, while others were dismissive.

GIRLS

Adolescent girls did not elicit the same concern as boys. Working-class girls usually acquired domestic responsibilities at an early age, and did not experience such a clear-cut period of adolescence. They were also less visible to the reforming agencies and posed much less of an apparent threat. Nevertheless, by the late nineteenth century, signs of independence and 'precocity' in young girls were being viewed with disfavour.[103] They were increasingly perceived as the future wives and mothers of the Empire, whose moral and domestic standards must be raised to a suitable level.

The first major organisation to work specifically with adolescent girls was the Girls' Friendly Society (GFS), an Anglican association which was founded in 1874. The foundress was Mrs Townshend, a lady who had been involved in moral rescue work among young women and who saw the need for an association to prevent girls from 'falling'.[104] In the GFS she created an organisation which aimed at preserving the morality of respectable young girls by separating them from the non-respectable and training them in womanly virtues. The association was established in the Carlisle diocese in 1878, with Lady Lawson as its first president, and branches were quickly begun in many parishes throughout Cumbria. New branches were still being formed in the early twentieth century and the organisation was still thriving in Cumbria in the 1920s, when decline was becoming apparent elsewhere. Decline seems, however, to have been quite rapid in the 1930s, although there were societies in existence in the region until the Second World War and, apparently even later.

The GFS was highly conservative and intended 'to promote friendship and harmony across class boundaries'.[105] As mentioned in the discussion of the YMFS above, it had a bipartite structure of associates and members. From 1879 there were also candidates, younger girls who were waiting to become members. In the early years, the policy was that associates should be upper-class ladies, while the members were all working-class girls. We are told that a very clear line was drawn between the two categories. 'Upper class Lady Associates were to adopt a protective motherly role towards unmarried working girl members.'[106] How far Cumbria fitted into the standard pattern in this respect is unclear. The only known associates from the early years were the wife and daughter of the vicar of Orton, who were acting in that capacity in 1887.[107] Given the social structure of the region, it seems likely that there would have been a general shortage of genuinely upper-class ladies to take on the work. Of the class of the early members in the region, nothing is known. Nationally, domestic servants predominated. In 1891, 57 per cent of the employed membership were working in service.[108] In that year, domestic service was by far the largest employer of women in both Cumberland and Westmorland, but how many of those so employed were GFS members must at present remain a matter for conjecture.[109]

By the mid-1890s, the society's policy was shifting towards recruiting more middle-class girls as members and appointing associates from the ranks. By the early twentieth century, more middle-class girls were being enrolled, but, suggests Harrison, the society never really 'succeeded in shaking off its servant image'. In 1906 the percentage of the membership in service was still as high as 49 per cent, while 10 per cent were employed in the professions and 19 per cent in business. The GFS, says Harrison, repelled 'many self-consciously superior shop, clerical and business girls'.[110] If this was true of the earlier years in Cumbria, it seems to have ceased to be so by the 1920s. GFS members among oral informants were predominantly lower-middle class and include shop assistants and a clerical worker, although there were also working-class girls who were members. Informants speak of it very much as an organisation for refined and respectable girls. This may in part account for the organisation's success in the region, although it did, in any case, flourish best in rural areas.

One informant, a working-class woman from Workington, went on to become an associate,[111] but in the main the role seems to have been filled by any respectable woman in the parish with the leisure to take it on. Another Workington GFS member said that associates in the 1930s 'just belonged to the Church. They'd be older people . . . . Maybe retired people that had been teachers and things like that . . . and knew how to control children.' In Dalton a doctor's wife and the vicar's wife took on the task during and after the First World War.[112] Harrison has suggested that the democratisation of the society and the consequent loss of the 'aristocratic cachet' which had aided its popularity in the early years was a factor in the decline of the GFS, but it is not possible to assess the relevance of this argument to Cumbria without knowing more about the early structure of the society.

Under GFS rules members need not be Anglican, although this was compulsory for associates. In Cumbria, members were apparently all Anglican, and the organisation was thought of as specifically Church of England. Nonconformists, although they possessed no comparable organisation of their own, never attended. A Roman Catholic girl did attend meetings in Penrith until she was prevented from continuing by her priest, but this seems to have been an isolated instance.[113]

Central to GFS ideals was rule 3, which required members to bear a spotless character. As a Dalton informant put it: 'you'd to have a very clean living life before you could go in! And while you *were* in. If there was any babies or anything came on the scene you were hooked out.'[114] No informant could remember any girl being ejected, however, and as girls could, and often did, become members from the age of twelve there was little time for loose living beforehand. Candidates could even be admitted from the age of eight. The GFS girl, declares Harrison, was 'expected to be devout, kindly, serious minded, uncomplaining and (by modern standards) relatively uninterested in the opposite sex'.[115] The improving ethos was apparently accepted unquestioningly by informants, but the determinedly single-sex nature of the organisation's activities did rankle a little with some. 'I'd been in it for years and years before we were allowed any boys at a social evening,' said one lady, 'and then it had to be the Boy Scouts! As if they weren't as bad as all the rest of 'em.' The demise of the society in

Penrith was blamed by another informant on the starting of a mixed Church Fellowship which supplanted the GFS as a recreational society.[116]

Although membership of the society had practical benefits for girls leaving home or seeking work,[117] it was the recreational aspects of the GFS which led many Cumbrian girls to continue as members from the age of twelve or thirteen until they married. As one informant said, 'it was a night out'. There was a very wide range of activities. The girls performed plays, gave concerts and were taught country dancing.[118] They had socials and parties, went on outings and organised garden parties and fêtes. At Penrith after the First World War, the GFS had a noted choir, which competed in musical festivals and gave at least one young contralto a voice training which brought her success as a soloist. At Workington in the early 1930s, the girls took part in sports and athletics, although sport was not a usual part of GFS activity.[119] At the weekly meetings there were speakers on various religious and non-religious subjects, and the girls did practical work for the church, knitting and sewing for sales of work and embroidering altar cloths and such like. The GFS also had annual festivals at which the girls competed for prizes awarded for talents as various as knitting, reciting, playing the piano, cookery and thrift.[120]

Harrison has suggested that the GFS gave young women 'self-confidence and self-respect in a predominantly masculine world,'[121] and the activities of the GFS in this region can be seen as tending to produce this result. Self-confidence would have been gained from activities such as amateur dramatics and competitive singing and sport, while the society's stress on purity and its emphasis on the virtues of domesticity would have tended to 'exalt femininity'[122] and produce self-respect. Why then did the GFS decline? Probably because, both recreationally and in other respects, it had been outgrown. Harrison claims that for the GFS the First World War only accentuated trends previously established, and that the seeds of its decline had already been sown before 1914.[123] The war, however, hastened the decline of domestic service, the society's main occupational base, and extended the emancipation of women. It also shattered for a while the ideology of imperialism which underpinned the society's aims. In addition, I would suggest that the GFS had, in a sense, prolonged the period of adolescence in girls until marriage, but after the war this was a much less feasible aim. The inter-war period brought much wider recreational opportunities for women and girls. There were other places to go for 'a night out', where a girl could, if she so wished, be accompanied by her 'young man', while for younger girls the churches offered an alternative to the GFS in the Girl Guides.

In some respects the Guides were a natural progression from the GFS. While the emphasis on womanly accomplishment remained, the outdoor ethos of the Guides was more in tune with the expectations of young girls in the inter-war period if not, as we shall see, with those of some parents. The Girl Guides were founded in 1910 following the attempt by self-styled 'Girl Scouts' to participate in the 1909 Crystal Palace Scout rally. Baden-Powell would not allow his organisation to be infiltrated and 'contaminated'[124] by girls in this way, and he insisted that a separate organisation should be provided for them, with a different name. With his sister Agnes, he produced the book *Girl Guides: a suggestion for character training for girls* and the Guides were established. Until the leadership of the movement passed from the Victorian spinster Agnes to Baden-Powell himself, and then in 1916 to his young wife Olave, the Guides had a 'tepid and uninspiring programme' and the organisation grew slowly.[125] Thereafter, both the Guides and the Brownies (established in 1914) expanded rapidly. No specific figures are available for the organisation's growth in Cumbria, but there were already Guides in Barrow in 1910,[126] and the press and oral evidence make it clear that, if less so than the Scouts, the Guides were widespread and popular in the region by the 1920s. The organisation's expansion continued until and beyond the Second World War.

Both the Church of England and the Nonconformist churches ran Guides and Brownies, although they seem more often to have been attached to the former. The Catholic church again preferred its own piecemeal and sometimes non-existent organisations. Church membership was sometimes insisted upon, but not always. In Dalton, where the Guides were run by the Church of England, this was said to be the case,[127] but with the Brownies there was apparently some leniency. The Dalton Catholic Church ran a female counterpart to its Knights of the Blessed Sacrament, the Handmaids of the Blessed Sacrament, which offered similar activities to the Guides, but met only monthly.[128] As with the Band of Hope, Catholic girls were sometimes tempted by the other churches' organisations. A Catholic informant confessed that, one night in the 1920s, she and a friend attended the

Brownies. 'We seen all these kids going in and we joined them.' The organiser, she said 'let us join in with all the games'. However, when she arrived home and told her mother where she had been, 'Ooh dear, it was a tragedy!' "Shouldn't go in there!" ... She told me off.' In Barrow, however, a Catholic girl attended the Guides at St Mark's Church, apparently with her parents' blessing.[129] It seems that, as with many church activities, the exclusion of Catholics was at least partly self-imposed.

Religious affiliation was not the only possible obstacle to Guide membership. In the case of the Guides there is evidence that the cost of the uniform prevented some girls from joining. When asked if most of her friends attended the Guides with her, a Dalton informant replied, 'Some of them, their mothers couldn't afford the uniform you know ... you had to have the uniform.' A lady interviewed by Elizabeth Roberts in Barrow was herself prevented from joining for this reason. 'I think at that time it was money,' she said 'it would be uniform that would be the drawbback. They had to have their own uniforms and there just wasn't any money.'[130] No evidence has come to light of any leniency over the matter of uniform, or of any schemes to meet the cost as with the Workington Scouts. Some girls were also prevented from joining by parents who disliked the movement's ethos and activities. A Penrith lady (who was brought up by her aunt) said regretfully that 'No, I wasn't in the Girl Guides. I wanted to be. But ... my aunt was old and old-fashioned. She thought it was terrible, girls wanting to go and camp!' Another informant said that 'It was one thing my mother wasn't very keen on my joining. So I was never in the Girl Guides ... To her it was classed as army. You know, a military business. She didn't like the idea of it at all.'[131] Both these ladies were members of the GFS, whose ethos was found more acceptable.

The Guides did, of course, go camping and they spent much time in the open air, but otherwise their activities were not greatly different from those of the GFS. They, too, gave concerts and put on plays, and did their share of church work. In Raughton Head and Gaitsgill parish in 1932, for instance, it was reported that, while the GFS had 'renovated the most dilapidated of the cushions and kneelers ... the hymn and prayer books' had been 'neatly mended by the Girl Guides'.[132] Like the Scouts, the Guides worked for badges, but these were in many cases for the same accomplishments for which the GFS awarded prizes; piano-playing, thrift, cookery and so on. If Guides were permitted fresh air and exercise they were still expected to excel in the womanly arts.

Work with adolescents by the Cumbrian churches differed little in pattern from that undertaken elsewhere. The majority of oral informants were in a church youth organisation of some kind, and it is clear that religious bodies were successful in drawing in Cumbrian adolescents, who enjoyed the activities which were on offer. The organisations' success in character training is unmeasurable, although they cannot have been without influence. The writer of the 'Notes and Gossip' column in the *Barrow News* in 1930 placed the Scouts and Guides firmly among the beneficial influences which were at work in the town. Commenting on the decline in drunkenness, he said:

> The improvement in the habits of the people, the greater love for sport and rational enjoyment which is particularly noticeable in the rising generation are some of the best signs of the times, and reflect the success of the various agencies which are quietly and unostentatiously at work for the development of a higher manhood than was possible before the days of the Scouts and Girl Guides and various other organizations, which are having remarkable effects in the moulding of the characters of those who will be the men and women of the morrow.[133]

THE CHURCHES AND ADULT LEISURE

The various denominations were relatively successful in prolonging their influence over the recreational lives of those young people who had outgrown the youth organisations. There were those who, even if they had attended church activities as children, had no further contact with organised religion or its recreational provision after adolescence. A high proportion of the young and single seem, however, to have continued to avail themselves of the entertainment offered and of the opportunities for 'making suitable acquaintances',[134] and for self-improvement which the social life of the churches provided. There were few of my oral informants who never participated in church events at this stage in their lives, although not all were assiduous attenders. In later life the churches were less important in terms of entertainment, although every effort was made to retain the interest of mature adults.

One of the earlier successes in attracting adults were the mutual improvement societies which were run by many Anglican and

Nonconformist churches in the late nineteenth and early twentieth centuries. The Anglican societies seem all to have been restricted to males, and aimed at the young, having the words 'Young Men's' in their titles. A solitary exception was the society formed as a men's club at St Aidan's, Carlisle in 1902, which decided the following year to admit ladies as members. Thereafter, however, it quickly evolved into little more than a mixed rambling club.[135] Some of the Nonconformist societies seem also to have been all-male organisations, for instance that in existence at Appleby Wesleyans in 1875,[136] but the majority were open to both sexes. The societies' programmes generally consisted of weekly or fortnightly lectures plus musical entertainments and socials. Papers were read on topics as diverse as 'Iron', 'The Norman Conquest', 'Socialism', 'Christ an example for us', 'Water', and 'Travelling in South Africa'.[137] Referring to similar societies in Durham, Robert Moore has suggested that the wide variety of topics discussed is in itself less noteworthy than the fact that people were willing 'to subject themselves to what constitutes a rigorous intellectual discipline; that they did "endeavour to train or cultivate the mind"'.[138] Although most of the Nonconformist societies offered opportunities to mix with the opposite sex in a social environment, they would surely have deterred the frivolous-minded, and the success of mutual improvement suggests a genuine desire for self-education, perhaps reaching to lower social levels than membership of mechanics' institutes a generation earlier.

Most Anglican societies were still in existence until the First World War, but by the early years of this century many Nonconformist societies had given way to local branches of national organisations such as the Christian Endeavour and Wesley Guild. The Christian Endeavour movement, which arrived in Britain from the USA in 1887 and spread rapidly during the 1890s, was itself non-denominational, but in Cumbria it was usually associated with the Primitive Methodist church. The Wesley Guild was the Wesleyans' counterpart organisation, and other denominations similarly had their Young People's Guilds or Fellowships. All these organisations were aimed principally at young adults, although they were again open to both sexes.

Stephen Yeo has suggested that the Christian Endeavour was a part of the churches' resistance against 'vacuous amusements'.[139] Its aim was 'to promote an earnest Christian life among its members, to increase their mutual acquaintance and to make them more useful to the service of God'. It was, according to Yeo, 'devotional rather than for entertainment and ... determined not to sacrifice ends for means'.[140] The programme card of the society attached to Cecil Street Primitive Methodists in Carlisle in 1907 shows that the members met weekly for discussions on biblical topics, although there were also occasional socials. Between then and 1912, however, social events came increasingly to the fore, a rambles and picnics committee being formed in 1910.[141] The society nevertheless remained more biased towards religious matters than its counterparts. Workington Wesley Guild for instance preferred 'limelight lectures' on such topics as 'Ants' and 'Medical superstitions', only the limelight differentiating the meetings from those of Mutual Improvement Societies.[142] Despite the overall decline in Methodism, membership of the Wesley Guild and Christian Endeavour appears to have held up between the wars. In the Cumbrian circuits in 1923 there were thirty-six branches of the Wesley Guild, with 2,164 members. Ten years later there were sixty-eight branches with 3,359 members. The Primitive Methodists had forty-one branches of the Christian Endeavour in 1933, an increase of five over the previous year, but earlier figures are not known.[143] Only one Anglican organisation which was at all comparable to the Christian Endeavour and Wesley Guild has been encountered. This was the St Andrew's, Penrith Church Fellowship which was mentioned above in the discussion of the Girls' Friendly Society. Untypically for an Anglican organisation, this was open to both sexes. It aimed to promote 'worship, study, service and recreation'. An undated programme shows that, in addition to addresses by the vicar, its activities included play-readings, evenings of gramophone records and quizzes.[144] The society appears to have been less intellectual in tone than the Nonconformist societies. The Roman Catholic Church appears to have had no comparable societies, although in places it did have clubs for young men in the inter-war period. In Whitehaven, for instance, a Catholic Young Men's Society was reported to be flourishing in 1920, when its 'social study debating class' was making 'good progress'.[145] The Catholic Church believed in separate treatment for the sexes, and this was also the Church of England's general policy in the provison of leisure activities for adults. There were mixed parish socials and sometimes dances, but in the main the Church followed through the philosophy of the youth movements, and offered men and women separate social activities considered appropriate for their sex. The Church believed that men were deterred by the presence or influence of women, while women's recreational needs were perceived to be quite different from those of men. The activities offered to women were an extension of those provided for girls, but for men, militarism and woodcraft were put aside in favour of conviviality and, as we have seen above, the cultivation of the intellect.

The Church had a nationally organised society for men, the Church of England Men's Society, which was founded in 1904. By 1906 there were 350 branches nationally. This society was described by a secretary of a Reading CEMS as 'a real attempt by men to regain for the church those men who she has lost or who have never been within her influence'.[146] In Cumbria it was not a very widespread body, although it existed in a number of parishes where it was apparently well supported. None of my oral informants was a member, however. In Kirkby Stephen, a branch of the society was formed in 1905. The programme for the first month consisted of two church services, a smoking concert, a debate and a lecture on 'The new photography, illustrated by examples, demonstrations and a hundred limelight views'.[147] In the first quarter of 1907, the society had lectures on 'The Life of Our Lord' and 'The violin, its masters and makers' and a discussion on 'Disestablishment and Disendowment', as well as impromptu speeches, a smoking concert, an address by a visiting clergyman, and church services.[148] The society aimed to interest men generally and educate them in conservative Anglicanism. In common with others, this branch of the society was still in existence in 1910 when there was a 'capital attendance' at a lecture on the history of the Bible.[149] After the First World War nothing is however heard of the society in any parish.

The other major thrust of church activity for men was the organisation of Parish Men's Clubs or Institutes, which sought to provide an alternative meeting place to the public house, or, as the Kendal club's organisers said, to 'the temptations of the streets'.[150] Games such as billiards, whist and draughts were generally offered. A small number of Nonconformist and Roman Catholic churches also had clubs of this sort, but the Church of England clubs predominated. They appear to have been virtually indistinguishable from the secular village institutes and reading rooms which had proliferated in the region by the inter-war period. If a permanent club was out of the question, then an effort was sometimes made on one night a week, as at Arnside, in 1909 and 1910, where Men's Saturday Social Evenings were organised.[151] Most clubs seem to have been open to those over the age of sixteen, and many of them were aimed specifically at young men. They in any case usually failed in the attempt to draw in older men. In Kendal in 1911, it was complained that 'the idea seems to prevail that it is a club for boys only'. The membership list contained 'only a small proportion of the names of the men of the Parish Church Congregation', which the committee felt was 'not quite what ought to be'.[152]

Church activities for women were more conspicuously successful, although they did not appeal to all. Probably the most important women's association before the spread of the Women's Institute was the Mothers' Union. This was an Anglican body, restricted to communicants of the Church of England, which was founded by Mrs Sumner, an Archdeacon's wife and Girls' Friendly Society associate, in 1885. Her aim was to provide a follow on organisation for GFS girls who left that society on marriage. As with the GFS, purity was linked with the future well-being of the Empire. The objects of the Mothers' Union were:

1) To uphold the sanctity of marriage.
2) To awaken in mothers a sense of their great responsibility in the training of their boys and girls (the future fathers and mothers of the Empire).
3) To organise in every place a band of Mothers who will unite in prayer and seek by their own example to lead their families in holiness and purity of life.[153]

There is no evidence of the organisation's existence in Cumbria before the early twentieth century, but as there are few parish magazines available from the late nineteenth century, and the organisation's activities were not generally worthy of report in the press, it could be that branches were formed in the region at an earlier date. New branches were being established both before and after the First World War, for example at Selside in 1911, and at Dalton in the mid-1930s.[154] Some branches evidently had a flourishing membership. In 1910 Kendal branch had 117 members, an increase of fifteen over the previous year, and Upperby (Carlisle) branch had ninety-five.[155] In 1913, there were said to be 6,500 members in the Carlisle diocese.[156] No further figures are known, but the Mothers' Union was evidently in a very flourishing condition between the wars.

A number of Anglican informants, or their mothers, were Mothers' Union members. In most cases they had also been members of the GFS. Meetings were seen as an opportunity for respectable women, who were otherwise housebound with small children, to meet and socialise. Meetings were usually monthly and in the afternoon, and in most cases mothers took their offspring with them. 'You just kept them on your knee', or they 'were set on the mat to play', I was told.[157] A typical meeting consisted of a short service and readings from some suitable book, or a talk from a visiting speaker, 'a vicar from another church or something like that'.[158] Parish magazines reveal that there were also speakers on temperance.[159]Both middle- and working-class women were members, but there is no evidence of two classes of membership as suggested by Caroline Hallett in her instructions for organising a Mothers' Union branch. She suggests that the 'more educated class' should be subscribing members and pay a small yearly subscription, while the working class, as ordinary members, should pay nothing. She also suggests separate meetings for the two classes. In Cumbria, there appears, for the most part, to have been only one class of member and a nominal subscription, if any. In one or two places, however, the society had 'associates' like the GFS, and elsewhere there seems often to have been an upper-class president, who periodically entertained the mothers and took on a role similar to that of an associate.[160] The organiser was usually the vicar or his wife. By the 1930s, however, the society appears to have become more democratic. Two lower-middle-class informants then held office, one of them travelling to London twice a year as 'members' representative'.[161]

Preserving the sanctity of marriage was one of the society's basic aims and at a mass meeting of the Mothers' Union at Carlisle in 1913 the foundress, Mrs Sumner, 'besought the mothers to set their faces resolutely against any further extension of the Divorce Act, reminding them that faithful marriage is the first ideal of the Mothers' Union'.[162] Just as in the GFS, any girl who lost her good character was ejected, so with the Mothers' Union any woman who was in any way involved with a divorce was asked to leave. In Penrith, an informant told me that 'We had a person joined and she was an awfully nice person . . . . Her husband had been married . . . before and divorced. And when they found out they stopped her coming.'[163] The reactions of members to this are not known, but at the time of interview, my informant considered this to be very unjust.

The Mothers' Union would not appear to have very much to recommend it as entertainment, and its continued success perhaps reflects the social isolation of women at home caring for children. The organisation idealised their position, and perhaps helped to make them more comfortable in it. By the 1930s it also offered the possibility of gaining status within the Church community as an office holder, and provided an outlet for women's growing confidence in organisational matters. The imperialist ethos seems to have faded after the First World War, and this was doubtless an asset in the organisation's continued success.

Many Anglican parishes had other meetings for women, such as Mothers' Meetings and Young Wives. These had no national organisation, but they existed in different parishes in a very similar form, sometimes in addition to the Mothers' Union and sometimes instead of it. Young Wives was an inter-war innovation in Cumbria, and it was more modern in outlook than the Mothers' Union. At meetings, children were usually looked after in a separate room to allow their mothers to enjoy the proceedings undisturbed, while the meetings themselves offered a wider variety of speakers (informants mentioned child-care, first aid and flower-arranging), and there were also outings and Christmas parties for mothers and children together.[164] The Mothers' Meetings were simply social meetings for women, without any high-flown aims, although the emphasis was still on improving and useful activity. They also, like the Young Wives, had excursions and Christmas parties. For much of the time the women were engaged in sewing to raise money for church funds, and they had a close parallel in the sewing meetings of the Nonconformist churches.

Apart from the occasional women's Bible class, sewing meetings were the only Nonconformist activities restricted to, or, in the nature of things only attended by, women. Women seem to have given unstintingly of their time in this work, which reflects the generally accepted rule that women's leisure should be not only productive, but subject to the needs of others. The Minister of South William Street Wesleyans in Workington said in 1914 that 'He sometimes thought the Christian Church did not realise how great was its indebtedness to sewing meetings.' That of his own chapel had 'been working for a considerable time every day with most praiseworthy enterprise', for the annual sale of work, 'and when the day was not sufficient they had extended their labours to an advanced hour of the night'. They had, he said, 'worked late every night for weeks'.[165] Sewing meetings were the mainstay of chapel funds, and the first to be called on in a financial emergency. Penrith Wesleyans, for instance, found it necessary to ask for the assistance of their sewers in paying off the debt on the Sunday school buildings in 1902.[166] The women agreed to hold a sale of work. Even 'the nameless heroes of calico and flannel'[167] decided enough was enough occasionally, however. In 1923 the women at South William Street passed a resolution that they would 'in future refuse to help in the case of debts acquired on schemes concerning which they have not been previously consulted'.[168] Clearly, the increasing confidence and independence of women between the wars was making itself felt. Probably, also, the increasing availability of mass-produced clothing was making needlework less effective as a means of fund-raising.

Speaking of a Cambridgeshire village in the 1970s, Mary Chamberlain said that 'social activities for women must do and be seen to be doing something for the improvement of the community or of themselves as well as providing incidentally, a social outlet'.[169] As far as the denominational communities were concerned this was, as we have seen, equally the case in Cumbria during our period. The enormous growth and popularity of the Women's Institute in Cumbrian villages in the 1920s and 1930s suggests further that this rule also had a more general applicability in married women's recreational lives.

At the church socials and dances it was invariably the women who were responsible for the supper and, it may be supposed, for cleaning the hall afterwards. These events were, however, well supported by both sexes. Methodist churches did not allow dancing during our period, and theatrical entertainments were generally frowned upon. Not all Methodists accepted the prohibition gracefully. A Barrow Wesleyan interviewed by Elizabeth Roberts confessed that 'We did dance and were caught dancing', whereupon the minister 'came up and told us that we'd go to hell and that was the end of that'.[170] The Church of England and the Catholic Church did allow both these activities, although some cautiousness about dancing lingered among Anglicans. By the inter-war period, Church dances were held annually, or rather more frequently in a number of places. In Workington at 'the Church annual "do" (in the 1930s) they danced till about 1 and 2 in the morning . . . . The mothers used to go to help with the suppers. And we were there all night . . . '. All the young people connected with Church organisations would attend, 'And they used to sell tickets and outsiders could buy one, you know.'[171] In other places, however the dances had to be intermixed with games. In Barrow, in the 1920s, 'They didn't call them dances, they were socials and they had to have so many games in as well . . . the vicar insisted that they had three or four games at least. The vicar was always there . . . of course, as soon as the vicar went the games finished, it was all dancing.'[172] Evidently, in both the Methodist and Anglican churches, the views of congregaton and hierarchy did not always coincide.

If Nonconformists lagged behind in the matter of dances, they did have Pleasant Sunday Afternoons. The PSA was a non-denominational, but Nonconformist organised association, which was founded in West Bromwich in 1875. Like other church organisations which have been mentioned above, it spread rapidly in the late nineteenth century, becoming established in a number of places in Cumbria. Although its heyday was before the First World War, it was still flourishing in Penrith and Workington at least, during the 1920s. The organisation's motto was 'Brief, bright and brotherly', and an alternative name for it was the Brotherhood.[173] As this title suggests, it was aimed principally at men. It aimed to draw in those men who no longer, or who had never, attended church, and reflecting Church of England policy, it aimed to do this by excluding women. The Cumbrian PSAs seem to have differed from the norm, however, as, by the inter-war period at least, meetings were open to all, and attended by whole families and people of all ages.[174] Whether earlier PSAs were restricted to men is not known, as press reports of meetings do not make it apparent. Women did, however, take part in the entertainment. This consisted usually of hymn-singing, and performances by a band or orchestra and one or more soloists. Byles suggested in his booklet on PSA organisation that, ideally, the orchestra should be formed from the members, and this was the case in inter-war Workington.[175] Sometimes, but not always, there were one or more addresses. In Blennerhasset in 1902 the PSA was addressed on the subject of 'Born again Christianity'. In Workington, however, 'there weren't any speakers'.[176] The meetings lasted for one hour, in order that people should not become bored, hence the word 'brief' in the motto. The meetings remembered by informants were certainly popular. In Penrith, 'they used to pack the picture house on

Middlegate ... . Every seat packed', while in Workington an estimated 600 to 700 people attended the PSA at the Hippodrome Theatre.[177] There is no evidence that the PSA served to win people back to the chapels, however. Although it was, as it were, a kind of adult Sunday school, prizes being given for regular attendance, the PSA was viewed simply as entertainment, as, quite simply, a pleasant Sunday afternoon.

Apart from women's sewing meetings, which perhaps should not be considered as leisure activities at all, Nonconformist recreational organisations for adults were for the most part open to both sexes. With the exception of a minority of mutual improvement societies, there were no organisations for men only. Even the PSA, which might originally have been for men, was open to all by the 1920s. The chapel organisations were primarily a part of chapel social life, and they had a different ethos from most Anglican organisations. It was mutual improvement rather than improvement of the working classes by their social betters. The Church of England had its mutual improvement societies as well, of course, but the main thrust of Church activity with adults was an extension of its work with adolescents. This was particularly the case with its women's organisations, which were concerned with purity, duty and womanly accomplishment. With men, the aim, as with boys, was to draw them off 'the streets' and into the Church's sphere of influence, though the methods were necessarily modified. Even so, Church organisations for men were not markedly successful. Both church and chapel found it difficult to retain the interest of older men, and except for the devout, or those who sang in a choir, religious organisations scarcely figured in their recreational lives. Older women, perhaps because of their more restricted leisure opportunities, more often found church organisations agreeable, although they were not attractive to all.

CONCLUSION

Attendance at church or chapel, and at the leisure activities attached to them, demonstrated that a person belonged to a particular denominational or parish community. Attendance also demonstrated respectability. All Protestant churches were more or less respectable, and members of different denominations would, to some extent support one another's events, participating in a general culture of respectability. Catholics, however, generally kept themselves separate, and their church seems to have figured less importantly in their lives in a recreational, though not, of course, in a religious, sense.

The intimate and local culture of the chapel or parish community gave way during our period to a more cohesive national culture. The arrival of branches of national and international bodies, the Christian Endeavour, Mothers' Union and others mentioned above, broke down the cultural isolation of church communities. Those organisations which were interdenominational also helped to break down the divisions between different Protestant churches, which were united in a common aim. Anglican Boy Scouts were likely to have closer links with other Scouts in the area, from whichever denomination, than with other organisations in their own church. The separation of Catholics, who had their own organisations, was probably thereby reinforced.

All the churches offered an alternative to public house culture, but this was more readily taken up by those who would not or could not have gone in a public house anyway – children, and the majority of women. The churches' association with the temperance movement grew out of the long-standing Nonconformist condemnation of drink, and the increasing social conscience of the Church of England in the late nineteenth century. It was probably difficult to base recreational organisations on the negative principle of abstention, and the use of recreation to promote temperance objectives was found in the main to be only appropriate for children, for whom the pledge had little meaning.

Church work with children and adolescents was on the whole the most successful. Almost no other agencies worked with children in a recreational way, and they were usually keen to avail themselves of what was on offer. Women's activities were also successful, probably because they were quite accurately aimed at women's social and cultural position. Because of the exclusion of men, women in the Mother's Union and the sewing meetings necessarily gained organisational experience and abilities, and probably gained confidence as a result. The churches were least successful in providing leisure activities for men. The view that men were deterred by the presence of women may well have been erroneous, since activities such as choirs, the Wesley Guild, parish socials and the PSA were successful in drawing in both sexes. It was 'men only' events which tended to fail.

There is, however, no doubt about the overall importance of church-based leisure activity. It usually cost little, it was available almost everywhere, and at the chapels in particular, it provided opportunities for the young to make 'suitable acquaintances'. Nonconformists, if they were prepared to give their minds to improving pastimes, had ample opportunity for mixing with the opposite sex in circumstances of the utmost propriety. The Church of England, with the same need in mind was, by the inter-war years, in many places, running dances. The young had more leisure time than older people, and they took the fullest part in the recreational life of the churches, although the needs of women were also generally catered for. Men, however, usually had a network of workplace and possibly public house acquaintances, and had less need of what the churches could offer.

NOTES

Place of publication London unless otherwise stated.
1 See J. D. Marshall and J. K. Walton, *The Lake Counties from 1830 to the mid-twentieth century, A study in regional change*, Manchester, 1981, p. 149; 1851 Religious Census, P.P. 1852–53, LXXXIX. It is not possible to give a more precise figure for attendance as there is no way of knowing how many people, if any, were present at more than one service.
2 H. McLeod, 'Class, community and religion: the religious geography of nineteenth-century England' in *A Sociological Yearbook of Religion in Britain*, 6, 1973, pp. 46–7; W.C.T., 20.12.1902. The Whitehaven figures were for the town, not the registration district or Poor Law Union as in 1851; 1851 Religious Census, P.P. 1852–53, LXXXIX.
3 W.C.T., 20.12.1902.
4 John Burgess, *A History of Cumbrian Methodism*, Kendal, 1980, *passim*.
5 John Burgess, 1980, p. 146.
6 E. Royle, seminar paper given 13.11.86 at Centre for Social History, University of Lancaster.
7 K. S. Inglis, *Churches and the Working Classes in Victorian England*, 1963, p. 74.
8 Hugh Cunningham, *Leisure in the Industrial Revolution*, 1980, p. 180.
9 Inglis, 1963, p. 79.
10 See, for instance, *Congregationalist*, Vol. 8, July and August 1879, Congregational Symposium Report.
11 Revd. H. T. Smart, 'The recreations of the people', *Wesleyan Methodist Magazine*, 1890, p. 664.
12 Second Ecumenical Conference, pp. 582–4, quoted in M. Edwards, *Methodism and England. A Study of Methodism in its Social and Political Aspects during the period 1850–1932*, 1943, p. 219.
13 Edwards, 1943, p. 220.
14 Respondent 7.
15 Vic Gammon, 'Babylonian Performances; the Rise and Suppression of Popular Church Music, 1660–1870' in E. and S. Yeo (eds.), *Popular Culture and Class Conflict 1590–1914*, Sussex, 1981, pp. 62–88, *passim*.

16 J. W. Nicholson, *History of Crosby Garrett, Westmorland*, Kirkby Stephen, 1914, pp. 96–7; Gammon, 1981, pp. 63–4.

17 S. H. Scott, *A Westmorland Village*, 1904, p. 178.

18 Gammon, 1981, p. 65.

19 Respondents 26 and 28; *Parochial Magazine* for Penrith, Kirkoswald,, Lowther, Appleby and Kirkby Stephen Deaneries, 1910, C.R.O. PR/110/1/307.

20 Respondents 11 and 30.

21 Gammon, 1981, p. 83.

22 Respondents 23, 28, 26 and 30.

23 *Workington Wesleyan Circuit Magazines*, C.R.O. FCM/7/1/16.

24 Robert Moore, *Pitmen, Preachers and Politics. The effects of Methodism in a Durham mining community*, 1974, p. 116.

25 See Anthony P. Cohen, *The Symbolic Construction of Community*, Chichester, Sussex, 1985, p. 19 and Ch. 1, *passim*, for discussion of the symbolic representation of communities.

26 Stephen Yeo, *Religion and Voluntary Organisations in Crisis*, 1976, p. 177.

27 Quoted in James Walvin, *Leisure and Society 1830–1950*, 1978, p. 97.

28 Minute book of choir committee, Sandgate Head Primitive Methodists, Penrith, C.R.O. FCM/3/4/33.

29 *The Monthly Record*, Wesleyan Methodist Magazine for Penrith and Kirkoswald circuits, C.R.O. FCM/4/1/36.

30 Respondents 30 and 31.

31 *Workington Wesleyan Circuit Magazines*, C.R.O. FCM/7/1/16.

32 Walvin, 1978, pp. 97–8.

33 *The Monthly Record*, Wesleyan Methodist Magazine for Penrith and Kirkoswald Circuits, April 1920, C.R.O., FCM/4/1/36.

34 Respondent 8.

35 Respondent 6.

36 James Obelkevich, *Religion and Rural Society – South Lindsey 1825–1875*, Oxford 1976, p. 212.

37 Respondents 9, 8 and 13.

38 Richard Hoggart, *The Uses of Literacy*, 1960, p. 92.

39 See for instance Flimby Wesleyans roll books 1896–1900, C.R.O. FCM/2/68B, 69 and 70.

40 Respondents 14 and 19.

41 Respondents 9 and 12.

42 Burgess, 1980, p. 111.

43 Kenneth Young, 1972, *The joyous days and prayerful nights of the nonconformists in their heyday*, c 1850–1950, 1972, p. 93 (information of an un-named respondent); p. 17.

44 Moore, 1974, p. 130.

45 Respondents 8 and 26.

46 W.G., 1.1.1870. Respondent 30; Mr PIB.

47 *Workington Wesleyan Circuit Magazine* November 1914, C.R.O. FCM/7/1/16.

48 Brian Harrison, *Drink and the Victorians*, 1971, p. 184.

49 See N. Longmate, *The Waterdrinkers*, 1968, pp. 78–80; W.G., 19.2.1910.

50 Respondent 6; local press, *passim*.

51 See Harrison, 1971, p. 187.

52 Harrison, 1971, p. 183.

53 *P.O.*, 26.5.1885.

54 Membership Certificate of Juvenile Band of Hope, C.R.O. WDX/276; *C.J.*, 7.6.1870; *C. Pacq.*, 16.8.1870; *P.O.*, 23.6.1885.

55 Respondents 7 and 24.

56 Lilian Lewis Shiman, 'The Band of Hope movement; respectable recreation for working class children', *Victorian Studies*, Vol. XVIII, No. 1, September 1973, p. 52.

57 Respondent 20 (information concerning her sister).
58 Respondents 22 and 24; Shiman, 1973, p. 68.
59 Shiman, 1973, p. 67.
60 Respondent 9.
61 Shiman, 1973, p. 51.
62 Respondent 32.
63 Harrison, 1971, p. 193.
64 Sammy Tate, in Melvyn Bragg, *Speak for England*, New York 1977, p. 425; Respondent 25.
65 Respondents 24 and 18.
66 Respondent 25.
67 Respondent 26.
68 Respondent 25.
69 Peter Burke, *Popular Culture in Early Modern Europe*, 1978, pp. 199–200.
70 Burke, 1978, p. 200.
71 Respondent 25.
72 John R. Gillis, *Youth and History, Tradition and Change in European Age relations, 1770–present*, 1974, pp. 98, 133.
73 Gillis, 1974, pp. 128–9.
74 John Springhall, *Youth, Empire and Society*, 1977.
75 Gillis, 1974, pp. 121, 129.
76 *The Church Monthly*, Holy Trinity, West Seaton (Workington), 1894–96, C.R.O. PR/14.
77 Respondent 1.
78 *The Quarterly Messenger*, Parish Magazine of Upperby (Carlisle), 1886, C.R.O., PR/76/77/1.
79 *The Quarterly Messenger*, 1887, 1888, C.R.O. PR/76/77/ 2 and 3.
80 *Penrith Ruridecanal Magazine*, 1893, C.R.O. PR/110/1/229.
81 Gillis, 1974, p. 111.
82 For clergy attitudes see *W.G.*, 10.2.1900, address of vicar of Bowness at 'patriotic concert', and *W.G.*, 12.8.1914, Canon Rawnsley's sermon at Grasmere rushbearing.
83 John M. Mackenzie, *Propaganda and Empire*, Manchester, 1984, p. 242.
84 St James's Church, Whitehaven, *Parsh Magazine*, January and November 1907, C.R.O. PR/82/52.
85 Respondent 30.
86 Springhall, 1977, p. 40.
87 St James's Church, Whitehaven, *Parish Magazine*, October 1914, C.R.O. PR/82/52.
88 See Springhall, 1977, pp. 30, 40–1.
89 Bundle of Circuit Returns, Carlisle Primitive Methodists, C.R.O. FCM/1/1/28.
90 Respondent 25.
91 Respondents 36 and 32.
92 Respondent 32.
93 Respondents 2 and 20.
94 Springhall, 1977, p. 91, quoting Ian Niall, *A London Boyhood*, 1974, p. 115.
95 Respondent 32.
96 Respondent 25.
97 Springhall, 1977, p. 124, quoting Robert Baden-Powell, *Scouting for Boys*, 1909 ed., p.293.
98 Mackenzie, 1984, p. 243.
99 Respondents 26, 32 and 25.
100 Respondent 26.
101 Respondent 23.
102 Respondents 34 and 32.

103 See Carol Dyhouse, *Girls Growing up in late Victorian and Edwardian England*, 1981, p. 113.
104 Mary Heath-Stubbs, *Friendship's Highway, Being the History of the Girls' Friendly Society, 1875–1925*, 1926, p. 4.
105 Dyhouse, 1981, p. 108.
106 Dyhouse, 1981, p. 108.
107 *Orton Parish Magazine*, 1887, C.R.O. WDX/194/Z5.
108 Brian Harrison, 'For Church, Queen and family: the Girls' Friendly society 1874–1920', *Past and Present*, 61, 1973, p. 117.
109 See Marshall and Walton, 1981, Appendix 3, pp. 244–7.
110 Harrison, 1973, pp. 117, 120.
111 Respondent 11.
112 Respondents 17, 28 and 12.
113 Respondent 13.
114 Respondent 12.
115 Harrison, 1973, p. 116.
116 Respondents 12 and 13.
117 See Harrison, 1973, pp. 125–6.
118 Respondent 9. Great Salkeld Girls' Friendly Society minute book, C.R.O. PR/116/57; Respondent 1.
119 Respondents 13, 14 and 17.
120 See Great Salkeld GFS minute book, C.R.O. PR/116/57.
121 Harrison, 1973, p. 135.
122 Dyhouse, 1981, p. 110.
123 Harrison, 1973. p.137.
124 See Dyhouse, 1981, p. 110.
125 Springhall, 1977, p. 132.
126 Mrs M3B, interviewed by Elizabeth Roberts. Transcript in Centre for North-West Regional Studies.
127 Respondents 9 and 2.
128 Respondents 2 and 20.
129 Respondent 20; Mrs M3B, interviewed by Elizabeth Roberts. The date of attendance is not given in the interview.
130 Respondent 9; Mrs A2B.
131 Respondents 13 and 12.
132 *Raughton Head and Gaitsgill Parish Magazines*, 1932, C.R.O. PR/22/56.
133 *B.N.*, 15.2.1930.
134 Congregational Symposium, *Congregationalist*, Vol. 8, August 1879.
135 St Aidan's Parish Young Men's Mutual Improvement Society, Carlisle, minutes, C.R.O. PR/68/2/44.
136 *P.O.*, 2.11.1875.
137 Penrith Wesleyans Mutual Improvement Society minutes, C.R.O. FCM/3/1/105; *W.N.*, 6.2.1890 (Cleator Moor and Millom Wesleyans).
138 Moore, 1974, p. 105, quoting a paper on mutual improvement classes by John Harrison.
139 Yeo, 1976, p. 176.
140 Yeo, 1976, pp. 171–2.
141 Cecil Street Christian Endeavour, Carlisle, minutes, C.R.O. FCM/1/1/55.
142 Whitehaven Congregational Church Guild, C.R.O. DFC/C1/1/89; *Workington Wesleyan Circuit Magazines*, 1914–15, C.R.O. FCM/7/1/6.
143 Bundle of Circuit Reports, Returns, etc., Carlisle Primitive Methodists, C.R.O. FCM/1/1/28.
144 St Andrew's Penrith, Fellowship, papers, n.d., C.R.O. PR/110/1/22/8.

145 *W.N.*, 8.1.1920.
146 Quoted in Yeo, 1976, p. 172.
147 *Kirkby Stephen, Crosby Garrett, Ormside, Ravenstonedale and Soulby Parish Magazine*, October 1905, C.R.O. WDX/370/Z3.
148 *Kirkby Stephen, etc., Parish Magazine*, 1907.
149 *W.G.*, 19.2.1910.
150 *Parish Gazette*, December 1911, C.R.O. WPR3.
151 *Parish Gazette*, 1909 amd 1910, C.R.O. WPR3.
152 *Parish Gazette*, December 1911, C.R.O. WPR3.
153 Caroline M. Hallett, *How to begin and carry on a Branch of the Mothers' Union*, n.p., 1909, pp. 3–4.
154 *Parish Gazette*, C.R.O. WPR3; respondent 28.
155 *Parish Gazette*, 1909 and 1910, C.R.O. WPR3; *Upperby Parish Magazine*, 1910, C.R.O. PR76/78.
156 *Allhallows, Torpenhow, Parish Magazine*, July 1913, C.R.O. PR 86/36.
157 Respondents 16 and 37.
158 Respondents 9 and 16.
159 *Parish Gazette*, November 1909, C.R.O. WPR3; *St James, Whitehaven, Parish Magazine*, August 1909, C.R.O. PR/82/52.
160 There were associates at Kendal and Upperby in 1910. *Parish Gazette*, January 1910, C.R.O. WPR3; *Upperby Parish Magazine*, January 1910, C.R.O. PR76/78. For presidents, see *Parish Gazette*, September 1909 and September 1911.
161 Respondents 9 and 28.
162 *Allhallows, Torpenhow, Parish Magazine*, July 1913, C.R.O. PR86/36.
163 Respondent 14.
164 Respondents 14 and 28.
165 *Workington Wesleyan Circuit Magazine*, January 1914, C.R.O. FCM/7/1/16.
166 Penrith Wesleyans Ladies' Sewing Meeting minutes, 1896–1927, C.R.O. FCM//3/1/82.
167 Penrith Wesleyans Ladies' Sewing Meeting minutes, 1896–1927, C.R.O. FCM/3/1/82.
168 Workington Wesleyans South William Street Church Ladies' Sewing Association minutes, 1919–26, C.R.O. FCM/7/1/69.
169 Mary Chamberlain, *Fenwomen*, 1975, p. 144.
170 Mrs M1B (born 1898).
171 Respondent 16.
172 Elizabeth Roberts's respondent Mrs M10B.
173 See Arthur Holden Byles, *The P.S.A. What it is and how to start it*, 1891, p. 6.
174 Respondents 13 and 25.
175 Byles, 1891, p. 25; respondent 25.
176 *W.C.T.*, 20.12.1902; respondent 25.
177 Respondents 13 and 25.

CHAPTER VI

The arts: music, dancing, drama and cinema

INTRODUCTION

It will be apparent from the foregoing chapters that music was ubiquitous in Cumbria during our period. There was music and singing in both the middle-and working-class home, and despite magisterial disapproval, it was an established part of public house culture. It was an integral part of many popular festivals, and social occasions such as hunts, and from the late nineteenth century on, it was increasingly fostered by the churches and chapels. David Russell has suggested that 'a 19th century working class communal event without music was inconceivable'[1] and, certain sporting occasions apart, this was very largely true of not only the working class, but the middle class as well in Cumbria throughout the period of this study. Amongst all classes there was also a great deal of public music-making for its own sake, and amateur music of all kinds will be discussed in the first part of this chapter. The music might be informal or formally organised by a club or society, and choral and operatic societies were to be found in the region in significant numbers. There were also orchestral societies, and numerous communities possessed brass or silver bands. Concerts and competitions brought this music to a wide audience, which was also exploited by touring professional musicians.

Music is inevitably linked with dancing, and this was also an essential component of the region's culture which was enjoyed by all classes, despite the, at best, ambivalent attitude of the churches towards it. The style of the dancing changed quite dramatically during the period and this process will be examined below, as will the role of semi-professional, and ultimately commercial, interests in its promotion.

Commercial interests had long been responsible for the promotion of drama in the region. Although permanent theatres were confined to the major towns, touring companies utilised public halls, and they also performed in collapsible booths, taking plays to all parts of Cumbria. Music halls had also appeared in the region's major centres by the 1860s. Beginning in public houses, they evolved, in accordance with the national pattern, into purpose-built Palaces of Variety, in which the region's audiences were occasionally able to see the 'big names' of music hall. Some of the legitimate theatres also went over to varieties. Our period saw both the rise and decline of the music hall, however, and Cumbria was no exception. By the First World War it had been ousted in the popular estimation by the cinema, which had quickly become established in the region, becoming the most popular form of entertainment among all classes by the inter-war years.

AMATEUR MUSIC AND DRAMA

Cumbrians exercised their musical talents at home, at concerts and soirées linked to churches, schools and sports clubs and in the public house. Those who were known to be performers would be called upon to entertain and, where appropriate, to lend their support to the cause. It should not be thought that the songs sung were 'folk-songs', however. A minority of them were. There were old hunting songs (and new ones in the traditional idiom), and a number of the songs which had circulated on broadsides during the early and mid-Victorian years were still being sung. Other songs had probably been in oral circulation for much longer, and competitors in the folk-song competitions which were organised as part of the Westmoreland Musical Festival in the early years of this century offered songs in all these categories, as well as demonstrating that the dialect compositions of Robert Anderson had not completely fallen from favour.[2] Elsewhere, Cumbrian singers and their audiences eschewed the distinction drawn by the Edwardian collectors between 'folk-song' and other, in their view, less worthy forms of popular song, and the competitions which were sometimes held at sports days made no such value judgement. At Egremont Crab Fair in 1920 the competition was divided into the following categories, the prizes awarded perhaps being an indication of the esteem in which a particular type of song was held:

Best sentimental song	5/–
Best comic song	5/– and a box of kippers
Best sung old hunting song	10/–
Best sung scotch song (for lady competitors only)	£1[3]

Most competitions were not subdivided in this way, however. A folklorist who was present at a competition at Winster Sports in 1937 tells us that

the first singer . . . sang a few verses of one of the old hunting songs. He
was followed by . . . singers of Victorian ballads in the old style, a choir
boy who sang 'Cherry Ripe', an Irishman who sang 'The Mountains of
Mourne', and various crooners of modern sentimental ditties. An old
man of seventy sang 'John Peel', (and finally) . . . the carpenter from a
neighbouring parish . . . pulled his cap down over his eyes and sang in
an impersonal voice the 'Ballad of Balaclava', which was recently
republished in a collection of Victorian broadsheets.[4]

By 'Victorian ballads', Wilson probably meant what are usually
referred to as 'parlour ballads', the popular song of polite society in
mid- and late Victorian England, much of which owed its origins to
English opera and musical comedy.[5] Evidently he did not mean
broadsides. He suggested that the adoption of non-traditional forms of
song 'showed how the folk can absorb things that are alien to their
lives'.[6] Culturally alien, in a narrow sense, some of the songs may have
been, but they were evidently not alien to people's lives, or they would
not have been found attractive and learned. The songs sung were
suited to the contexts in which they were generally performed, and
apart from the public house, the most usual platform for singers was the
parish concert.

Apart from the 'crooners', which were an inter-war phen-
omenon, the songs sung at Winster are representative of the vocal
part of the programme at almost any village concert during the period
of this study. To the songs would be added renditions on various
instruments. The music chosen tended to reflect the availability of
cheap sheet music rather than the 'folk' tradition and, if the instrument allowed, it was likely to be of a 'light classical' nature. Dance
music was also played, however, and the influence of nigger minstrels
and ragtime was sometimes apparent, the banjo being occasionally
encountered. Pearsall suggests that this was a middle-class instrument,[7] and there is no reason to suppose that Cumbria was exceptional
in this respect, although no banjo players have been identified. Dialect
or other humorous readings or recitations would usually complete the
evening's entertainment.

The same songs were also typical of the vocal offerings at 'penny
readings' in the region. The penny reading movement was, said a
writer in the 1870s, 'designed to bring about a fusion of classes'.[8] The
intention was to improve working-class musical and literary taste by
offering morally unexceptionable entertainment of a high artistic

standard, and though Thomas Wright, the 'Journeyman Engineer', asserted that no patronage of the working classes was associated with them,[9] C. M. Davis, the writer quoted above, thought that they perhaps involved 'too much of an assumption that the "working man" had to be lectured to, or read to, by his brother in purple and fine linen.'[10] Penny readings were 'everywhere and often' in Cumbria in the mid-Victorian period,[11] and in places they persisted until the 1890s. Here, as elsewhere, they appear to have been middle-class organised, known chairmen being a local vicar, a solicitor and a grammar-school headmaster,[12] though the class of performers is for the most part unknown. Some at least were middle-class.[13] The readings were extremely popular. At Sawrey, in December 1869 upwards of 200 people were said to have been present, while at Troutbeck a new village institute, provided by local gentlemen, was opened in the same month, as no previously existing room had been large enough to contain all who wished to attend the penny readings.[14] Songs far outweighed readings in the programmes, and it may be that the assimilation of parlour ballads, a quintessentially middle-class style of song, into the popular repertoire was facilitated in this way.

By the inter-war period the tradition of amateur concert per-formances had to some extent been formalised by the advent of 'concert parties'. Bands of amateurs would combine to put together and rehearse a concert programme which would usually then be offered to any organisation which wished to raise funds.[15] Alternatively a concert party might be arranged to raise money for a specific purpose. For instance, Dalton Rose Festival owed some of its funds to a concert party of that name.[16] Both the middle and working classes were involved in concert parties. It seems likely that they were a response to the need for higher standards as, with the advent of radio and a wider range of commercial entertainments, audiences became more sophisti-cated. Mackerness has suggested that radio 'unquestionably made listeners more critical', especially where singers were concerned.[17] Perhaps, also, professional concerts, the variety theatre, and above all the cinema, had given rise to audiences whose members expected to be entertained, rather than to make a contribution to the proceedings themselves. Amateur musical life as a whole was becoming more formalised during our period, as choral and operatic societies, brass bands and amateur orchestras came into being. David Russell has suggested that, in the textile district of the West Riding of Yorkshire, such societies were formed because 'existing modes of music making were endangered by processes of industralization and urbanization',[18] and it is probable that in Cumbria these processes also had some impact on the social networks which provided the environment for amateur music.

In the West Riding, musical societies flourished best in small towns where there were few counter-attractions. They were stimulated by 'the intensity of local pride'.[19] In Cumbria, musical societies appear to have flourished in all types and sizes of community, from the region's major centres to small villages. In the case of the former, there were always counter-attractions, though probably not as many as in the Yorkshire towns, and it is clear that there was no simple relationship between commercial entertainments and amateur music. Local pride was probably a more important factor. It was at stake every time a musical society performed in public, and it gained an institutionalised outlet in the competitive festivals which were probably an important factor in the development of the choral movement and, to a lesser extent, the brass band movement in Cumbria.

CHORAL AND AMATEUR OPERATIC SOCIETIES

Cumbria has not generally been considered an important area for choral singing, and it is true that it was surpassed by areas such as Yorkshire and South Wales in this respect. Nevertheless, there were numerous societies in existence in the region during our period. David Russell found that the most important decades for the formation of choral societies in the West Riding were the 1880s and 1890s, although there were societies in existence before 1850, and new societies continued to be formed up until 1914.[20] In Cumbria there was a moderate growth in numbers in the 1870s and 1880s, but no great expansion until the 1890s and early 1900s, particularly in the case of village societies. As in Yorkshire, some societies were formed much earlier. Ulverston was able to boast a Philharmonic Society by 1850, for instance, and a Barrow Choral Society and Keswick Choral Society were in existence by 1859.[21]

In the West Riding, the societies drew their membership largely, but not exclusively, from the lower middle and skilled working classes,[22] and Cumbria's choral societies seem, from the limited number of members whose occupations could be traced, to have been predominantly of the same strata.[23] There may have been variation from this norm in some choirs, however. Barrow Madrigal choir was said by a member to have had 'a good social mix',[24] which could indicate the involvement of a wider range of classes. Unless singers were brought in from elsewhere, this seems likely to have also been the case in choral societies in small villages such as Blennerhasset, Calthwaite and Great Salkeld, all of which had choirs entered in the Carlisle festival in 1912.[25] In West Cumberland and Furness, Welsh and Cornish mineworker immigrants would doubtless have involved themselves in the local choral societies. In addition, there were in the 1930s male voice choirs attached to the unemployed clubs in West Cumberland, for instance at Frizington and Cleator Moor.[26] Conductors of choirs seem, from available information, to have been uniformly middle class. There were no exceptions among those traced. The Triphena Choir from Penrith, for instance, was trained by a 'private resident' who also acted as Girls' Friendly Society associate, and Windermere Choral Society by a JP.[27]

Choral societies were mixed sex bodies, sopranos and contraltos always being women rather than boys. This may have been a musical preference, but it seems more likely that it was so because the societies were formed as leisure organisations for adults. They were an important recreational outlet for lower middle and middle-class women, whose range of socially permissible leisure activities was somewhat limited. There were also male voice and ladies' choirs, but these were never as numerous as those for mixed voices.

The audience at choral concerts can, for the most part, only be assessed from the price of tickets which, throughout the period, usually ranged from 1s up to 3s or more, suggesting a middle-class and possibly skilled working-class audience. Concerts by church and chapel choirs tended to be cheaper, and they may have attracted more working-class enthusiasts. The cheapest price of 1s had been reduced in real terms by the inter-war period, however, and it may have been that, by that time, more working-class people were attending choral concerts. The audience at musical festivals has proved impossible to assess. The press appears to carry no advertisements, and the price of entry to competitions and end of festival concerts is unknown, although a letter to the *Westmorland Gazette* complaining about the hardness of the better, 7s 6d, seats at a concert at the Mary Wakefield festival in 1912 suggests that, although cheaper seats were available, 'popular prices' were not the order of the day.[28] The only oral informants to have attended festivals were members of competing choirs, and a (working-class) man who acted as steward at Workington.[29]

The Mary Wakefield Festival, which was begun in Kendal in 1885, is often claimed to have been the first competitive musical festival in England, although Miss Wakefield herself made no such claim. It was, in fact, pre-empted in Cumbria by the Workington Eisteddfod which was started by the expatriate Welshman William Ivander Griffiths, the manager of Barepot tinplate works at Seaton, in 1872.[30] The Kendal festival was, however, very influential nationally, and gave rise to a number of similar competitions elsewhere in the country. Within Cumbria, a second festival was begun in Carlisle in 1895, and there were, later, others in Keswick and Barrow. Workington, or its counterparts in Wales, also had influence, however, and in 1897 and 1899 Eisteddfodau were begun in Dalton and Ulverston, although these only continued for a few years.[31] The festivals and Eisteddfodau differed in philosophy. At the latter, cash prizes were awarded; for instance, £16 was given at Workington in 1890.[32] At the festivals, on the other hand, honour alone was at issue. The aim of the Kendal festival is said to have been 'musical education through emulation and appreciation of one's rivals'.[33] Miss Wakefield was the musically gifted daughter of a wealthy Quaker family, and a trained singer and composer. She was also a political radical, a friend of Ruskin and a supporter of the Suffragettes. Her objective in starting the festival was to 'create the love and in consequence the demand for the greatest music by the greatest number'.[34] The festival can, says Russell, 'be seen as a compounding of her love of music and her social and political philosophy'.[35]

Both the Kendal and Carlisle competitions were principally directed at the encouragement of singing in their local areas, and both imposed geographical limits on competition. At Carlisle, competitions were open to anyone resident in Cumberland or in adjacent counties within thirty miles of Carlisle. It was, however, complained in 1902 that the festival was not achieving its objective of encouraging the spread of the choral movement, as the 'same handful of choirs' entered the competitions every year.[36] West Cumberland choirs appear not to have travelled to the Carlisle Festival, and it may have been that, given the geographical restrictions, saturation point had been reached in east Cumberland by the early twentieth century. Numbers of choral societies are not capable of infinite expansion. Church choirs excepted, there do not seem to have been a significant number of choirs which did not take part in competitions. Only by competing (and hopefully winning) could a choir acquire status for itself, and only then would its concerts acquire cachet and draw the crowds. Despite the objectives of the Kendal and Carlisle festivals, they functioned like the Eisteddfodau as arenas for competition. At both festivals, concerts of massed competing choirs were organised in an attempt to try and overcome this tendency. These drew large audiences, and oral evidence suggests that performance in them became another source of status for choirs, as they were usually conducted by someone famous. Sir Henry Wood conducted at Kendal in 1912, for instance.[37]

Musical literacy appears to have become more general as the choral movement spread, but whether this resulted from musical education in school or training at choir practices is impossible to assess. In the early part of our period there is some evidence that the Tonic Sol-fa system of notation was in use. In Barrow, a Tonic Sol-fa Choral Society was begun in 1869.[38] A great deal of interest was clearly aroused, as sixty people enrolled at the first meeting, and a further twenty at the second, and this suggests that the level of conventional musical literacy was low. Curwen's system was also in use in Carlisle in 1870,[39] but no further references to it have been discovered. By the early twentieth century, adjudicators were attaching great importance to the ability to read ordinary staff notation, and there were competitions for sight reading at festivals and Eisteddfodau. However, at Workington in 1906, the only entry for the competition was a school choir from Penrith. At Carlisle in 1912, when there were four competitors, all except the winners 'only managed to flounder through the text'. At Kendal that year, all competing choirs were obliged to enter the sight-reading competition, but again the adjudicator complained that 'a large proportion of the work that morning had been guess work – stumbling and mumbling'.[40] It may be that these classes are not a valid indicator of musical literacy. Sight-reading an unpractised piece would not be easy for a large group of singers even when the level of musical literacy was adequate, and the result for any but the highest quality choirs was likely to be ragged. The ever-widening range of music performed, which can only have been acquired from printed sources, does argue for a fairly high level of musical literacy among choirs by the early twentieth century. The fact that sight-singing was a compulsory class at Kendal further underlines this.

The mainstay of the choral repertoire was religious oratorio, but increasingly during our period this was widened to include a great deal of secular oratorio and other non-religious music. Choirs also occasionally performed opera and operetta, which became enormously popular in the region in the twentieth century. Carlisle Choral Society performed *Carmen* in 1930, for instance.[41] For the most part, however, separate operatic societies were formed for this purpose, although they seem often to have shared singers with the choral societies. A Barrow informant was in the town's amateur operatic society and also its choral society between the wars, while in 1912 three soloists in Penrith Musical Society (choral) were also taking leading roles in the operatic society.[42]

Most amateur operatic societies were established in the early years of this century. They appear to have flourished better in the south and east of the region than in West Cumberland, and to have been more middle-class in following than the choral societies, although not exclusively so. Rather more information is available on the membership of operatic societies than of choral societies, as newspapers occasionally name the soloists in a particular production, and this evidence suggests that operatic societies were basically middle-class bodies with a small minority of members from the lower middle class and labour aristocracy. However, I was told by a respondent that Ulverston Amateur Operatic Society, of which he was a member, contained people from 'every walk of life. From bank managers to labourers ... and everything in between. As long as they could sing or act ... .'[43] It is possible that elsewhere there were working-class members among the un-named singers in the choruses. Particular vocal merit would have been required to supplant the local elite as soloists. Possibly also some societies were more socially exclusive than others.

The class of the audiences is more difficult to assess. Ticket prices receive less advertisement than the casts and no pre-1914 prices are known. Admission to a production at Ambleside in 1920 cost 1s 6d, 3s and 5s. Ten years later at Holker, the prices ranged from 1s to 4s.[44] The 1s tickets were, however, only available on the opening night, Thursday. Friday and Saturday were to be more exclusive. It appears, then, that a mixed, but predominantly middle-class audience was expected, as 1s or 1s 6d would have been within working-class means, for an occasional event, between the wars. The limitation of 1s tickets to the opening night at Holker does indicate, however, that a working-class audience was not always actively sought.

Amateur operatic societies doubtless drew inspiration from the professional companies which occasionally brought opera to the region. With the exception of Barrow, the most flourishing societies appear to have been in villages or towns without permanent theatres, and the amateur performances probably filled something of a void. The mainstay of the repertoire was Gilbert and Sullivan, but a great deal of musical comedy was also performed. As in the West Riding;[45] the Gilbert and Sullivan style inspired local composers. The oriental theme of *The Mikado* was particularly influential. In Appleby, a local doctor wrote and produced a musical comedy, *Okiitoko*, in 1906 and in Dalton, *The Rose of the East*, the work of a local journalist and an ex-bank manager, was performed in 1932.[46]

The societies set themselves high standards, and many companies employed, or were fortunate enough to have the services of, professional producers. At both Ambleside and Grange, the company was trained by Madame Forbes-Wilson, a member of the D'Oyly Carte Opera Company who had retired to the latter place.[47] At Penrith, for the society's first production in 1912, Mr W. Simms Bull of The Savoy Theatre, London was employed as coach. The Ulverston society always employed a professional.[48] Costs of performances, which in most cases also required elaborate costumes and scenery, were consequently high. The performance of HMS *Pinafore* at Penrith in 1912 cost £150, but this was more than met by receipts of some £200.[49] At Ulverston, the costs were clearly also met, as in 1929 and 1930 the society had balances of £40 and £42 respectively.[50] It seems that the services of professionals were a good investment. Profits seem always to have been handed over to charity, principally to hospitals and nursing associations.[51] People involved themselves in opera for their own enjoyment and the entertainment of others. It was a socially acceptable pursuit for those of the respectable classes who were not strict Nonconformists, and it marked their community as a respectable and cultured place in which to live. Any sharing-out of the proceeds would have been unthinkable to the classes concerned, and respectable opinion dictated that the money should be given to charity. The charities chosen were, however, invariably those which benefited all classes of the community, including those involved in the amateur operatics.

ORCHESTRAL SOCIETIES AND BRASS BANDS

Operatic societies were, in a number of cases, linked with or instrumental in the formation of local orchestral societies as, if it aspired to professional standards, opera needed orchestral accompaniment. The Ulverston Operatic Society, for instance, called a meeting in 1930 to discuss the formation of an amateur orchestra to save the expense of paying professionals.[52] A number of instrumental ensembles long predated the development of amateur opera, however. Workington's Orchestral Union made its debut in 1889, and Maryport had a well established orchestral society by 1890.[53] Nevertheless, orchestral societies were always few in number in comparison with choral or operatic societies.

Nothing is known of the membership or instrumentation of the early societies. Three lists of performers have come to light from the early twentieth century, two of them because of their association with opera. These are for Ambleside in 1913, Grange in 1912 and Penrith in 1906.[54] The names have proved more than usually difficult to trace, suggesting that members may have been drawn from other towns and villages in the area. Oral evidence confirms that this was the case in an orchestra in Dalton.[55] The minority who have been identified were predominantly middle or lower middle-class. Only among the handful of brass players do we find a bootmaker and a billposter. Working-class people are more difficult to trace from trade directories, however, and their presence in other sections of the orchestra cannot be discounted. David Russell found that, in the West Riding, there was a minority of working-class players in all sections,[56] and the only amateur orchestra on which I have oral evidence, that at Dalton, was apparently socially quite diverse.[57]

At Grange there were only three female musicians out of a total of fourteen. At Penrith there were thirteen out of thirty, and at Ambleside, six out of twenty-one. All of them played strings or piano. Only three of them have been identified, two the wives of 'private residents' and the other the wife of the music teacher who was conductor at Penrith. Like choral and operatic societies, the orchestras would have been suitable recreational outlets for middle-class women, many of whom were made to learn the violin or, more particularly, the piano, but the presence of working-class women must not be totally discounted.

Amateur orchestral concerts were not frequent occurrences and, although they were occasionally reported in the press, I have no information on prices or audiences. At Penrith in 1906, the orchestral society gave a 'popular concert', which included a local choir, solo singers and a 'humorist from Manchester', as well as orchestral selections.[58] This was doubtless an attempt to attract larger numbers and create interest in their activities, and it seems to have been successful, as the hall was reported to have been well filled. There was, of course, little point in an orchestra existing if the public did not wish to hear it play, but widespread public support was probably not the financial necessity it was for brass bands. A predominantly middle-class orchestra, whose members owned their own instruments and could afford to buy music, would not have needed to rely for its continuance on public support.

It has been suggested that brass bands had their origins in town waits and church bands, and that their development was influenced by military bands.[59] The early nineteenth century bands were 'wind bands', using mostly reed instruments, but by mid-century, when the introduction of valves and other technical advances had widened the range of brass instruments and made them quicker and easier to master, the use of brass instruments was becoming the norm.[60] Thereafter, brass bands proliferated. By 1860, unspecified brass bands are occasionally reported as leading friendly society processions in Cumbria although on one occasion at least, a military band, 'the cavalry band', was doing the honours, and it seems likely that there were comparatively few bands in the region at that date.[61] As in the West Riding,[62] there was phenomenal growth in numbers between the 1880s and 1910. Bands were attached to communities of every description. Towns, villages, workplaces and temperance societies all had bands. As David Russell has stressed for the West Riding, workplace bands were not the most numerous type, though there were, for instance, bands attached to both the iron and steelworks, and the shipyard in Barrow, and Tebay had a Railwaymen's Brass Band.[63] Many bands, again as in the West Riding, were in small towns and large villages, but there were also bands in the larger industrial centres, and even occasionally in rural areas such as Patterdale and the Leven Valley.

Bands occasionally had middle-class sponsorship, from an employer, a temperance organisation or, as at Appleby, from the Town Council.[64] In the earlier part of our period there seems also to have been more general middle-class and gentry support for brass bands. At a concert given at Dalton in 1860 by 'a brass band from Keighley', the hall was 'crammed with a highly respectable company' including all the clergy and gentry in the neighbourhood.[65] Perhaps at that date brass bands were still associated in the minds of the gentry with the military. Later, when brass bands had acquired a solidly working-class image, the gentry appear to have deserted their concerts. When the famous Besses o' th' Barn gave a concert in Penrith in 1912, 'there were many vacant places in the front', in the 3s seats, although 'the hinder parts', at 6d and 1s, were extremely well filled'.[66]

As far as can be ascertained, brass band players were, in Cumbria as elsewhere, mainly working-class men. No women are known to have played in bands in the region during our period. Brass instruments would doubtless have been considered unfeminine, and the bands had a reputation for, in Mackerness's words, 'masculine gaiety' and (most temperance bands excepted) for an excessive consumption of alcohol.[67] Because of the working-class playing membership, the financing of brass bands was always a headache. Brass instruments, and the *de rigueur* uniforms, were expensive, and a great deal of money had to be raised before a band could be started. When a group of men in Seascale wished to form a band in 1885, they began by holding a public meeting to discuss how the money might be raised. The meeting resolved that 'an appeal should be made to the public', and in particular that the gentry should be canvassed for support.[68] Although brass bands were considered to be rational recreation, and deserving of encouragement, one doubts whether gentry support would in itself be adequate. Rising real wages for many workers, allowing contributions to be made, were undoubtedly an important factor in the development of the brass band movement. At Penrith, the band's financial basis is indicated by the word 'subscription' in its title, but that band and others also held prize draws to raise funds. Numerous prizes were donated for the purpose by members of the community.[69] Once established, bands added to members' subscriptions (3d a week at Ambleside) by playing in the park or street and making a collection.[70]

Bands were also paid for engagements such as playing at sports days, although in Ambleside it was the rule that this money was shared out among the band,[71] and there may have been similar customs elsewhere. As Russell has pointed out, the opportunity for earning a little money was one of the attractions of band membership.[72] There were others. The camaraderie and drinking have already been referred to, and members also acquired status in the community due to their central role in sports, processions, rushbearings or other events which required their services. Even those bands which did not take part in competitions represented their town or village to hearers from elsewhere, and there was friendly rivalry between bands in an area.[73]

In contrast with choirs, there seem to have been a large number of brass bands which did not take part in formal competitions, although these were held in the region.[74] They were already taking place at Workington and Whitehaven in the 1870s although, in the former place at least, they did not last the decade.[75] In the 1880s, Barrow became the major competition centre, and the August Bank Holiday Monday contests drew enormous crowds,[76] although they too were apparently discontinued by the turn of the century. By then, a contest was being held at Carlisle,[77] and by the 1930s, brass band competitions had been added to the programme of the Workington Eisteddfod.[78] All of these contests drew in bands from outside the region, and the competition was probably sufficiently fierce to deter smaller village bands from competing.[79] Only four Cumbrian brass bands are known to have taken part in first-class competition, all of them between the wars. They were Dalton, Workington Town, Barrow Shipyard, who took second at Belle Vue in 1921 and, most noted of all, Carlisle St Stephen's, who won the London national championships in 1927 and 1929.[80] It is not known whether Cumbrian bands were already unsuccessfully involved in major competitions before the First World War, as the names of those who fall by the wayside in preliminary rounds are not recorded. Similarly, the bands mentioned above may be just the tip of the iceberg as far as inter-war competition is concerned. If competition was not new, the achievement of championship quality was, and while this could be fortuitous, it might indicate a change of emphasis in response to industrial depression. The towns involved would have badly needed a focus for working-class pride at the time. All Cumbrian bands faded from first-class competition during the 1930s, however. Workington, who came sixth at London in 1934, were the last band from the region to achieve national success. By that time the brass band movement, both in Cumbria and in the country as a whole, was declining perceptibly and Cumbrian bands were not the only ones to disappear from the competition dircuit.

Although many of the region's brass bands ceased to exist during the First World War, some struggled on with greatly reduced numbers, or brought old members out of retirement.[81] Their continuance was clearly of importance in their communities. After the war, most bands were re-formed, and despite the changed recreational environment with increased numbers of counter-attractions, brass banding was still in an apparently healthy state during the 1920s when, as we have seen, some competition bands came to prominence. The bands' ceremonial functions were steadily being eroded, however, with the demise of friendly societies, and the decline of the Band of Hope and village sports. In addition, as we shall see below, dance bands were becoming an alternative and more lucrative outlet for working-class musicians. Counter-attractions became ever more enticing, and by the 1930s it was no longer easy to recruit members to brass bands. An Ambleside bandsman explained that it was difficult 'to get people to take the time to learn instruments'.[82] Unemployment may have further weakened bands as members left the area to find work elsewhere. Some brass bands collapsed entirely. St Bees Village Band, which was formed in 1912 in a blaze of enthusiasm, was disbanded at the end of 1929, for instance, due to 'a lack of playing members'.[83] Many others continued, and it should not be thought that brass bands became a thing of the past in the region. By the 1930s, however, their heyday was over.

AMATEUR DRAMATICS

Music in its various forms dominated participation in the performing arts in Cumbria during our period. Nevertheless, there are known to have been amateur dramatic societies in existence by the 1880s in West Cumberland and in Penrith.[84] Between then and the First World War, performances by a growing number of societies are reported, but it was not until the inter-war period that amateur drama groups really proliferated. Before 1914, amateur dramatic societies appear to have been middle-class bodies, though few participants have been positively identified. The word 'fashionable' was commonly used to describe audiences,[85] and the proceeds of the performances were given to charity. At Whitehaven in 1885 the 'distressed poor' were the beneficiaries, but in the early twentieth century, as in the case of operatic societies, charities which benefited the whole community, such as nursing associations, were generally chosen.[86]

Many people must have been deterred from involvement in amateur dramatics by their religious affiliations. As mentioned in the previous chapter, Methodists in particular frowned on acting, and although the denomination were a minority in the region as a whole, this may go some way towards explaining the apparent lack of working-class involvement. There was, for instance, a conspicuous lack of amateur drama groups in the Methodist strongholds of east Westmorland.

By the 1930s there were numerous drama groups existing in their own right, and attached to a multifarious array of organisations. They drew in performers of all classes, from the professional middle classes to the unemployed, although individual clubs seem still to have been class specific. Oral evidence suggests, for instance, that Penrith Players were still basically a middle-class group at this period, although they were beginning to become less so. A lower middle-class informant who joined in the 1930s said that 'the doctors in Penrith were in it, you know, and we thought they were so classy! Oh all the posh folks were in it in those days.'[87] In Carlisle, around the same time, there was a Theatre Club, which likewise appears to have had a middle-class ethos. It functioned as 'a social rendezvous' as well as 'encouraging drama study and acting'.[88] By then Carlisle offered drama to all classes, however. Those who would not have felt at home at the Theatre Club could have joined drama groups at Charlotte Street Centre for the Wives of the Unemployed, the WEA or the Currock Community Centre.[89] By 1936 there was even a Methodist Guild of Players, attached to Cecil Street Church.[90] A Cumberland Drama League was established in 1934, and this body successfully ran drama festivals from then until the end of the 1930s. In 1937 and 1938, unemployed clubs from places such as Distington, Frizington and Cleator Moor competed against drama groups from schools, the Women's Institute and the YMCA and YWCA, as well as bodies such as Penrith and Brampton Players, which existed purely as dramatic societies.[91]

The plays performed by the amateur groups seem predominantly to have been modern, and in particular comedies, although Shakespeare was being performed at Penrith by the end of the 1930s.[92] The standard of performance seems from press reports to have been generally high, and an oral informant asserted that 'Penrith Players were absolutely marvellous.'[93] Professional theatres were often used for performances, suggesting that large audiences were drawn by the better amateur companies.[94] Venues had to be licensed for stage plays, of course, and this may have been another reason for using professional theatres, although the region's magistrates do not seem to have been loath to grant theatrical licences. The 'New Rooms' in Milnthorpe were licensed without demur in 1890 for use by an amateur company,[95] and there does not appear to have been a general shortage of performance space, parish rooms and institutes being generally utilised.

The influence of professional theatre on amateur dramatics is difficult to assess. Two of the earliest drama groups were in Whitehaven and Workington, both of which had theatres in the nineteenth and early twentieth centuries. Penrith, however, never had a permanent professional theatre at all, although touring companies occasionally visited. Nevertheless, there was an amateur dramatic society there by 1880, and activities continued until the Second World War. Where amateurs and professionals existed side by side, the two probably reinforced one another, both fostering a public interest in playgoing, although amateur performances for charity, often involving members of the local elite, perhaps attracted a slightly more respectable audience than the professional companies, which in some minds were still tainted with impropriety. In towns without theatres, or in villages at a distance from the major centres, the amateurs, like the operatic societies, perhaps compensated for the general lack of professional entertainment. After the First World War, when the cinema had forced the professional stage into retreat, the focus of popular interest in drama probably shifted to the amateur companies which were then proliferating. By the thirties, Methodism was losing the power to censure and proscribe such activities, and many schools and voluntary bodies were actively promoting drama. What had been mainly an interesting pastime for the middle classes was apparently becoming evidence of culture and an appreciation of the arts among all classes.

Amateur music and drama undoubtedly flourished in Cumbria during our period. In the 1870s brass bands and choral societies were the most widespread assocations, although they had not yet reached their peak of popularity, which came between the 1880s and 1914. These bodies were truly popular and central to their communities. By the inter-war decades the period of expansion was over, however, and brass bands in particular were being adversely affected by new recreational patterns. Public taste in vocal music had by then shifted somewhat from religious oratorio, and amateur operatic societies, which first appeared in the Edwardian period, became enormously popular. Opera and operetta were more spectacular than choral singing, and better equipped to compete with the cinema and other inter-war attractions. It was not however as 'popular' in a class sense, and the bulk of the participants, if not their audiences, were apparently middle class. The closely related field of amateur dramatics was also a largely middle-class preserve until the inter-war years,[96] when acting became for the first time a truly popular pastime. Amateur orchestras could probably never have been so described. There do appear to have been a minority of working-class players, especially when a 'full' orchestra with a brass section was aspired to, but amateur orchestras were themselves a minority interest, fostered by the operatic societies, but as far as can be ascertained, existing only intermittently.

DANCING

Frances Rust's assertion that, during the nineteenth century, 'dancing was unlikely to have played much part in the lives of the under-privileged',[97] is clearly erroneous as far as Cumbria is concerned. There is ample evidence that in this region, people of all classes danced at every available opportunity. Speaking of the early nineteenth century, T. Sanderson said that 'Dancing has so many advocates among the lower, as well as among the higher classes of the community, that to censure it would probably be to incur the charge of puritanical austerity.'[98] Later in the century, a witness giving evidence before a Royal Commission on the conduct of hiring fairs in the region claimed that 'the "acomplishment" of dancing is universal. A day labourer with a large family may declare that he is too poor to pay the weekly pence for his children's schooling, but he seldom fails to find money enough to pay for the lessons of the itinerant dancing master.'[99] Methodists, of course, frowned on dancing, and the growth in the denomination's following in the region in the second half of the nineteenth century must have been a negative influence, particularly in Methodist strongholds such as the Eden Valley, though its precise impact is impossible to measure. Certainly it was not sufficient, even in strongly Methodist areas, to prevent the continuance of dancing. Throughout our period it remained an important aspect of social life in both the towns and the rural areas. The Fletts tell us that 'It was the accepted thing that most young people were taught to dance.' The dancing masters were, they assert, 'part of the traditional life of Lakeland'[100] from the beginning of the nineteenth century, if not earlier, and as their book goes on to show, their importance was not diminished until the First World War.

A great deal of information on the dancing masters active in the region during the late nineteenth and early twentieth centuries was gathered by the Fletts, in part from oral evidence, during the 1960s.[101] The masters came from a wide range of social backgrounds and might teach either full- or part-time. 'Old Jos' Robinson (1838–1908), whose family taught dancing in the region for three generations, was the son of a shoemaker, who became a bobbin turner and later rose to be manager of a bobbin mill.[102] One of his sons was licensee of the Lakeside Hotel, and his grandson was a taxi-driver. All taught dancing 'part-time', which seems to have meant part of the year rather than part of the week. Other dancing masters known to the Fletts include the son of a surveyor of highways, who became a full-time 'professor' of dancing; the licensee of the Punch Bowl at Crosthwaite, who also later taught full-time; the son of a sweet manufacturer in York, who became manager of a drapery store in Workington, and then first violin at the town's Opera House before becoming a full-time dancing master; a music hall singer and dancer; a railway worker; and a mason. The last two taught dancing part-time in addition to their normal work. The Fletts totally ignore the numbers of female teachers of dancing who regularly advertised their services in the press throughout our period. These women do not usually seem to have taught step-dancing, in which the Fletts were particularly interested, but nor did all dancing masters, and there seems overall to have been litle difference in the range of dancing taught by men and women. All taught the popular ballroom dances of the day, and some also taught fancy exhibition dances. Nothing is known about the class background of any of the women teachers.

Most dancing teachers, male and female, had one or more permanent bases where they held classes and public dances. None of the women appears to have operated on the itinerant basis, which had been usual in the early nineteenth century, but some of the dancing masters still did. The Robinson family did most of their teaching in this way. Operating mainly between September and Easter (when the hotel and taxi business would have been slack), they would stay in an area for a period of about ten weeks, teaching in a different village each evening. Oliver Cowper (1854–1922), who taught in Workington, was itinerant during the summer months. It was said of him that 'They knew him so well round Cumberland, they used to write to him to ask him to come, and he had a job to decide which village was the best to go to.'[103] At the end of the course there would be a 'finishing ball' to show the parents how much their children had learned. Many non-itinerant teachers held similar balls periodically. They consisted of a performance by the pupils lasting some two or three hours, followed by a general ball until the early hours of the morning. Traditionally the performance was stylised and almost ritualistic in form. The youngest pupil of each sex (commonly aged about four) were made 'king and queen' of the proceedings. If there were a number of very young children there might be two 'kings' and two 'queens', or they might be titled princes and princesses. These children, dressed in appropriate costume, led the procession of dancers on to the floor and took part in the first dance. They then sat on thrones for the remainder of the performance, until the last dance, which they again took part in, before leading the dancers off.[104] By the late nineteenth century not all teachers seem to have adhered to this ritual, but the Robinsons, and one or two others at least, still did. The Fletts suggest that it was simply a way of keeping small children 'happy and still',[105] and it is true that such young children would not be able to take part fully in the display, but this nevertheless seems to me to be an inadequate explanation. It was the usual practice to send children to the classes at a very early age, when their ability to participate would have been limited, and the proceedings should perhaps be seen as a 'rite of passage' to mark a child's introduction into the social life of the community.

Some teachers were clearly more exclusive than others. The Robinsons, for instance, seem not to have catered for the poorest classes. The son and grandson of 'Old Jos' Robinson charged 10s 6d per family, irrespective of the number of children, for the course of lessons, and 1s or 1s 6d for parents and others at the 'finishing ball'. They insisted that, at the latter, the pupils should all wear black patent shoes of a specified style, and that the boys should wear white gloves. Costumes for speciality dances were also usually provided by the parents, although the Robinsons did supply some 'for those pupils who could not provide their own'.[106] The Robinsons themselves wore full evening dress for the balls. The only informant who was taught by the Robinsons was the daughter of a farmer, and this would seem to have been the class aimed at.[107] Oliver Cowper charged 6d per lesson for children and 1s for adults. He insisted that white gloves were worn at his town classes, but not in the villages. Miss Ellie Anderson, who taught in Barrow, Dalton, Ulverston and Grange before the First World War, also insisted on white gloves at her balls. Her Dalton class was described by an informant who attended it as 'rather a select dancing class'.[108] Other classes were probably less select. Richard Allen, a railway worker, who held regular Saturday classes in the Assembly Rooms at Langwathby between 1910 and 1915, charged 3d for children at the class, and 6d for adults at the dance which followed it.[109] Similarly, a Mr Bryden, who taught in a room over his wife's dressmaking shop in Workington in the early 1900s, charged 6d for dances. The cost of lessons is unknown, but they were attended by an informant from a poor family.[110] As far as is known, no stipulations were made about shoes or gloves at either of these classes.

Tremenheere may not have been right, however, to suggest that universal expertise in dancing necessarily reflected the diversion of money from more important objects to the dancing masters' pockets. Their skills spread to a greater number of people than those who actually paid for lessons. An informant who went to school in Kendal remembered that a girl who attended a 'rather posh' dancing class taught the steps she learned there to the other girls during the dinner hour.[111] Dancing expertise was also passed on informally without the recent involvement of a teacher. Parents taught their children, and farm servants learned steps from one another to while away the time after supper. The respondent cited above, for instance, remembered that on her parents' farm 'the maidservant and lads' would do step dancing in the evening in an outside wash-house with a flagged floor. The acquisition of dancing skill was considered important, and the teachers were highly regarded, but dancing was such an essential part of the popular culture of the region that learning it did not depend on access to a dancing master.

The Fletts have shown that the repertoire of dances taught did not change greatly between the early nineteenth and early twentieth centuries.[112] All teachers seem to have taught country dances such as the Cumberland Square Eight, Long Eight and Circassian Circle. They also taught the (old style) waltz with all its variants, and other fashionable ballroom dances within a year or two of their introduction. Quadrilles, including the Lancers, were as popular in Cumbria as they were elsewhere,[113] and some teachers specialised in these – numerous 'quadrille classes' are mentioned in the local press before the First World War[114] – but they formed part of the repertoire of all teachers. Some of them, as already mentioned, also taught traditional Lakeland step-dancing, for which there was still a great demand in the latter part of the nineteenth century. Oliver Cowper, an incomer to the region, who did not himself know or teach step-dancing, sent his teenage son to learn from a noted local dancer so that he could meet demands for tuition.[115] The step-dancing was often incorporated into a number of 'fancy' dances which seem to have been derived from stage dances, such as 'Horse to Newmarket', done in jockey costume, a skipping rope dance, a hoop dance and Irish, Welsh and 'nigger' dances. 'Horse to Newmarket' was performed in the theatre in the eighteenth century, while the skipping rope dance was twice featured at the Star Music Hall in Carlisle in 1880.[116] In the latter case, of course, the dance could have been performed by pupils of the dancing masters. The 'nigger' dances undoubtedly owed their origin to the troupes of nigger minstrels which were popular in the region, as elsewhere, during the mid- and late nineteenth century. These dances, together with straightforward step-dancing, formed the greater part of the display at the finishing balls. The cheaper teachers seem not to have taught these 'fancy' dances, perhaps because costumes would have been out of reach of their pupils, although some of them did teach step-dancing.

As new dances became fashionable, the teachers included them in their programmes, and between the 1890s and the First World War the Tango, American Two-Step and One-Step were to be found as items on programmes which might otherwise have dated from the 1850s. The One-Step required very little expertise, as dancers merely 'walked' in time to the music, and it could quickly be learnt by anyone.[117] It also required syncopated music, very different from anything which had been played for dancing before, and it must have fitted very uneasily into the established format of a 'finishing ball'. In 1914 the Foxtrot, another ragtime dance, arrived in Britain, and then, towards the end of the First World War, came jazz.[118] These made an appearance in Cumbria after the war, and later, in the 1920s, the Charleston arrived.[119] These developments marked a revolution in social dance. The gulf between jazz dancing and the dancing of the previous century was enormous.[120] The dances of the 1920s were essentially for young adults, displaying freedom from inhibition rather than practised skill, and dancing masters of the old school found themselves becoming redundant. 'Young Jos' Robinson gave up teaching just after the First World War, for instance, because there was no longer sufficient demand.[121] Tommy Cannon, who was based in Underbarrow, left to teach ballroom dancing in Carlisle in 1925 because the number of his pupils had so diminished. Declining numbers there shortly forced him to give up teaching altogether.[122] By the 1920s the practice of making children 'kings and queens' of the ball had also fallen into abeyance. Children now seem only to have been present at dances which were specifically for them,[123] which was probably another facet of the growing tendency to treat them as a separate category of human beings which has been identified elsewhere. Dancing teachers still existed, but they were now almost all women. It is difficult to suggest why this should have been so, but there does appear to have been a growing tendency to regard dancing as a feminine accomplishment in the inter-war years.

The old time social dances did not completely disappear from programmes. The Lancers and other quadrilles continued to be danced, as did the Barn Dance, Veleta and so on,[124] although by 1930, in the towns at least, their inclusion in a programme in any numbers was becoming sufficiently unusual to provoke comment.[125] The waltz, which by the end of the First World War had acquired its modern, slow form remained very popular. The occasional folk-dance was also still featured, and interest in them was fostered by the mainly middle-class folk-dance revival. A number of folk-dance evening classes were organised by local authorities, and two informants attended these,[126] although this was, as now, a minority interest. By the 1930s, when the Charleston and the like had faded, a typical dance programme consisted of waltzes, quicksteps and foxtrots, with the occasional 'old time' or folk-dance for variety.

The range of social dances in Cumbria, as elsewhere, differed little between the middle and working classes. All classes waltzed and took part in the Lancers and quadrilles, and all danced Two-Steps and sequence dances such as the Veleta. Similarly, this century, the ragtime and jazz dances were enthusiastically taken up by people of all classes. There was, however, very little class mixing at dances.

Ticket price was the most usual means of controlling entry, though between the wars this might not have been as effective as it had previously been. An Ambleside respondent said that the Fire Bridade, Conservative, Liberal and other balls held in the Assembly Rooms there in the 1920s drew a mixture of classes, although these still managed to keep aloof from one another.

> It was very funny there was three classes of people at these dances. There was probably [the local elite] all at the very top against the orchestra. Then there was . . . farmers and such like, and then down at the very bottom . . . was what they called 'the laundry clique', a lot of girls [laundry workers] . . . and they always had the bottom of the floor . . . they always stuck together down there.[127]

Perhaps in a small place like Ambleside, the participation of all classes was encouraged at fund-raising events such as those mentioned. Evidently the local social hierarchy was not disturbed.

No town seems to have been without one or more halls which could be utilised for dancing. Some of them were apparently more used for middle-class balls, perhaps reflecting hiring costs. The large hotels also catered for and promoted dances for the middle classes and gentry.[128] There was no shortage of venues for lower middle or working-class dancing, however, and these increased in numbers and probably in quality during our period. As we have seen, rooms attached to public houses were sometimes used for dancing, and by the inter-war period scarcely a village was without a hall or institute where dances could be held. In many places they were a weekly occurrence.[129] Some of the halls owed their origins at least in part to middle- and upper-class paternalism, but many were paid for wholly or in part by the sustained fund-raising activities of the local inhabitants.[130] The acquisition of a hall was clearly seen as important by communities, and this may have been linked with public house closures which reduced the number of rooms available for recreational activities. The halls were normally run by committees, who booked bands, arranged for late buses home, and so on.[131] Although they were also used for other activities, dances were the most common use to which the halls were put, and an important source of funds for their upkeep.

In one or two towns there were Co-op dance halls. That in Dalton early this century was described by an informant as 'a lovely ballroom'.[132] Elsewhere, commercial interests also offered dancing facilities, although these were sometimes rather makeshift. Before the First World War in Maryport, the dance hall was just 'a hall that was let out', which an entrepreneur had hired, arranging for music and charging for admission on the door in much the same way as the village hall committees.[133] By the 1930s, however, the *palais de danse* had arrived in West Cumberland. It is not clear whether they were all purpose built, but by 1934 Whitehaven had its Empress Ballroom, and Workington its Albert and Hippodrome Dance Halls, the latter being a sideline of Williams' Cinemas Ltd. By 1937, the Palace Ballroom in Maryport was open.[134] Other places still apparently used their existing public halls for dancing, however, and the region's entertainments industry probably paid less attention to the provision of dancing facilities than was the case elsewhere. It is probable that as dancing was already such a highly organised activity, there were few gaps in the market to be exploited.

In the 1870s few dance bands existed in Cumbria. Music for dancing seems to have been supplied mostly on an *ad hoc* basis by local individuals. There were, however, a small number of 'quadrille bands', based in towns such as Kendal, Maryport and Carlisle.[135] Nothing is known of the social composition of these bands, or of the instruments in use, nor do we know whether the musicians were full-time professionals, although this would seem to be unlikely. By 1890 a number of 'string bands' had appeared alongside the 'quadrille bands', but again, nothing more is known about them than their names and some of the places they played at. There is no apparent difference in the kind of events the two types of band played for, and they may have differed only in instrumentation, or merely in title. Neither type seems to have been able to satisfy the requirements of the fashionable classes in the late nineteenth century, and bands for high-class events were often brought from a distance. In January 1890, a band was brought from Manchester for a subscription ball at the Hydropathic Establishment in Bowness and for a Primrose League ball the following evening.[136] By the end of the century, however, there was a very fashionable and high-quality band in Carlisle, Felix Burns's Band. Felix Burns was organist and choirmaster at St Mary and St Joseph's Roman Catholic Church, bandmaster to the First Battalion, the Border Regiment, a teacher of instruments of all types, and a noted composer of dance music.[137] His band was playing at events in Carlisle by 1900, and by 1910 it was travelling as far afield as Ulverston, where it supplied the music for a charity ball attended by 'a fair representation of local gentry'.[138] Nothing is known of Mr Burns after 1914, and it may have been that he left the district. He is of particular interest as an embodiment of the interrelatedness of music of all kinds in the period before the First World War.

By the early years of this century the number of dance bands in the region had increased phenomenally. This may have been a response to increased demand as village halls proliferated, and associations of all kinds took to holding dances as a means of raising funds. The gramophone and the ubiquity of brass bands may also have raised expectations of quality in dance music, so that something more than a local fiddler was required. 'Quadrille bands' were still numerous, but 'string bands' had given way to 'orchestras'. There is no evidence to suggest that these were anything other than ordinary dance bands, and the title may at the time have implied strings, whereas the word 'band' implied brass. None of the dance bands appears to have travelled far from its home base, which suggests that most performers were part-time semi-professionals. Holiday seasons apart, most dances were held on a Friday or Saturday, and it would probably not, in any case, be possible for a dance band to operate on a professional basis on one or two engagements a week. Transport difficulties would have been a further limiting factor.

Between the wars bands were even more numerous, and thanks to oral evidence rather more is known about them. The instruments in use varied. 'They could have a string orchestra. Or they could have brass as well,' said a lady speaking of dances at Penrith Drill Hall in the late 1920s and 1930s. 'There was pianists, and trombones . . . . Fiddles, and drummers. There was always drummers.'[139] 'Accordions, violin and saxophone as a rule,' said another informant, 'and a drummer. Always a drummer.'[140] Other informants broadly agreed. Piano or accordion, drums, violin and a brass instrument was a typical line-up, but there were variations from this. A band at Kirkby in Furness in the late 1930s consisted of piano, two accordions and drums.[141] and there were, as the first informant said, still string bands in existence. The drums were a response to the rhythmic needs of inter-war dance styles, and were almost certainly absent in earlier bands. Before 1920 the modern 'drum kit' did not exist, although drums had earlier been in use in, for example, music hall bands.[142] Coniston Quadrille Band in 1920, which may perhaps be taken as an example of an earlier type, consisted of piano, violin, cornet and piccolo.[143]

Only a small number of dance band musicians are known, and these were working- and lower middle class. Three such among oral informants were an (at the time) unemployed miner, a motor engineer and an office worker at Barrow Shipyard.[144] The latter was a member of the Kirkby Band already referred to, the other members of which were a butcher, a farmer's son and a dental mechanic.[145] The three informants were all in run-of-the-mill village bands, however, playing in village halls and public houses, and higher-class bands could have had middle-class members. The question of the class background of bands must therefore remain an open one.

All three of my informants, coincidentally, played the accordion. These were expensive and had to be saved up for. One respondent paid £14 for his first in the 1930s, and then acquired a larger one for £25.[146] The cost of other instruments of course varied, but in no case would it have been an insignificant amount of money. Another informant said that 10s per person was the usual fee paid for playing for a dance in the thirties, but a band engaged for a season at Urswick village hall was paid £1 a night in total, which would presumably have been rather less per person.[147] Five or ten shillings a night would have been a useful supplementary income, but the cost of instruments and music needs to be set against it, and it seems likely that most band members played as much for pleasure as for the money they earned. Playing for dancing may have allowed people to own instruments they could not otherwise have afforded. The money was however important to the informant who was unemployed.

Motor transport was allowing bands to work over a rather wider area by the 1930s, but many of them, including those that informants were involved in, still mainly confined themselves to their own locality. No area seems to have been short of bands, the majority apparently being general dance bands playing for all the modern and old-time dances which were than in vogue. There were also jazz bands in the region, however. Mr L. Twists's Jazz Band was already playing in Barrow in 1920, and in the same year there was a Parton Jazz Orchestra in existence.[148] Ten years later, Lupton's Orphean Syncopators from Kendal were apparently on a wave of popularity.[149] Many bands by this time had fanciful names, rather than just being named after their leader.[150] This was probably intended to give them a more glamorous and, sometimes, exotic image, and underlines the great change that had taken place in dancing in the region during the twentieth century.

Throughout the nineteenth century, Cumbria was influenced in its dancing by developments in London. New dances were generally taken up only a year or two after becoming popular in fashionable circles, and the programme at a dance in Cumbria would have differed little from that at a similar occasion elsewhere in the country. This was probably due to the activities of the dancing masters and mistresses, though public demand may have compelled them to keep abreast of the latest, terpsichorean fashions. The new dances were integrated into the established framework of dancing in the region which, so far as I am aware, did not, in its more formal aspects, have parallels elsewhere in the country.[151] The practice of making children 'king and queen' of the ball was apparently confined to the region. It was probably undermined in the end by widespread changes in attitudes towards children which affected Cumbria in common with the rest of the country. In the twentieth century, and particularly after the First World War, the prevailing influence on dancing was American. Ragtime and jazz arrived via the gramophone and wireless, which brough the outside world to Cumbria at first hand. The new dances were seen at the cinemas, bypassing the mediation of the dancing masters. Local bands quickly absorbed the new rhythms, and with them the aura of cosmopolitan glamour. Instead of being integrated into the pre-existing pattern of dancing, the American influences dominated, and older styles of dancing, although not entirely abandoned and forgotten, had to find a less central place in a changed milieu.

THE THEATRE, MUSIC HALL AND CINEMA

In late nineteenth and early twentieth-century Cumbria, permanent theatres offering either 'legitimate' drama or varieties existed only in Carlisle, Workington, Whitehaven and Barrow. Even in these towns the theatrical business was always insecure. Closures were common, and there was a rapid turnover in owners and lessees. Whitehaven's Theatre Royal, built in 1760, was the oldest still in operation in the late nineteenth century. It survived until 1932 or 1933, although it was closed for two periods at least before then, in 1891 and 1892 and 1908–09, when first the lease and then the freehold were for sale.[152] Apart from a period around 1890 and another between 1909 and the First World War when varieties were on offer, the theatre confined itself for the most part to plays and opera.[153] The town is also known to have had two music halls, although very litle can be discovered about them. One was attached to the Shakespeare Hotel in the 1860s, and the other was operating at the Royal Standard Hotel by 1885, when the music hall trade's journal *Era* reported that it had been seriously damaged by a fire.[154] It was still in business in 1891 when a firm of billposters and advertising contractors listed it among their clients,[155] and in 1910 and 1914 it was still listed in local directories as a going concern.[156] Thereafter no more is heard of it. At no time does the Royal Standard music hall appear to have advertised in the local press, which totally ignored the hall's existence. No reviews of the entertainment on offer ever appeared. This raises the possibility that there may have been music halls attached to public houses elsewhere in the region which have left no trace for the historian.

In Carlisle, theatres existed only intermittently before 1879, when Her Majesty's was opened. This became the city's main venue for stage plays until after the Second World War, although between 1895 and 1904 it operated mainly as a variety theatre, there being very little 'legitimate' drama presented during that period.[157] The Oxford, probably the city's first music hall, opened in 1866, but it appears to have been short-lived, there being no evidence of its existence in subsequent years. By 1880 the building was in use as a Salvation Army Citadel.[158] Meanwhile, the Star Music Hall was opened in a converted bacon warehouse in Peter Street in 1877. It continued for five years before changing over to plays, in competition with Her Majesty's. The date of its final demise is not known, but by 1893 it, too, had become a Salvation Army Citadel.[159] There was further competition for Her Majesty's between 1900 and 1903 when Algie's Circus was permanently in Carlisle offering a programme which, at most times, differed little from that of a music hall.[160] In 1906, when Her Majesty's had ceased to offer varieties, the Palace Music Hall opened in a purpose-built theatre. Originally run by Signor Pepi in conjunction with the Tivoli at Barrow, and other halls, it lost money and the lease was sold in 1909 to the Frank McNaughton chain of halls. It continued in existence until 1933, when in common with a number of other McNaughton Halls, it became a cinema.[161]

The history of the theatre in Workington is rather less clear. In 1869, a Lyceum Theatre was in existence in Washington Street and this was still open the following year. By 1885 it had been renamed the Theatre Royal and was being used by the town's amateur players.[162] In 1890 it was operating as a 'legitimate' theatre alongside the much larger Queen's Opera House, which had been opened in 1887.[163] It is not known whether both remained open continuously, but both were in operation in 1897 and in 1914, when they and the Whitehaven Theatre Royal were all leased to the same man, one Stanley Rogers. Both survived the First World War, and the Theatre Royal was reconstructed and refurbished in 1925. By 1934, however, the Opera House was the only theatre in the town.[164]

Barrow-in-Furness was very much the theatre capital of the region. Its first theatre, the Theatre Royal, later to become His Majesty's opened in 1868, as soon as a town of any size existed, and by the following year the Alexandra Music Hall was also in being.[165] His Majesty's survived to the inter-war years, though at times it did not advertise and may have been closed, but the fate of the Alexandra is not known.

In 1872 the Royal Alhambra Theatre and the Star Music Hall were opened. Renamed the Royalty and the Tivoli, these two like His Majesty's, continued in business until the inter-war years, the Tivoli becoming a cinema in 1931.[166] A venue known as the Amphitheatre was also opened in the 1870s.[167] Sometimes known as the Stadium, this housed resident circuses until just before the First World War, when it was demolished to make way for the Coliseum Cinema. Two more variety theatres were opened before and after the First World War, but were quickly converted into cinemas.[168] From the 1870s until the 1930s there were thus always at least two theatres open in the town, and at times there were four or possibly more.

'Late trains' were often arranged to allow people living in nearby towns and villages to attend the theatres,[169] and the drama and other shows were taken to towns without permanent theatres by travelling companies, who gave performances in Town Halls, market halls or any other suitable premises.

Opera was performed in Appleby market hall in 1906, and in the same year a touring Shakespearean company played in Penrith Drill Hall.[170] In Kendal, the Town Hall was utilised and St George's Hall, opened in 1880, was regularly used by touring companies from the end of the century.[171] Until the beginning of this century, travelling theatres also played in the region in semi-permanent wood and canvas structures like those used by circuses. These would stay in a town for several weeks at least, performing a number of different plays. Lawrence's Theatre, for instance, arrived in Maryport in June 1890, intending to stay for three months.[172] Travelling theatres ('just something they used to build up on spare ground') were still visiting Maryport at the beginning of this century, when they were occasionally patronised by an informant.[173]

It is not on the whole easy to discover the type of drama which was offered in the region's 'legitimate' theatres, as many of the titles advertised are now unknown. The *Whitehaven News* is, however, quite informative about performances at the Whitehaven Theatre Royal in the late nineteenth century, and some of the theatre's accounts and other papers from the same period survive.[174] From them we can see that the theatre offered programmes comparable to those performed in London.[175] This might, of course, have been expected, as many of the touring companies were London based, and all were probably London influenced. The same companies also played elsewhere in the region, and it seems likely that programmes in all theatres were broadly similar, a supposition which is supported by the information which can be gleaned from other newspapers, and, for the later period, from oral evidence. Spectacle was favoured, and music was very much to the fore, the greater part of the repertoire in the late nineteenth century being melodrama, burlesque and English light opera. In the early twentieth century these were superseded by musical comedy. Spectacle was still in vogue, and many productions had enormous casts, children sometimes being used to reduce the expense.[176] There were also 'straight' plays without music throughout our period, and Shakespeare was regularly featured, drawing crowded houses.[177] 'Straight' drama was also presented in a spectacular manner. One play, *Still Alarm*, performed at Whitehaven in 1889, featured two real horses which, during the course of the play, were 'harnessed to a fire-engine and despatched to the scene of a fire'. The *Whitehaven News* reported loyally that 'the piece is shown to as great an advantage as could possibly be wished for upon such a small stage'.[178] Between the wars, spectacle faded from the legitimate stage, and more sophisticated 'straight' plays were the order of the day. These seem to have predominated over musicals, perhaps due to the competition from cinema musicals.[179]

Although the various theatre lessees and owners had different pricing policies, all the 'legitimate' theatres in the region throughout our period catered in some measure for a popular audience. Nowhere was the lowest admission price greater than 6d, and at times, especially between 1890 and 1914, a ticket for the gallery cost only 3*d* or 4*d*. At Her Majesty's in Carlisle in 1910, a musical comedy could be seen for as little as 2*d*, although the more spectacular productions cost 3*d*.[180] Even the very poor amongst oral informants went to the theatre, both before and after the First World War, but there is little concrete evidence of the extent to which the working classes availed themselves of the accessible admission prices during the nineteenth century. It may be supposed that those fixing prices knew their audience, and that many working-class people did attend. At the opening night of the Star Theatre in Carlisle (previously the Star Music Hall) in 1882, it was said that 'smoking was indulged in by all parts of the house, from the cigar and meerschaum in the front seats to the cutty clay at the back',[181] indicating that the audience on that occasion was socially mixed and, it would seem, predominantly male. On other occasions reports of crowded houses presumably include the gallery, while travelling theatres using booths were probably aimed principally at the working and lower middle class.

Before about 1890, all theatres seem to have had a top price of between 2*s* and 3*s*, evidently aimed at the middle classes, and 'the cigar and meerschaum' were probably to be found in all theatres. The various classes may not have been equally represented at all performances, however. Douglas Reid has shown that in mid-Victorian Birmingham popular attendance fell off later in the week, particularly on Friday night, which was 'a good night for the best company'.[182] Although there is no direct evidence, it seems likely that this was also the case in Cumbria, Saturday generally being pay day. Gentry patronage at theatre performances in early nineteenth century Bolton has been noted by Robert Poole,[183] and in this region it remained common practice for a Friday evening's performance to be under the patronage of some respectable body in the town until about 1890. The patrons might, typically, be 'the officers of the 12th Regiment', or 'the officers and members of the 1st Cumberland Artillery and 2nd Cumberland Rifle Volunteers', but on other occasions, the Freemasons, a Master of Harriers and an athletic and football club did the honours.[184] The intention might have been to change the social composition of the audience on the night in question, or, if there were in any case few working-class people there, to bring the respectable classes out in force, making the evening more of a 'society' occasion. The patrons would have been making the theatre part of their sphere of influence and boosting their social image, while the theatres would probably have benefited from increased attendance. 'A packed house' was expected on the night the Master of Harriers presided, for instance.[185]

Between the 1890s and the First World War, the 2s and 3s tickets were continued as before by some theatres, but others were by then catering only for popular audiences. Two such were His Majesty's in Barrow and Her Majesty's in Carlisle, both of which in 1910 had a usual top price of 1s. The middle classes, as we have seen, were involving themselves in amateur performances a great deal at this time, and of course not all theatres were beyong the pale to them, but it does nevertheless appear that *fin-de-siècle* and Edwardian playgoers in this region were more solidly working and lower middle class than their earlier Victorian counterparts. This situation may have been altered in the inter-war years by cinema competition for the working-class audience, although prices remained within the reach of all.

As far as can be ascertained, the programmes at the region's music halls were also, by and large, comparable with those on offer in London. Jeremy Crump, speaking of music hall in Leicester, has argued that the 'music hall, far from being a focus of local and regional popular cultural expression, served as a conduit for the further permeation of national standards of performance and national imagery'.[186] Music halls in Cumbria, like those in Leicester, were relatively late on the scene, and they were able from the start to draw artistes from an established entertainments industry.[187] There were, however, some local performers. It has already been mentioned that a local dancing master, Will Wright of Seaton, was a music hall singer and dancer. He appeared at halls in Scotland and Cumberland in the early years of this century.[188] There were also, as we have seen, more general links between the dances taught by the dancing masters and those performed on the stage, and at Carlisle Star there appear to have been rather more dancing acts than we might expect to find.[189] The popularity of clog dancing, in particular, suggests that there was, to some limited extent, a north-west regional music hall tradition linking the Lancashire and Cumbrian halls, as this type of act was not favoured in London.[190] There is though, no evidence that stars of the Tyneside music hall appeared in Cumbria, even though there were other cultural links between the two northern regions. The majority of the artistes who played Cumbria's halls never became famous, and their names are now forgotten, but all the recognisable 'big names' were stars of the London halls. The three great *lions comiques*, George Leybourne, Charles Coborn and 'Jolly' John Nash, all topped the bill at the Star in Carlisle. Vesta Tilley appeared there at Her Majesty's in the 1890s, and she and Dan Leno played Barrow Tivoli in the same decade, as, this century, did G. H. Elliott ('the Chocolate Coloured Coon'), Harry Tate and Marie Kendall.[191] The only exceptions to this London domination were the appearances of George Formby and Gracie Fields at Barrow between the wars, and these, despite their Lancashire roots, were very much a part of the national varieties scene, and as popular in London as they were in the north.

The audience at the region's music halls is overall difficult to assess, as no information is available on admission prices at the short-lived Oxford Music Hall in Carlisle, or on the Alexandra and Star in Barrow. It may probably be supposed, however, that the clientele of the two halls attached to Whitehaven public houses did not include those with aspirations towards gentility. Admission prices at the Star in Carlisle between 1878 and 1882 also suggest that there were no wealthy patrons, although the hall was apparently not uniformly working class. A 'stage box' cost 2s and a 'side box' 1s 6d, while the balcony and body of the hall, presumably containing the majority of seats, cost 6d and back seats cost 3d.[192] This was not particularly cheap by music hall standards, but it was on a par with prices at the theatre, and most people could have afforded a back seat. The Star was evidently keen to establish its respectability. In October 1878 the hall held a 'ladies' week', when 'more than usually refined acts' were featured, including a troupe of Spanish acrobats who gave a 'most marvellous and original *drawing-room* performance'.[193] The presence of respectable women, and particularly the wives of patrons, was seen by music hall proprietors as the ideal answer to the accusation of impropriety.[194] Whether the 'ladies' week' had any effect on the subsequent clientele is not known, but in 1880 it was still evidently necessary for the Star to stress its orderliness by stating on handbills: 'Persons creating a disturbance will be immediately expelled', and 'No dogs or disorderly characters allowed'.[195]

It has been suggested that in the country as a whole, middle-class patronage of music halls increased during the 1890s.[196] This, it is argued, resulted from the evolution of the morally questionable tavern music hall into the stylish and respectable palace of varieties.[197]

Although the Royal Standard in Whitehaven remained open, it is possible that a similar process occurred in Cumbria. The well-appointed Her Majesty's Theatre in Carlisle was showing varieties in the 1890s. Really palatial variety theatres seem not to have arrived in the region until the early twentieth century, however. The Palace, opened in Carlisle in 1906, was a variety theatre of great style, elaborately decorated and elegant. A patron (of unknown class) interviewed by Joanna Felc said that a visit 'was like entering fairyland'. The theatre nevertheless lost money,[198] and it is possible that the middle classes were not being attracted. Signor Pepi's other hall in Barrow, the Tivoli (the glamorously reappointed Star) was said by an informant to have had a mixed audience before the First World War, although it was then 'rougher' and less sophisticated than it was to be during the 1920s.[199] Even then it had a risqué reputation in some quarters. A Dalton publican's daughter told me that in her youth, just after the First World War, 'we weren't allowed to go to the Tivoli because there was *cheeky* men on'.[200] There was no consensus about the non-respectability of variety theatres, however, and a number of working- and lower middle-class informants or their parents did attend, although others including members of the middle class, told me that they only visited the 'legitimate' theatre. This, of course, was as much a matter of personal taste as it was of perceptions of respectability, and education seems to have had some bearing on the matter, though it is difficult to separate its effects from those of class background.

If the middle classes were not, for much of our period, catered for by the music halls, they were occasionally able to enjoy entertainment of a similar, if more refined, kind at concerts in morally neutral venues such as drill halls. 'Nigger' minstrels, for instance, were appearing regularly in the region between 1860 and the end of the century. Michael Pickering has suggested that these, 'in contrast to the early music hall ... quickly established a reputation for respectability and propriety that was long maintained'.[201] In 1860, a performance by the Ethiopian Serenaders, one of the best known troupes, at Kendal Town Hall, was described as a 'Fashionable entertainment of refined Negro Music ... under the patronage of Her Majesty the Queen', and admission prices indicate that the concerts were aimed principally at the middle classes.[202] There was a morning matinee priced at 3s and 2s, while the evening performance cost 2s and 1s. Some minstrel shows did have a lowest price of 6d[203] and, as Pickering has made clear, there was also a popular following for black-face acts which were, of course, featured at music halls. Nevertheless, minstrel shows were, throughout the later nineteenth century, a species of entertainment which the Cumbrian middle classes could safely patronise. While the earliest troupes were principally comic, the Ethiopian Serenaders introduced sentimentalism into their act, and this was copied and gradually came to predominate in separate minstrel shows, while the comic elements remained at the forefront in music hall black-face acts. Harold Scott has suggested that the Ethiopian Serenaders and their imitators 'charmed principally by their gentility and this impression was heightened by the fact that they appeared in conventional tail coats and white waistcoats'. Their songs were 'of a melodious and artistic nature', and their comedians succeeded in entertaining 'without resorting to vulgarity in any form'.[204] Tuneful sentimentality, polite convention in dress, and a complete absence of vulgarity were obviously consonant with the prevailing standards of the mid- and late Victorian middle classes. In addition, performances before royalty made minstrels fashionable and this, together with the above attractions, would appear to be a superficially adequate explanation for the popularity of minstrel shows with the middle classes. The underlying psychological reasons for the success of black-face acts have been recently analysed by Pickering, and these cannot be fully discussed here.[205] He suggests, however, that 'What was being symbolically worked out in minstrelsy . . . were questions about the status of white Victorian society in the whole human social and biological order. These questions were posed within a framework of class differentiation.' 'Negroes' were classed with Jews, the Irish, 'working class roughs' and criminal groups as 'a perpetually lower order that was defined by its antithetical contrast with English gentility'.[206] If this is so, then there are obviously connections between 'nigger' minstrels and the performances given to middle-class audiences by the coster comedian Albert Chevalier, who twice appeared at the County Hall in Carlisle in the early years of this century.

Chevalier was a popular music hall performer in the 1890s, but he is said to have had no high opinion of his audiences, and in 1898 he gave a series of matinee recitals at high-class venues in London and Brighton, and at the Free Trade Hall in Manchester. He played before audiences who had never visited a music hall, including members of the royal family, and when it became known that the future Queen Mary enjoyed his songs, he became the social vogue.[207] Seats at his 'recital' in Carlisle in 1902 cost 4s reserved and 2s unreserved, though admission (presumably standing?) was available to 'a limited number' for 1s. The hall was crowded 'as many people had pleasant recollections of Mr Chevalier's last visit',[208] and I would suggest that the cockney songs and monologues (such as 'My Old Dutch' and 'The Future Mrs 'Awkins') were approached like the minstrel shows, with feelings of sentimentality and condescending affection towards a foreign, lower social category. Chevalier's caricature of a cockney was perhaps not far removed from his audience's perception of the genuine article.

Middle-class audiences were also able from the start of our period to see the shows which ultimately evolved into the cinema. Dioramas, otherwise known as panoramas or myrioramas, were already on show by 1860 in the region's public halls.[209] These were 'immense vertical scrolls, upon which scenes were painted', or, as in Whitehaven in 1885, photographs were reproduced. They were illuminated and 'unwound to present changing panoramic views'.[210] Gompertz's Diorama, which visited Carlisle in 1860, featured views of Canton, Delhi and other exotic locations, and overall, travel was the most usual subject matter, the shows being presented as, for instance, excursions to Scotland, or 'trips abroad to all parts of the Globe'.[211] The dioramas were accompanied by music or, depending on the show's emphasis, used as 'backdrops' or illustrations to musical performances. At Whitehaven in 1890, for instance, Birrell's New Great Diorama of Scotland was shown at a performance by the Royal Caledonian Minstrels.[212] This show was largely aimed at a respectable public, as admission prices ranged from 3s to 6d, and this also seems to have been the case with other shows using photographic effects which visited the region. Professor Pepper's Ghost and Gompertz's Spectrescope and Spectral Opera Company, which played in Whitehaven Market Hall in 1885, again had tickets priced from 3s to 6d, with half prices for children only in the better seats, for which family tickets to admit six were also on sale. Clearly aimed at the middle-class family, the entertainment claimed that its aim was 'to refine, instruct and amuse, and . . . not merely to beguile a fleeting hour'.[213]

Shows similar to these reached a working-class public via fairground shows, and Cumbria was presumably no exception in this respect, although no evidence can be cited. The music halls also featured them. The *Carlisle Star* in March 1880, for instance, advertised a 'Scientific and Novel Photoscope of Eminent Statesmen and Public Characters'.[214] When film proper was shown by the Lumière brothers and Robert Paul in 1896, this too was immediately taken up by showmen and variety theatre proprietors. The cinema pioneer showman Randall Williams caused a sensation with his bioscope show at Hull fair in October that year, and as, by the early years of this century if not before, his shows regularly appeared at Dalton Whitsun fair,[215] and presumably elsewhere in the region as well, it is probable that fairground film shows were not slow to reach Cumbria. A number of informants remembered seeing them in the early 1900s.[216]

The shows were cheap (1d or 2d, according to one informant),[217] and they reached many who, for one reason or another, did not attend music halls. Bioscope shows toured with the fairs until the outbreak of the First World War, by which time they were in competition with permanent cinemas. A number of showmen then settled down to become cinema proprietors themselves. Two such were Relph and Pedley, who had established themselves at the Hippodrome in Cleator Moor by 1913.[218]

The date of the first music hall film show in the region is not known, but 'Mr Chalmers' World Famed Cinematograph' was being advertised at the Star Palace of Varieties in Barrow in 1900, and when that theatre was bought by Signor Pepi in 1902, 'Topical events on the Pepi-Scope' became a regular feature of the shows.[219] In the latter year, Algie's Circus in Carlisle was advertising 'Seiver's Bioscope' with coloured films. Presumably at that date these would be monochrome films coloured by hand.[220] Other variety theatres which are known to have shown films before the First World War are Barrow Hippodrome, Carlisle Palace and Whitehaven Theatre Royal.[221] Barrow Hippodrome became wholly a cinema in 1912, setting the pattern for the inter-war years when Barrow Tivoli, Workington Theatre Royal and Carlisle Palace were to follow suit.[222]

The third means by which film was popularised in the region were the touring shows which, like the Dioramas before them, played in public halls throughout the region. Scott's Cinematograph, for instance, occasionally visited Ambleside Assembly Room, a local pianist being called in to accompany the films.[223] These shows seem to have been aimed at a more popular audience than their forerunners. Messrs Archers of Liverpool's Kinematograph Exhibition, which played in Carlisle Drill Hall in 1902, offered 500 seats at 1s, and 1,000 at 6d. The audience was said to be 'numerous'.[224]

Perhaps partly due to the nature of the films which were then being made, many of the early film shows at all types of venue were of an 'improving' or informative nature. An informant remembered that the first film he saw at Dalton Co-operative Hall was 'In the Grip of Alcohol'. 'It was a dreadful thing', he said. 'This poor fellow was coming home ... and we were bored to tears watching.'[225] The Archers' show in Carlisle in 1902 mainly featured films of the King and royal family, such as 'The Coronation Procession' and 'The King's Visit to the Isle of Man', but there were also films of other topical events.[226] Another show, at the city's Public Hall in 1906, included a film about the construction of a railway, which apparently met with great public approval, and in 1910 film of King Edward's funeral was shown at a number of venues throughout the region, including the Tivoli Music Hall in Barrow.[227] By that date, some lighter subjects were also on offer, however. Barrow Hippodrome in August 1910, for instance, was showing 'Buffalo Bill' and 'Saved by her Dog'.[228] Topical events apart, many films shown before the First World War were either American, French or Italian, and it is unlikely that those shown in Cumbria differed in any way from those on offer in London or Manchester.[229] One notable exception to this general rule were Manders Local Living Pictures which visited Carlisle hirings in 1902. They advertised films of 'Daily Life at Carlisle', including 'Employees leaving Carr's Works at dinner hour'. The invitation to 'Come and See Yourselves' must have been compelling.[230]

By the end of the Edwardian period, film was no longer a novelty in the region, and permanent cinemas were fast being established. The first was probably over Whitehaven Market Hall, although it may have been preceded by that of Sidney Bacon, a Newcastle cinema owner, who began showings in the Public Hall in Carlisle in 1907. He was so successful that he was able to build the City Cinema in 1912.[231] Victor Brandford, the Whitehaven promoter, was also sufficiently successful to go on to build that town's Gaiety Cinema.[232] Barrow acquired its first cinema, the Electric, in 1910 or 1911 and this was quickly followed by two others,[233] while Workington could boast two, the Carnegie Hall and the Hippodrome, by 1912. Smaller places, too, were not backward in acquiring cinemas. By 1914, Dalton and Millom each had two, while Aspatria had its Queen's Hall and Frizington its People's Palace. The region as a whole probably had over twenty cinemas by that date.[234] Many of these, although primarily cinemas, also featured varieties. Relph and Pedley at Cleator Moor were advertising a 'Pictorial and Vaudeville Show' in 1913, and in the same year trained cockatoos, a male impersonator and a weightlifter shared the billing with films at the St James Cinema in Whitehaven. Others, for instance Millom Picture Palace, appear from the beginning to have offered only films,[235] and the variety element quickly died out after the First World War. In 1929, *Kelly's Directory* listed thirty cinemas in Cumberland and Westmorland, and there were probably about ten more in Barrow and the other Furness towns.[236] Numbers continued to increase in the 1930s, and *Kelly's Directory of Cumberland and Westmorland* for 1938 lists thirty-five.

In this region, as elsewhere, the earliest cinemas were converted halls and other makeshift premises, but the purpose-built cinemas, in conformity with the national pattern, were splendidly appointed. 'Oh it was lavish!' said an informant speaking of Dalton Empire, 'it was posh!'[237] Admission prices were, however, low. Before the First World War 'People's Popular Prices' were advertised, ranging from 2d to 9d, or 3d to 1s, and during the 1920s and 1930s, 3d to 1s appears still to have been usual.[238] No 'middle-class prices' were anywhere apparent. By the inter-war years, cinema attendance amongst oral informants was almost universal. Most of those who lived within easy reach of a cinema attended regularly, once or twice a week being usual. One informant claimed that he attended every night in the 1930s, while another said that he was 'never away from it'.[239] No other form of entertainment was so widely and generally participated in, and it seems that Cumbria was no exception to the statement made by the Commission on Educational and Cultural Films in 1932 that 'The cinema has become the staple entertainment of the average family'.[240]

Among oral informants, both sexes appear to have attended equally often, and it was a favourite outing for courting couples. There was much cinema-going by the unemployed. A Workington informant, recalling that town's Carnegie Cinema, said; 'I can remember us being unemployed and standing outside, many times . . . we used to stand outside and wait until the little films were over. Then (the proprietor) would come out at the front and if he'd any seats left . . . he would let us all go in.'[241] A Dalton informant's unemployed father for a time acted as unpaid steward on one of the exits in order to be able to see the film free.[242]

Perhaps the most avid cinema-goers of all were children. Children's matinees appear to have been on offer everywhere, and the great majority of working and lower midle-class informants who spent their childhood within reach of a cinema attended them. One informant said that 'you usually got the feature film that was on during the week, and also a serial, which you went to see week after week'. The hapless Pearl White tied to railway lines or danging from windows was one serial which was remembered.[243] Admission, seemingly everywhere, cost 1d or 2d and children were accordingly separated into 'roughs' and 'respectables'. In Dalton, 'All the roughs used to be sitting at the front and we used to sit at the back', and similarly in Penrith, 'if you were very . . . poor you were in the fleapit . . . . And if you had a bit more pocket money you were in the stalls.'[244] Behaviour reminiscent of mid-Victorian theatre galleries[245] was not however confined to the penny seats. One denizen of the tuppennies admitted that 'we had . . . pea pistols, which shot pigeon peas. And we used to sit in the tuppences and fire pigeon peas down into the pennies'.[246] Both pennies and tuppenies were noisy and boisterous. In the days of silent pictures, 'the kids could make as much noise as they liked, because it come up on the screen, the words. And you were always egging, telling the goody where the baddy was.' The reading of captions out loud for the benefit of those not able to read them for themselves contributed to the noise.[247] The long-suffering pianist was also habitually taunted and assailed with missiles, and this treatment was not, it seems, confined to children's matinees. In Workington, 'on a Saturday night, people used to go who'd had a pint or two . . . and used to shout [the pianist's] name, and when he turned round they used to throw an egg at him or something like that'.[248] Audiences could also exert a very direct influence over the films which were shown. It is related that, on one occasion in Dalton, the film 'Dante's Inferno' was being shown. One scene showed the Devil 'eating a man, with only the lower half of the man's body visible hanging from this huge mouth. The women in the audience were shocked and started stamping their feet and shouting for the film to be stopped.' The proprietor did stop it and went on stage to speak to the audience, and the film was then replaced by 'a sort of documentary showing swans swimming round a park lake', which apparently satisfied the audience.[249] The theatre tradition of audience involvement clearly passed, alive and kicking, into the inter-war cinema.

Favourite types of film mentioned by informants were Westerns – 'I would go anywhere or do anything to see a cowboy picture', – horror films and musicals. Two said that they 'always followed up the serials'.[250] Stars mentioned included Charlie Chaplin, Al Jolson, Gracie Fields and Mary Pickford. Jeffrey Richards has suggested that 'the bulk of cinema-goers chose a film for its star or its story or both', but that there were differences in taste between working-class and middle-class audiences.[251] No conclusions about preferences can be drawn from the oral evidence, and in small towns with one or two cinemas the audiences were probably mixed, and any class differences are impossible to discern. However, in Carlisle at the beginning of 1937, four cinema proprietors were questioned by the *Carlisle Journal* about the most popular films shown by them during the previous year.[252] The answers given suggest that, in a town with a choice of cinemas, class differences arose and were catered for. The manager of the Palace (advertised as 'Carlisle's most comfortable cinema'), said that he had found 'by experience that local audiences prefer musical productions and strong dramas with plenty of movement'. This statement echoes that of the manager of a 'select' cinema in an unanmed southern town, which was investigated around the same time by Winifred Holmes.[253] He said that his patrons preferred 'musicals . . . and thrillers, but not horror films . . . . Modern witty sophisticated drama appeals to our patrons.' This similarity and the advertised comfort suggest that this cinema might have been mainly middle-class in clientele. The most popular films included 'Rose Marie', 'Captain Blood', Hugo's 'Les Misérables', 'Sanders of the River' and 'The Call of the Wild', while the list of favourite stars was Jeanette McDonald, Ronald Colman, Charles Laughton, Jack Buchanan, Errol Flynn, Paul Robeson and Ann Harding. These names echo those in the Bernstein Questionnaires, which were conducted in better-class cinemas.[254] The Lonsdale Cinema, on the other hand, appears to be closer to the working-class cinemas investigated by Holmes. Its manager listed 'Queen of Hearts' starring Gracie Fields, 'First a Girl' with Jessie Matthews, 'The Littlest Rebel' with Shirley Temple, 'Stormy Weather' with Ralph Lynn and Tom Walls, and 'Boys will be Boys' featuring Will Hay, among its biggest successes. The most popular stars at this cinema were Gracie Fields and Shirley Temple. More difficult to classify, but probably not a middle-class venue, was the City Picture House, whose manager said that films were 'judged on their merits', success not being dependent on the star. His list of 'winners' ranged from Laurel and Hardy in 'Bonnie Scotland' and Charlie Chan in 'Shanghai' to the lurid melodrama 'A Free Soul'. The fourth cinema surveyed, the Botchergate Picture House, only named its favourite stars, who were Fred Astaire and Ginger Rogers, and Shirley Temple. These two, together with Gracie Fields, were the three greatest attractions on film in Britain in 1936, and audiences at the Lonsdale and Botchergate were to that extent in line with the rest of Britain in their preferences. Richards had also suggested that working-class audiences preferred American films, while British films appealed more to the middle-class audience,[255] and the information on Carlisle does, on the whole, appear to support this argument.

The American influences projected by films had their effect on Cumbrian popular culture. We have already seen that, together with the gramophone and wireless, film was altering the style of music and dancing in the region, and Thomas Park Benson tells us that following the showing of 'Broadway Melody' at Barrow Coliseum in 1929 'young people learned a whole new language from the script': "O.K. baby", "Gosh oh gee", . . . and "Hi ya babe"'.[256] It seems likely that films, both British and American, had the effect of making older and more local forms of recreation appear passé. Neither the 'legitimate' nor the variety theatre could offer comparable glamour or escapism. As Howkins and Lowerson have argued, however, 'localism died hard'.[257] The region's culture was brought full circle by the film made at Ambleside Rushbearing in 1930. This drew a crowded house at the local cinema before 'doing the rounds' of others in the region.[258]

CONCLUSION

The performing arts, music, drama and dancing, were in a very flourishing condition in Cumbria between 1870 and 1939. New art forms rose to popularity during the period, and although some of them peaked and declined by the 1930s, others retained their popularity into the post-war years. On the amateur front, choral and operatic societies and brass bands all rose to prominence during the period, and a knowledge and appreciation of a much wider range of music than hitherto was spread, while many communities were provided with a new focus for their local chauvinsim and pride. Amateur orchestras were also established during the period, and these were perhaps the equivalent of brass bands for the middle classes, who seem to have provided most of the members. By the 1930s brass bands were showing an appreciable decline, in common with the brass band movement as a whole, but the other musical societies were, by and large, still flourishing. The music hall was another art form which rose and declined during our period, its demise being mainly occasioned by the most important entertainment to appear before the Second World War, the cinema. This rapidly eclipsed all other forms of entertainment, and by the 1930s cinemas had mushroomed throughout the region.

The two older art forms, the drama and dancing, experienced mixed fortunes. The professional theatre saw some expansion in the late nineteenth century when new permanent theatres were opened in the main towns, but it appears to have lost most of its high-class audience by the end of the century, when it was at a peak as popular entertainment. When it began to lose the working classes to the variety theatre and cinema, its position became shaky, and by the 1930s the professional stage was at a low point. Amateur dramatics, on the other hand, developed from a middle-class hobby into a popular pastime with all classes during that decade. Dancing was as central to the popular culture of the region in 1939 as it had been in 1870. It had, however, changed quite markedly in style. Although some of the dances in use in the 1930s had been danced a century earlier, the predominant influence was by then American, and the old formal skills had given way to modern glamour.

The region's arts had always been subject to outside influences; new dances had come from the continent via London, the theatre was London influenced, and broadsheets had spread the same songs throughout the country. The outside influences increased markedly during our period, however. Sheet music and competitions established a national repertoire for brass bands and choirs, and London artistes brought metropolitan attitudes to the music halls, while 'nigger' minstrels introduced the first American music. This century, the cinema greatly added to the American influences which were being brought to bear by the gramophone and wireless, and horizons were widened dramatically.

NOTES

Place of publication London unless otherwise stated.

1 David Russell, 'The Popular Musical Societies of the Yorkshire Textile District, 1850–1914', PhD thesis, University of York, 1980, p. 2.
2 See E. D. Mackerness, *A Social History of English Music*, 1964, pp. 143, 204; *Westmorland Musical Festival 1902. Words of Folk Songs entered for competition*, Kendal, 1902. Much faith was pinned on 'folk-song' as a means of reforming the musical preferences of the working class.
3 *W.N.*, 23.9.1920.
4 E. M. Wilson, 'Folk traditions in Westmorland', *Journal of the Folklore Institute, Indiana*, Vol. 2, 1965, pp. 287–8 (paper given originally in 1938).
5 Ronald Pearsall, *Victorian Popular Music*, Newton Abbot, 1973, pp. 72, 159–60.
6 Wilson, 1965, p. 288.
7 Pearsall, 1973, p. 192.
8 Hugh Cunningham, *Leisure in the Industrial Revolution*, 1980, p. 123, quoting C. M. Davies, *Mystic London*, 1875, pp. 172–8.
9 H. P. Smith, *Literature and Adult Education a Century ago: Pantopragmatics and Penny Readings* Oxford, 1961, p. 29.
10 Cunningham, 1980, p. 123.
11 *W.N.*, 22.1.1920 (retrospective article).
12 See *W.G.*, 1.1.1870 (Sawrey); *B.H.*, 27.1.1869 (Kirkby); Ambleside respondent D.
13 Ambleside respondent D.
14 *W.G.*, 1.1.1870.
15 Respondents 21 and 24.
16 Respondent 2.
17 Mackerness, 1964, p. 256.
18 Russell, PhD thesis, p. v.
19 Russell, PhD thesis, p. 90.
20 Russell, PhD thesis, pp. 104–5.
21 J. D. Marshall and J. K. Walton, *The Lake Counties from 1830 to the mid-twentieth century. A study in regional change*, Manchester, 1981, pp. 165–6; *C. Pacq.*, 3.1.1860.
22 Russell, PhD thesis, pp. 66–77.
23 A moulder/debt collector, a secretary, a clerk, a cycle dealer, a colliery proprietor, a miner, a schoolteacher and three private residents have been traced.
24 Elizabeth Roberts's respondent Mr H2B.
25 *P.O.*, 20.2.1912.
26 *W.N.*, 14.1.1937.
27 Respondent 13 (*P.O.*, 20.2.1912); *W.G.*, 27.4.1912; *Kelly's Directory of Cumberland and Westmorland*, 1910, 1914..
28 *W.G.*, 27.4.1912.
29 Respondents 13, 14 and 25.
30 See Mackerness, 1964, p. 203; Marshall and Walton, 1981, p. 166.
31 J. E. Walton, *A History of Dalton-in-Furness*, Chichester, 1984, pp. 98–9.
32 *W.N.*, 2.1.1890.
33 Russell, PhD thesis, p. 157.
34 A. M. Wakefield, *The aims and objects of musical competition festivals and how to form them*, Kendal, n.d., quoted in Mackerness, 1964, p. 205.
35 Russell, PhD thesis, p. 156.
36 *C.J.*, 18.4.1902.
37 Respondents 14 and 26; *W.G.*, 27.4.1912.
38 *B.H.*, 9.10.1869.
39 *C.J.*, 10.6.1870.
40 *P.O.*, 9.1.1906; 27.2.1906; 20.2.1912; *W.G.*, 27.4.1912.

41 *C.J.*, 14.2.1930.
42 Elizabeth Robert's respondent Mrs P2B; *P.O.*, 2.1.1912; 23.1.1912.
43 Respondent, 23.
44 *W.G.*, 3.1.1920; 4.1.1930.
45 Russell, PhD thesis, p. 201.
46 *P.O.*, 24.4.1906; respondent 2.
47 Ambleside respondent V; *W.N.*, 9.1.1913.
48 *P.O.*, 23.1.1912, 13.2.1912; respondent 23.
49 *P.O.*, 13.2.1912.
50 *B.N.*, 15.2.1930.
51 E.g. Ulverston, *B.N.*, 15.2.1930; Grange, *W.G.*, 17.2.1912.
52 *B.N.*, 15.2.1930.
53 *W.N.*, 4.4.1889; *C.J.*, 4.3.1890.
54 *W.N.*, 9.1.1913; *W.G.*, 17.2.1912; *P.O.*, 27.3.1906.
55 Respondents 30 and 31.
56 Russell, PhD thesis, p. 164.
57 Respondents 30 and 31.
58 *P.O.*, 27.3.1906.
59 A. R. Taylor, *Brass Bands*, St Albans, 1979, pp. 14–17.
60 See Mackerness, 1964, p. 167.
61 See *C.J.*, 6.1.1860, Temple Sowerby Free Templars, Keswick Oddfellows.
62 Russell, PhD thesis, pp. 104–5.
63 Elizabeth Roberts's respondent Mr B1B; *W.G.*, 14.6.1930.
64 *W.G.*, 3.5.1890.
65 *C.Pacq.*, 5.6.1860.
66 *P.O.*, 2.1.1912, 16.1.1912.
67 Mackerness, quoted in Russell, PhD thesis, p. 252; Elizabeth Roberts's respondent Mr B1B.
68 *W.N.*, 22.10.1885.
69 See *P.O.*, 10.7.1906; *W.N.*, 2.1.1913, 28.5.1885, 1.1.1920.
70 Elizabeth Roberts's respondent Mr B1B; Ambleside respondent L; *B.N.*, 9.6.1900; *P.O.*, 2.10.1906.
71 Ambleside respondent L.
72 Russell, PhD thesis, p. 264.
73 Ambleside respondent L.
74 Ambleside respondent L.
75 Marshall and Walton, 1981, pp. 164–5.
76 Marshall and Walton, 1981, p. 165; *B.H.*, 5.8.1890.
77 *B.N.*, 21.4.1900.
78 Respondent 25; they were also on the programme of the Welsh National Eisteddfod by 1936. J. F. Russell and J. H. Elliot, *The Brass Band Movement*, 1936, p. 157.
79 Marshall and Walton, 1981, pp. 164–5; Russell and Elliot, 1936, p. 131; Taylor, 1979, p. 86.
80 Taylor 1979, Appendix of competition results; respondents 5 and 12.
81 *W.G.*, 1.1.1916, Langdale, Coniston, Endmoor (no bands), Kirkby Stephen (eleven men short); *W.G.*, 5.8.1916, Ambleside (old members out of retirement); *C.J.*, 7.8.1917, Grasmere (no band).
82 Ambleside respondent L.
83 *W.N.*, 2.1.1913; *B.N.*, 4.1.1930.
84 *C.J.*, 2.1.1880; *W.N.*, 12.3.1885.
85 See *W.N.*, 26.3.1885; *C.J.*, 2.1.1880.
86 *W.N.*, 12.3.1885; *W.G.*, 30.11.1912 (Kirkby Lonsdale).
87 Respondent 13.
88 *C.J.*, 1.1.1937, 8.1.1937.

89 C.J., 4.2.1938.
90 C.J., 1.1.1937.
91 C.J., 4.2.1938; W.N, 14.1.1937.
92 Respondent 21.
93 Respondent 13.
94 See W.N., 12.3.1885; C.J., 4.2.1938, 18.2.1938.
95 W.G., 4.1.1890.
96 Except, of course, for mummers' plays.
97 Frances Rust, *Dance in Society*, 1969, p. 79.
98 Quoted in Marshall and Walton, 1981, p. 160.
99 Report of Commission on Employment of Women and Children in Agriculture, P.P. Vol. XIII, 1868–69, p. 141. Tremenheere's evidence.
100 J. F. and T. M. Flett, *Traditional Step-Dancing in Lakeland*, 1979, p. 3.
101 Flett and Flett, 1979, pp. 5–7, 11–14.
102 Or owner. His descendants were not sure.
103 Flett and Flett, 1979, p. 12.
104 Flett and Flett, 1979, p. 9.
105 Flett and Flett, 1979, p. 9.
106 Flett and Flett, 1979, p. 9.
107 Respondent 1.
108 Flett and Flett, 1979, p. 12; respondent 30.
109 Flett and Flett, 1979, p. 14.
110 Flett and Flett, 1979, p. 13; respondent 29.
111 Ambleside respondent A.
112 Flett and Flett, 1979, dance programmes, pp. 80–103.
113 Nicholas Temperley, 'Ballroom and drawing-room music' in N. Temperley (ed.), *Music in Britain. The Romantic Age 1800–1914*, 1981, p. 112.
114 E.g. Cleator Moor, W.N., 23.10.1890; Kendal, W.G., 3.1.1880.
115 Flett and Flett, 1979, p. 13.
116 Flett and Flett, 1979, p. 9; Star Music Hall posters 1880, C.R.O. DX46.
117 See Rust, 1969, p. 84.
118 Rust, 1969, pp. 84–6.
119 Respondent 21 remembered Charleston competitions organised by a travelling theatre company in Penrith.
120 See M. R. Marrus, 'Modernization and Dancing in Rural France. From "La Bourrée" to "Le Fox-trot"' in J. Beauroy, M. Bertrand and E. T. Gargen (eds.), *The Wolf and the Lamb. Popular Culture in France from the Old Regime to the Twentieth Century*, California, 1976, *passim*, for discussion of a similar process of change in rural France.
121 Flett and Flett, 1979, p. 7.
122 Flett and Flett, 1979, p. 11.
123 E.g. Children's New Year ball in Longtown, C.J., 3.1.1930.
124 Respondents 6, 8, 21 and 27.
125 See B.N., 9.8.1930, dance at Ulverston.
126 Respondents 12 and 28; minute book of Urswick Recreation Hall Management Committee, in possession of Mr T. Stable, Urswick.
127 Ambleside respondent W.
128 George and Crown Hotels, Penrith, C.Pacq., 3.1.1860, respondent 6; Grand Hotel, Whitehaven, W.N., 2.1.1890; Tufton Arms, Appleby, C.J., 10.1.1890.
129 Respondents 6 and 24.
130 E.g. Urswick, respondent 24; Troutbeck, W.G., 1.1.1870; Greenodd and Flookburgh, W.G., 6.1.1900.
131 Respondent 6; minute book of Urswick Recreation Hall Management Committee.
132 Respondent 12.
133 Respondent 16.

134 *Kelly's Directory of Cumberland and Westmorland*, 1934; *W.N.*, 7.1.1937.
135 See *W.G.*, 1.1.1870, 12.2.1870; *C. Pacq.*, 4.1.1870; *C.J.*, 11.2.1870.
136 *W.G.*, 4.1.1890.
137 *C.J.*, 10.1.1902.
138 *C.J.*, 2.1.1900; *B.H.*, 12.2.1910.
139 Respondent 13.
140 Respondent 6.
141 Respondent 3.
142 *The New Oxford Companion to Music*, Vol. 1, pp. 581–2.
143 *W.N.*, 8.1.1920.
144 Respondents 14, 6 and 3.
145 Respondent 3.
146 Respondent 3.
147 Respondent 6; minute book of Urswick Recreation Hall Management Committee.
148 *B.N.*, 3.1.1920; *W.N.*, 1.1.1920.
149 See *B.N.*, 4.1.1930; *W.G.*, 4.1.1930.
150 Such as Arcadian, Lyrical and Savannah Bands, *B.N.*, 4.1.1930, *C.J.*, 14.2.1930, *W.G.*, 4.1.1930.
151 There are interesting, though not exact, parallels with the 'veglia' dances of Tuscany. See Alessandro Falassi, *Folklore by the Fireside. Text and Context of the Tuscan Veglia*, 1980, Ch. 6. It is possible that further research might bring to light a more general pattern of ritualised form in social dance.
152 Papers relating to Whitehaven Theatre Royal, C.R.C. D/BT/11/61, D/BT/11/75; Daniel Hay, *Whitehaven*, Beckermet, Cumbria, 1966, p. 122; *Kelly's Directory of Cumberland and Westmorland*, 1934.
153 Papers relating to Whitehaven Theatre Royal, C.R.O. D/BT/11/59, 68; local press, *passim*.
154 Marshall and Walton, 1981, p. 174; L. Senelick, D. F. Cheshire and U. Schneider, *British Music Hall 1840–1923 – bibliography and guide to sources*, Hamden, Connecticut, 1981, p. 101; the local *Whitehaven News* merely reported it as a public house fire, *W.N.*, 4.6.1885.
155 Papers relating to Whitehaven Theatre Royal, C.R.O. D/BT/11/72.
156 *Kelly's Directory of Cumberland and Westmorland*, 1934.
157 Joanna Felc, 'A History of Theatre in Carlisle', unpublished dissertation (unspecified) in C.R.O., n.d. pp. 22–5.
158 Felc, dissertation, p. 24.
159 Felc, dissertation, pp. 27–9.
160 Felc, dissertation, p. 31; *C.J.*, 1902, *passim*.
161 Felc, dissertation, pp. 36–7; G. J. Mellor, *The Northern Music Hall*, Newcastle, 1970, p. 188; *Kelly's Directory of Cumberland and Westmorland*, 1934.
162 *Mannix and Whellan's Directory of Cumberland*, 1847; *Slater's Directory of Cumberland and Westmorland*, 1869; *C.Pacq.*, 4.10.1870; *W.N.*, 26.3.1885.
163 *C.J.*, 7.1.1890.
164 *Kelly's Directory of Cumberland*, 1897, 1914; *Kelly's Directory of Cumberland and Westmorland*, 1929, 1934.
165 *B.H.*, 2.1.1869, 23.1.1869; Elizabeth Roberts's respondent Mr M8B.
166 Elizabeth Roberts's respondent Mr M8B; local press, *passim*.
167 Marshall and Walton, 1981, p. 175.
168 Elizabeth Roberts's respondent Mr M8B; *B.H.*, 13.8.1910; G. J. Mellor, *Picture Pioneers. The Story of the Northern Cinema 1896–1971* Newcastle, 1971, pp. 42, 46.
169 See for example, *B.N.*, 30.12.1899; *W.N.*, 9.1.1890; *C.J.*, 11.2.1910.
170 *P.O.*, 24.4.1906, 25.9.1906.
171 Marshall and Walton, 1981, p. 175; *W.G.*, 6.1.1900 and *passim*, in early twentieth century.

172 *W.N.*, 19.6.1890.
173 Respondent 6.
174 C.R.O. D/BT/11/58.
175 See M. R. Booth, *Victorian Spectacular Theatre 1850–1910*, 1981; George Rowell, *The Victorian Theatre 1792–1914*, 2nd edn, Cambridge, 1978; R. Pearsall, *Victorian Popular Music*, 1973, Chs. 4 and 10.
176 See *C.J.*, 11.2.1910; *W.G.*, 1.1.1910; compare Robert Poole, *Popular Leisure and the Music Hall in Nineteenth-Century Bolton*, Lancaster, 1982, p. 62.
177 For Shakespeare see *C.Pacq*, 4.10.1870; *W.N.*, 12.3.1885; *B.H.*, 1.1.1910; *W.G.*, 21.12.1912.
178 *W.N.*, 17.10.1889.
179 See *C.J.* and *B.N.*, *passim*; also respondents 9. 1 and 3.
180 *C.J.*, 4.1.1910, 11.2.1910, 20.5.1910.
181 Felc, dissertation, p. 28.
182 D. A. Reid, 'Popular Theatre in Victorian Birmingham' in D. Bradley, L. James and B. Sharratt (eds.), *Performance and Politics in Popular Drama*, Cambridge, 1980, p. 73.
183 Poole, 1982, pp. 44, 45.
184 C. *Pat.*, 7.1.1870; *C.Pacq.*, 4.1.1870, 3.1.1860; *W.N.*, 22.1.1885, 5.2.1885.
185 *W.N.*, 22.1.1885.
186 Jeremy Crump, 'Provincial Music Hall: Promoters and Public in Leicester, 1863–1929' IN PETER BAILEY (ED.), *Music Hall. The Business of Pleasure*, Milton Keynes, 1986, pp. 53–72.
187 Crump, 1986, p. 67.
188 Flett and Flett, 1979, p. 13.
189 Star Music Hall posters, C.R.O. DX/46.
190 Roy Busby, *British Music Hall. An illustrated who's who from 1850 to the present day*, 1976, p. 102. Dan Leno, one time 'champion clog dancer of the world', dropped it from his London act because it was unpopular.
191 Star Music Hall posters, C.R.O. DX/46: Felc, dissertation, p. 32; Marshall and Walton, 1981, p. 175; Elizabeth Roberts, *Working-Class Barrow and Lancaster 1890–1930*, Lancaster, 1976, p. 60; Elizabeth Roberts's respondent Mr M8B.
192 Star Music Hall posters, C.R.O. DX/46.
193 Star Music Hall posters, C.R.O. DX/46. My emphasis.
194 Dagmar Hoher, 'The Composition of Music Hall Audiences 1850–1900' in Bailey, 1986, p. 74.
195 Star Music Hall posters, C.R.O. DX/46.
196 See Hoher, 1986, pp. 85–6.
197 Peter Bailey, *Leisure and Class in Victorian England*, 1978, pp. 165–8; Hoher, 1986, pp. 85–6.
198 Felc, dissertation, p. 37; Mellor, 1970, p. 188.
199 Elizabeth Roberts's respondent Mr M8B.
200 Respondent 9.
201 Michael Pickering, 'White skin, black masks: "nigger" minstrelsy in Victorian England' in J. S. Bratton (ed.), *Music Hall. Performance and Style*, Milton Keynes, 1986, p. 73.
202 *W.G.*, 7.1.1860.
203 E.g. Queen's Minstrels at Whitehaven, *C.Pacq.*, 16.8.1870.
204 Harold Scott, *The Early Doors. Origins of the Music Hall*, 1946, p. 128.
205 Pickering, 1986, pp. 83–91.
206 Pickering, 1986, p. 84.
207 See Busby, 1976, pp. 33, 38.
208 *C.J.*, 28.2.1902, 14.3.1902.
209 *C.J.*, 31.3.1860; Mellor, 1971, p. 10 quotes a letter from a man named Hamilton claiming that dioramas were invented by his father in 1848.

210 Mellor, 1971, p. 10; *W.N.*, 29.10.1885.
211 *C.J.*, 31.3.1860; *W.N.*, 3.4.1890, 14.8.1890; *C.J.*, 4.3.1890, 7.11.1902.
212 *W.N.*, 3.4.1890.
213 *W.N.*, 8.1.1885.
214 Star Music Hall poster 8.3.1880, C.R.O. DX/46.
215 Respondent 31.
216 Respondents 30, 31, 4, 11 and 24.
217 Respondent 11.
218 Mellor, 1971, p. 11; *W.N.*, 9.1.1913.
219 *B.N.*, 17.2.1900; Mellor, 1971, p. 42.
220 *C.J.*, 11.2.1902.
221 Mellor, 1971, pp. 42, 46; *W.N.*, 1913, *B.H.*, 1910, *passim*.
222 Elizabeth Roberts's respondent Mr M8B; Mellor, 1971, p. 73; respondent 11.
223 Ambleside respondent W.
224 *C.J.*, 10.10.1902, 17.10.1902.
225 Respondent 31.
226 *C.J.*, 10.10.1902.
227 Felc, dissertation, p. 37; *B.H.*, 21.5.1910; *W.G.*, 21.5.1910; *C.J.*, 20.5.1910.
228 *B.H.*, 13.8.1910.
229 Margaret O'Brien and Julia Holland, '"Picture Shows". The Early British Film Industry in Walthamstow', *History Today*, 37, Feb. 1987, p. 10.
230 *C.J.*, 14.11.1902.
231 Mellor, 1971, pp. 23–4; Respondent 34.
232 Mellor, 1971, p. 41. Mellor gives the proprietor's name as Vic Branforth. *Kelly's Directory of Cumberland*, 1914.
233 Mellor, 1971, p. 42; Elizabeth Roberts's respondent Mr M8B.
234 *Kelly's Directory of Cumberland*, 1914; Respondent 31; Elizabeth Roberts's respondent Mr M8B. *Kelly's Directory of Cumberland*, 1914, lists sixteen in that county. There were probably in addition, three or four in Barrow, two in Dalton, one in Kendal, and possibly others.
235 See *W.N.*, 2.1.1913, 9.1.1913, 6.2.1913.
236 *Kelly's Directory of Cumberland and Westmorland*, 1929; oral evidence and local press.
237 Respondent 31.
238 *W.N.*, 9.1.1913, 6.3.1913; *W.G.*, 21.12.1912; T. P. Benson, *As I return to yesteryear* Ontario, 1983, pp. 65–6; Respondents 6, 18, 4, 26, 16 and 34 mentioned prices in this range. Prices between the wars were not advertised and were evidently well known.
239 The two addicts were Respondents 3 and 25.
240 Jeffrey Richards, *The Age of the Dream Palace. Cinema and Society in Britain 1930–1939*, 1984, p. 11.
241 Respondent 25.
242 Respondent 20.
243 Respondents 23 and 12.
244 Respondents 9 and 14.
245 See Poole, 1982, p. 67.
246 Respondent 23.
247 Respondents 20 and 13.
248 Respondent 25.
249 Walton, 1984, p. 112.
250 Respondents 25, 26, 21, 23, 18 and 1.
251 Richards, 1984, p. 24.
252 *C.J.*, 1.1.1937.
253 Quoted in Richards, 1984, pp. 28–9.
254 See Richards, 1984, p. 161.

255 Richards, 1984, p. 24.
256 Benson, 1983, p. 68.
257 Alun Howkins and John Lowerson, *Trends in Leisure, 1919–1939*, 1979, p. 26.
258 B.N., 9.8.1930.

CONCLUSION

A number of trends have become apparent in the development of leisure in Cumbria between c. 1870 and 1939. There was, first of all, a rise in the importance of domestic leisure. The cult of the fireside was undoubtedly very influential and this probably led to an increase in pet-keeping, and to a greater emphasis being placed on virtuous domestic pastimes such as needlework and gardening, interest in the latter being fostered also by improvements in working-class housing. The range of home entertainment also widened markedly during the period, and with the arrival of library books, the wireless and the gramophone, the home became more of a leisure centre and less of a place to merely 'eat, sleep and drudge in',[1] even though in some cases overcrowding and poor housing remained. Cumbrian society had always been unusually literate, chapbooks had long been available, and from the early nineteenth century on, the middle classes had been served by circulating libraries. The possibilities of reading for pleasure were, however, expanded considerably by universal education, the spread of cheap newspapers and children's comics, and rate-supported libraries, some or all of which enriched the lives of most informants. Phonographs and gramophones were also acquired, by the middle classes seemingly as soon as they became available, and by the working classes as soon as the price fell sufficiently. Between the wars the wireless spread very rapidly to all classes. Both provided a new focus for family entertainment and were integrated into the increasingly home and family-centred Christmas. Other festivals, especially Easter and Guy Fawkes night, also developed a domestic flavour for some, particularly the middle classes, although the tendency was much less marked than at Christmas.

The increased recreational importance of the home was closely linked to the growing child-centredness which is also apparent. Many domestic pets belonged to children, and much home entertainment was also aimed at them. Christmas became a children's festival *par excellence*, and the other festivals, although they were less closely tied to the home, also became, for the most part, occasions for children. Whitsuntide, which retained some importance as 'term-time', hiring week for farm servants, was the main exception in this respect, but even on that occasion children were by no means overlooked, and processions and treats proliferated. Cumbrians increasingly functioned as communities through their children, and much of the voluntary work which was undertaken in the region, from 'kiddies' treat' committees to the Boy Scouts, was aimed at them. The Band of Hope and the youth movements were, of course, concerned with the improvement of the rising generation, and while children were rightly considered easier targets than adults for education and reform, the proliferation of organisations for their benefit from the late nineteenth century on undoubtedly also reflected far-reaching change in the way children were viewed. Increasingly they were seen as a separate social category with different recreational and other needs from those of adults, and this change in perception was further demonstrated by the barring of juveniles from licensed premises. This new view of child-hood was very widely accepted by Cumbrians of all classes, and children were generally encouraged to participate in the improving pastimes which were offered. The commercial entertainments industry also quickly recognised children as a new market to be exploited, and this was done with the greatest visible success by the cinemas. Children's matinees were drawing crowds of juveniles all over the region from the end of the First World War.

The expansion in the range of domestic recreations also benefited women, who spent more of their time in the home than men, but the range of female leisure activities outside the home also widened considerably during the period. The precise extent of female involve-ment in mid-Victorian recreational life is difficult to assess, but it appears to have been relatively limited and predominantly passive. Women obviously took part in dancing and probably figured to some degree in theatre audiences, but the extent to which they participated in public house culture is unclear. Some women undoubtedly did make use of licensed premises at this time, but it seems likely that many did not. Mid-Victorian sport offered few possibilities for active female involvement and apart from hunting, which drew numbers of women followers, probably mainly middle class, the level of female participa-tion in sport was minimal. There were, however, always women spectators. The development of sports in which women could participate, notably swimming, tennis and cycling, changed this pattern, although progress was slow, and numbers of working-class women and girls in particular had no inclination or opportunity to become sportswomen before the Second World War. Financial outlay was one consideration, but prevailing ideas of propriety and respectability also continued to be a limiting factor, in sport as in other aspects of leisure. Church activities for women, which proliferated during the late nineteenth and early twentieth centuries, were unquestionably respectable, and this probably in part accounts for their success, although the paucity of other recreational outlets for women must also have been a factor. Church societies were not only respectable but also useful and improving, and hence embodied the guiding principles of women's leisure, at least until the First World War, although women's right to common enjoyment was increasingly recognised. The development of amateur musical societies, particularly choirs and amateur operatic groups, offered further scope for respectable and rational recreation by women. As there was little competitive female sport, choral singing was probably the first recreational activity which allowed women to compete with others and excel. Involvement in amateur operatic or orchestral societies similarly gave women the opportunity to achieve a degree of local fame, although starring roles seem frequently to have been the preserve of the local elite. Amateur dramatics, although mainly middle class before the 1930s, likewise gave women the chance to display talent and compete with others at drama festivals. Women also undoubtedly figured in the audiences at amateur performances, which had a slightly more respectable ethos than the professional stage, although in the twentieth century, variety theatres were evidently attended by very many women. The arrival of the cinema confirmed the right of women to enjoy escapist entertainment, and between the wars bolder spirits were also beginning to enter public houses. Although the question of respectability continued to direct women's recreational lives, its limitations were pushed back considerably during the early decades of this century, and there is no doubt that the pattern of women's leisure widened greatly during our period.

The range of recreational possibilities for men also expanded from the late nineteenth century on, even though men dominated the leisure culture of the 1860s and 1870s, especially the region's sport. By that time a strong sporting culture including wrestling and athletics, cockfighting and hunting was well established, and these sports continued to be part of the pattern of recreation, although they experienced varying fortunes. The unreconstructed game of football had disappeared from most of the region by the 1870s, however, surviving only in Workington, and other riotous customs faded into oblivion during our period as seasonal festivities were tamed, passing from masculine domination to child-centredness. There was a general movement towards respectability in leisure pursuits and many men found new recreational outlets in brass bands and other musical societies, and in playing the codified and social sports which became established alongside pre-existing recreations. Church activity for men was generally less than successful, however, perhaps because religious bodies could not compete with the many more enticing leisure options which were open to men. The camaraderie of the public house, in particular, remained a very real alternative, and except in strongly Methodist communities, a man was not debarred from it as a woman was by fear of losing her respectability. Men did not, at the end of the period, dominate leisure culture to as great an extent as they had at its start, however. Many of the pastimes enjoyed this century, from cycling and tennis to the variety theatre and cinema, were shared by both sexes.

A further trend in the history of leisure during the period is the extension of commercialisation. By the 1860s and 1870s there was already a small-scale leisure industry in existence in Cumbria. In part this was a sideline of the licensed trade, and here, as elsewhere, publicans promoted dances and social gatherings and sports of various kinds. There was also at least one public house music hall. Theatres, used by semi-permanent and touring professional companies, existed in four towns, although their trade appears to have been somewhat precarious, and travelling theatres, circuses and other shows using booths and tents also toured the region. In addition, a number of individuals obtained all or part of their livelihood as teachers of dancing or music, and others were supplementing their incomes with wrestling or other sporting prize money. During the late nineteenth and early twentieth centuries the profit-making element in leisure was extended, and its nature was, in part, changed from petty capitalism to larger-scale business, although the former continued to be important, notably in the large numbers of semi-professional dance bands which proliferated during this century. It is probable that most of the nominally professional football clubs which sprang up during the early years of the twentieth century should also be classed as semi-professional concerns, as few Cumbrian teams of either code were in the forefront of the game and able to pay high wages. Very few can have been profitable businesses. Primarily commercial recreations did increasingly appear in the region, however. Tennis courts and other sporting facilities were opened with an eye to profit, and the excursion trade was greatly developed. Between the wars, commercial interests brought the *Palais de Danse* to West Cumberland. Theatrical and variety entertainment was also expanded, and enjoyed a heyday in the early part of this century, although until the arrival of 'pictures and varieties' it was still confined to the four major towns. Theatres were increasingly run by businessmen who owned or leased a string of theatres within and outside the region. The Whitehaven and Workington theatres were all run by one man in 1914, for instance, and Carlisle Palace was built in the early years of this century as part of Pepi's chain of theatres, subsequently becoming part of Frank McNaughton's northern empire. Many cinemas were also part of major chains, although some were, and continued to be, small local businesses. Commercial forms of leisure never totally dominated the scene, due to the great expansion of amateur and voluntary organisations, and probably also to the limited number of large population centres in the region, but by the eve of the First World War there were five times as many people deriving their livelihood from recreational provision than there had been a generation earlier.

The final and perhaps most important trend in the region's leisure culture was its increasing penetration by outside influences and its closer integration into the national pattern of recreation. The region had never been totally insular. It had always been affected in some degree by national trends and prevailing fashions in sport and recreation, and some aspects of Cumbrian leisure in the 1870s were identical to those to be found in other parts of England. Theatres, for instance, necessarily performed plays from a general national repertoire, and cockfighting in Cumbria, if more openly continued, was essentially the same sport as practised elsewhere. There was, however, much in Cumbrian leisure culture which was inward-looking and unconcerned with opinion or developments outside the region, and popular recreation was, at the start of our period, dominated by a number of pastimes which were peculiarly local in form. Hunting on the Lakeland fells was not the sport practised in the shire counties, although it did have some parallels in the Yorkshire Dales. Wrestling was of a regional style, and fell-running was a form of athletics not to be encountered elsewhere. Hound-trailing, similarly, was unknown in other areas. Dancing, too, had a distinctive local style of stepping, and although the latest London fashions in dance also featured on programmes, the social organisation of dancing and the ritual of appointing little kings and queens were peculiar to Cumbria. Elements of public house culture, such as Auld Wife Hakes, were also local. The importance of this regional dimension in leisure declined from the late nineteenth century on, and although hunting and hound-trailing went from strength to strength, the other local pursuits were adversely affected by the arrival in the region of new forms of recreation, and new attitudes towards leisure.

The whole concept of sport was changed by the arrival in the region of codified and team games and new social sports such as cycling and swimming. These increasingly made the pattern of the region's sport comparable with that elsewhere, while the existence of leagues in football and cricket helped to integrate Cumbria into a northern or national framework of sporting activity. The region's distinctiveness was further weakened by the advent of whippet-racing, although hound-trailing did remain alongside it. Altered national attitudes towards sport also affected Cumbria, notably the rejection of professionalism in athletics, which had the effect of marginalising the Lake District sports, both nationally and in a sense locally, since, partly in consequence, they were self-consciously continued as a tourist attraction while ceasing to be central to the sporting life of the majority of Cumbrians. Cumberland and Westmorland wrestling may also have been adversely affected by the growing popularity of boxing.

Music halls and variety theatres also helped to further the acceptance of a wider national entertainment culture in the region, and this trend was continued this century by gramophone records and the wireless, the cinema, and subsequently, after the period of this study, by television. These brought an international as well as a national dimension to entertainment and greatly accelerated the acceptance of American music and culture which had been begun in a small way by the minstrel shows. The arrival of syncopated music and jazz greatly altered dance styles, and Lakeland step dancing virtually passed into oblivion by 1939. The great proliferation in the numbers of brass bands, choirs and other musical societies, on the other hand, brought very different musical influences to the region, and competitions and musical festivals further served to actively integrate Cumbria into the musical life of the nation.

The development of church societies during our period probably also helped to break down the region's insularity. An increasing number of organisations were branches of national or international bodies such as the Boy Scouts, the Mothers' Union or the Christian Endeavour, and these are likely to have made Cumbrians more outward-looking, as individual parish groups became units in an organisational network, sending delegates to national conferences, and attending rallies outside the region.

By the 1930s the average Cumbrian, if such a person existed, probably passed his or her leisure time in a very similar way to a person living in any other semi-rural region of England. No aspect of contemporary leisure culture was absent, and the most popular recreational pursuits were those which were enjoyed throughout the country, such as the cinema and dancing, and football, cricket and tennis. Cumbria may have lagged a little in some respects. Women were still largely debarred from public houses, for instance, but by and large the region was integrated into the national leisure culture. Interest in the primarily regional sports nevertheless continued, and local traditions such as rushbearing were maintained. Pride continued to be taken in Cumbrian culture, but, by the end of our period, this was no longer the mainstay of recreational life.

NOTE

1 *W.N.*, 9.9.1875.

APPENDIX
Biographical details of oral informants

Respondent 1 Female, born 1896. Anglican. Father's occupation: farmer. The informant became a teacher.

Respondent 2 Female, born 1917. Roman Catholic. Father's occupation: teacher. The informant became a teacher.

Respondent 3 Male, born 1913. Anglican. Father's occupation: painter at shipyard. The informant became a clerk at the shipyard.

Respondent 4 Female, born 1896. Anglican. Father's occupation: gamekeeper and subsequently licensee of beerhouse and iron-ore miner. The informant was in farm service and public house service, and during the First World War worked in munitions. Subsequently she kept a grocery shop.

Respondent 5 Male, born 1907, brother of Respondent 4. The informant worked at Barrow Steelworks.

Respondent 6 Male, born 1910. Family Methodist. The informant did not attend church after adolescence. Father's occupation: engineer and subsequently garage proprietor. The informant became a charabanc conductor and subsequently an engineer.

Respondent 7 Female, born 1896. Anglican. Father's occupation: teacher. The informant became a teacher.

Respondent 8 Male, born 1901. Family Anglican/Methodist. The informant was a Methodist occasional attender. Father worked at plaster works. The informant became a farm servant and subsequently a labourer at plaster works.

Respondent 9 Female, born 1903. Anglican. Father licensee of public house, which, after his early death, was kept by the informant's mother. The informant worked in the public house.

Respondent 10 Male, born 1920. Quaker. Father a snuff manufacturer. The informant became a doctor.

Respondent 11 Female, born 1897. Anglican. Father a steelworker and trade union official, and for a brief period kept a fish and chip shop. The informant did not work outside the home due to her mother's ill health.

Respondent 12 Female, born 1905. Anglican. Father an iron-miner, subsequently spent five years in New Zealand and on his return became a bus inspector. The informant became a clerk.

Respondent 13 Female, born 1912. Anglican. Brought up by aunt and uncle who kept an umbrella shop. The informant worked in a greengrocer's shop and subsequently in the umbrella shop.

Respondent 14 Female, born 1906. Anglican. Father's occupation: works manager, *Penrith and Cumberland Herald*. The informant worked in a tobacconist's, as a companion/help, and subsequently stayed at home due to her mother's ill health.

Respondent 15 Male, born 1894. No religion. Father's occupation: iron miner. The informant became a farm servant and subsequently an iron miner.

Respondent 16 Female, born 1887. Anglican. Father's occupation: collier. The informant never worked outside the home as her mother died young.

Respondent 17 Female, born 1918. Daughter of Respondent 16. Father's occupation: collier. The informant became a shop assistant.

Respondent 18 Female, born 1902. Anglican upbringing, later attended Seamen's Bethel. Father a steelworker. The informant worked at the steelworks during the First World War, and was subsequently in domestic service.

Respondent 19 Male, born 1888. Upbringing Anglican/Wesleyan, subsequently became a Baptist. Father's occupation: policeman. The informant was a clerk in a solicitor's office and subsequently a railway clerk and ticket inspector.

Respondent 20 Female, born 1916. Roman Catholic. Father a fitter at shipyard. The informant became a farm servant.

Respondent 21 Female, born 1921. Anglican. Father a shopkeeper, taxi proprietor and town councillor. The informant worked in a draper's shop and subsequently a jeweller's.

Respondent 22 Female, born 1921. Anglican. Father a farmer. The informant became a teacher.

Respondent 23 Male, born 1914. Anglican. Father a fitter and turner at iron mines and subsequently at shipyard. The informant became a brewer.

Respondent 24 Male, born 1904. Anglican. Father's occupation: farmer. The informant became a farmer.

Respondent 25 Male, born 1908. Baptist/Methodist upbringing. Became, in the late 1930s, a minister in the evangelical church. Father's occupation, ore miner and subsequently bricklayer's labourer. The informant worked at the shipyard and steelworks, but was often unemployed, before entering the church.

Respondent 26 Male, born 1899. Anglican. Father's occupation: engine driver. The informant worked in munitions, was in the army, and subsequently became a bus driver.

Respondent 28 Female, born 1906. Anglican. Father a clerk at iron mines and subsequently a local government officer. The informant became a teacher.

Respondent 29 Female, born 1892. Baptist. Father a ship's cook and subsequently a furnaceman. After her mother's death the informant was brought up by her aunt and uncle, the latter also being a furnaceman. The informant was in domestic service, and worked as a confectioner.

Respondent 30 Male, born 1901. Anglican. Father's occupation: master baker. The informant was apprenticed at Barrow Shipyard, but subsequently became a baker.

Respondent 31 Male, born 1901. Primitive Methodist. Father's occupation: gold miner (in Transvaal). The informant worked in the shipyard and, during the 1930s, on the roads.

Respondent 32 Male, born 1907. Anglican. Father's occupation: collier. The informant was apprenticed to a stonemason, but after a year left and became a collier.

Respondent 33 Female, born 1887. Anglican. Father's occupation: farmer. The informant became a travelling dressmaker.

Respondent 34 Male, born 1903. Anglican. Father's occupation: collier. The informant became a foundry worker and subsequently a builder's labourer.

Respondent 35 Male, born 1892. Anglican. Father's occupation: collier. The informant became a collier.

Respondent 36 Male, born 1908. Presbyterian. Father's occupation: grocer (shop owned by informant's uncle). The informant became a grocer working for the Co-op.

Respondent 37 Female, born 1903. Anglican. Father a signalman. The informant became a farm servant.

Interviews with Respondents 33–37 were, for a variety of reasons, cut short and not pursued further.

I have, in addition, used transcripts of interviews carried out in Barrow by Dr Elizabeth Roberts, which are available in the Centre for North-West Regional Studies at the University of Lancaster. I was also given access to the transcripts of interviews carried out by the Ambleside Oral History Project, which are in Ambleside Public Library.

INDEX